Cambridge Computer Science Texts · 6

Computing Systems Hardware

M. WELLS

Centre for Computer Studies
University of Leeds

Cambridge University Press
CAMBRIDGE
LONDON · NEW YORK · MELBOURNE

Published by the Syndics of the Cambridge University Press
The Pitt Building, Trumpington Street, Cambridge CB2 1RP
Bentley House, 200 Euston Road, London NW1 2DB
32 East 57th Street, New York, NY 10022, USA
296 Beaconsfield Parade, Middle Park, Melbourne 3206, Australia

First published 1976

Printed in Great Britain
at the University Printing House, Cambridge
(Euan Phillips, University Printer)

Library of Congress Cataloging in Publication Data

Wells, Michael.
Computing systems hardware.
(Cambridge computer science texts ; 6)
Includes bibliographies and index.
1. Computers. I. Title. II. Series.
TK7885.W42 001.6'4 75 27263

ISBN 0 521 29034 1 pbk.

Contents

Chapter 6 SYSTEMS ARCHITECTURE

Preface

The aim of this text is to introduce the concepts which underlie the structure of computing systems. The first chapter starts with basic principles and explores the important distinctions between encoding with digits and representations of digits; the simple kinds of operation possible with such representations; and the necessity of techniques for suppressing detail when describing a complex system such as a computer. The next four chapters describe some of the equipment currently in use for operations on information, laying emphasis on the economic factors that arise as a consequence of the internal design of individual units. These factors compel the use of devices which are not always those of highest performance in particular situations, and in the final chapter the compromises open to the system designer in his search for the most economic design of a system are discussed.

It is worth reminding the reader that computers are tools, meant to be used by people as part of information processing systems and that when assessing what is the 'cheapest' solution to a problem it is necessary to include all the relevant costs. The fact that this book makes no reference to costs outside the rather narrow confines of the internal details of the computing system should not be taken as an indication of the relative importance of those other costs.

In a subject such as this, where very rapid changes in technology are still taking place, and where the nature of courses dealing with the material also changes, it is difficult to aim a book at an audience; not only is the author aiming at a moving target, but the platform from which he aims is also moving. The book is intended for students in the second year of a course which includes a substantial element of Computer Science. The cautious wording recognises the fact that for most students Computer Science as a subject entire in itself may be a poor choice, and is better taught in conjunction with some other subject.

The reader is assumed to have some prior knowledge of concepts such as 'program', 'compiler', and the equivalent of A-level Physics. In the main, mathematical discussion is kept to a minimum, except for the material at the end of chapter 4 on Data Transmission, which can be omitted. The book is substantially a synoptic view of the technical situation as in 1974, and changes will arise from the advent of new devices, and from the continuing fall in the real price of semi-conductor devices. The reasons for the introduction of new devices are reasonably clear; less clear, but more interesting are the reasons for the fall in prices, and one day a book can be written on the development of the semiconductor industry in the mid-sixties and seventies. To keep pace with such a rate of change is very difficult - one solution, outlined in example 6 of chapter 2 is to have the reader reconstruct some of the factual material. The reader may also wish to discover those places where the forecasts made for future trends in the competitiveness of several devices are wrong!

It is a pleasure to record my indebtedness to all those who have helped in the production of this book; my colleagues Prof. Colin Reeves and Prof. Ewan Page for their helpful criticism; to Carol Gower and Joy Crowther who have patiently typed and retyped drafts; to the publishers; and to my wife without whose encouragement the work would never have been completed.

April 1976 M. Wells

1 · Basic aspects of digital systems

1.1 *Representations and encodings*

Information is an abstract concept, and from a very early age we are taught to associate symbols with many concepts. We do this to such an extent that there is a strong tendency to equate the symbol with the abstract concept which it represents. Thus we think of 8 as *being* the number eight, rather than as *representing* it; similarly we think of h as being the eighth letter of the alphabet rather than as representing it. In fact of course the abstract number 8 is a rather subtle concept. A very clear account of what a number is can be found in a book *The Psychology of Learning Mathematics* by Richard R. Skemp (Penguin Books, 1971).

We are taught to associate symbols with information so as to facilitate the processing of information. This symbolising of the information may well involve the use of a measure of some kind, where the information we wish to use involves a quantity which is not amenable to counting. For example one would normally count the number of passengers on an aeroplane, although for the designer of the wing a much more relevant factor might be the total weight of the passengers rather than their number. Whereas the number of passengers is simply a number, their weight is expressed in terms of a standard unit such as the kilogram or pound. This rather straightforward notion allows us a convenient classification of information processing systems into those which use quantities of one sort to represent quantities of a different sort, and those which use symbols; there are of course systems which use both methods.

Those systems which use quantities of one sort (usually electrical quantities such as currents or potential differences) to represent quantities of any sort are *analog* systems, while those which use symbols are *digital* systems; systems which use both methods are *hybrid* systems.

In this book we shall concentrate almost exclusively on digital systems, which manipulate symbols. This manipulation is (or ought to be) done in such a way that if we were to take some data about the real world and apply to this data some operation to produce a result, then the symbols which result if we perform on our digital system a representation of this operation on a representation of our original data will be a representation of this result. We can see this taking place in figure 1.1.

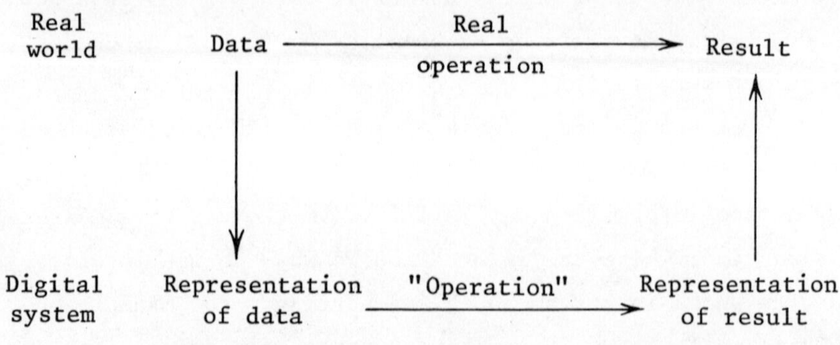

Figure 1.1 Operating on representations of data.

It is not in general possible to proceed directly from the data to an internal representation as figure 1.1 suggests. One reason is that the engineering of a digital system is a compromise between the requirements of extreme reliability and extremely high speeds of operation. The resolution of these requirements leads to the number of different symbols that can be represented within the system being as small as possible. This number of different symbols cannot be one and must obviously be an integer (notice that the absence of a symbol is itself a symbol). If you do not believe this, try to make sense of this, inwhichallthespaces (i.e. absences of symbols) havebeensuppressed!

It is instructive to consider how this situation arises, in rather general terms. A digital device has various stable states which can be recognised one from another. If we plot a graph of the potential energy of the device as a function of a 'displacement' the graph will have a number of local minima, each corresponding to a stable state of the device. The term 'displacement' here is used in a rather general way; typically for an electrically operated device the displacement would be the potential difference between two parts of the device, while for a mechanical device it might be the length of a spring or the angle between two ends of a component in torsion. Whatever the displacement, there will be a minimum for each stable state, and these minima will be separated by maxima in the energy/displacement curve. (Figure 1.2. See page 4.)

Switching the device from one state to another involves forcing the displacement from one value to another and this in turn involves performing work in climbing the potential energy hump between the two states. If W is the height of this potential hump and P is the maximum input power available then the switching time is in the order of W/P. We can make the device operate more quickly either by reducing W, or by increasing P. However, if we make W too small the device will become unreliable. In any system noise is always present, and this has the effect of introducing an uncertainty as to the potential energy of the device. If this uncertainty in energy is ΔW, then it is a standard result in thermodynamics that the system may switch from one state to another with a probability which is dominated by a term of the form $e^{-W/\Delta W}$. Since we have rather little control over ΔW, we can minimise this probability by increasing W. The choice of W is thus a compromise between our wish for maximum immunity to noise, and minimum operating time.

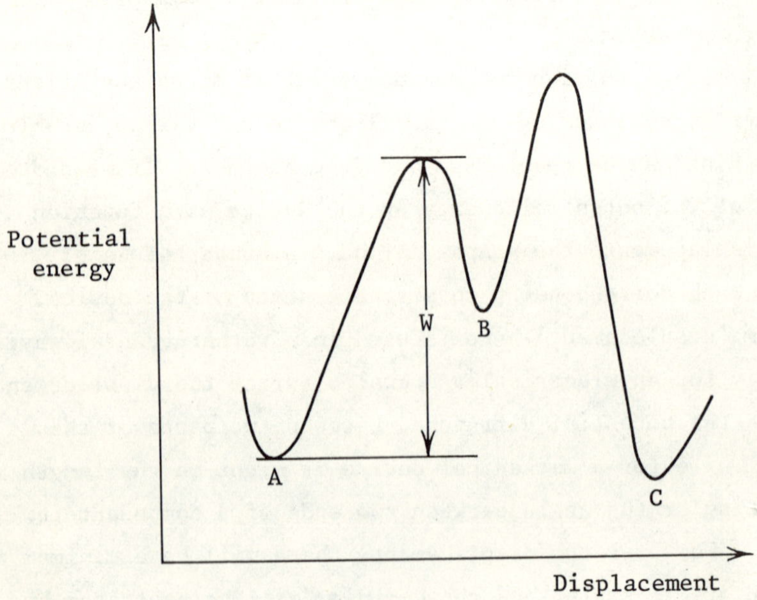

Figure 1.2 Energy/Displacement curve for a device with three stable states A, B, C.

As well as switching devices from one stable state to another, we must also be able to determine the state of a particular device. To do this we must determine the value of the displacement, and decide to which of the possible displacements this value corresponds. We must take into account two effects which serve to widen the displacement associated with a state from the discrete values indicated by the positions of the minima on figure 1.2 to a range of values. The first of these is again noise, which introduces an uncertainty in the energy level, and so into the value of the displacement for any particular device. The second is the effect of component tolerances. The devices when manufactured will not all be identical, and the energy/displacement curve for a given device will show small deviations from the curve for any other. When manufacturing devices there will be some form of quality control to ensure that the curves for all the devices agree to within some predetermined limits, which are the 'tolerances' mentioned above. The positions of the minima for a particular device may lie anywhere within these tolerance limits.

Both noise and tolerance limits widen the range of displacements which correspond to the energy minima from a single point to a probability distribution. It is essential that under no circumstances should the tails of any of these distributions overlap, for if they do wrong decisions as to the states of these devices will be made. The risk of this occurring is reduced by making the displacement from one state to the next as large as possible when compared with the spread of displacements possible for a particular state. Since the maximum possible displacement is limited, we can maximise the separation by using the smallest possible number of states and arranging for these to occur as near as we can to the ends of the range of possible displacements.

Thus virtually all modern digital systems use only two internal symbols, disguising this fact with varying degrees of success. It is therefore necessary to proceed in two steps:

(1) encoding, i.e. mapping the set of symbols that we wish to handle on to groupings of the (two) symbols the system can handle;

(2) representing, i.e. transforming the representation of the symbols the system can handle into a form convenient for the system.

Our simple picture of figure 1.1 now takes on a slightly more complex appearance, figure 1.3. (See page 6.) The data of the original problem are first encoded (using for example a card punch) and this encoding is then transformed into an internal

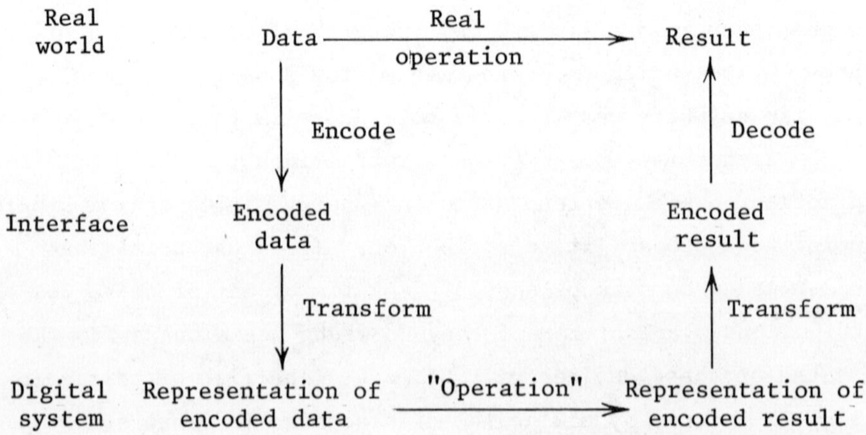

Figure 1.3 Operating on representations of encoded data.

representation (using now a card reader) in which form the data are processed. This internal representation can now be transformed again (using a card punch driven by the digital system) and then converted to a result (by interpreting the cards). It is of course arguable that by interpreting the cards we do *not* produce the result but merely yet another representation. It is also important to realise that what we have done is solely concerned with information, NOT with reality. If this point is obscure, consider applying the abstract operation of multiplication to the abstract data the numbers three and five; unless a mistake is made at some stage the system will produce a representation of fifteen. Now by contrast consider applying the operation of 'boiling' to 'a panful of potatoes'; the results of the manoeuvrings of figure 1.3 will NOT be a panful of boiled potatoes. Only the real operation in the real world will bring about this result. In such a simple case this point is obvious. However, as systems become more complex it is only too easy to confuse the representation of the situation which is maintained by the digital system with the real situation as it exists in the real world, and to suppose that actions within the real world will automatically bring about changes in the representation within the digital system or even more dangerous that changes within the representation will cause changes in the real world.

1.2 *Operations within digital systems*

As we have just seen a digital system holds physical representations of encodings of symbolic information, each symbol being represented by a grouping of several of the rather small number of distinct symbols possible within the digital system. If we take information in this way we find that there are five possible things that we can attempt to do with the information:

(0) leave it alone;

(1) retain it - i.e. keeping its position in space fixed, move it through time;

(2) change its representation - i.e. without changing the encoding, change the way in which the individual elements of the encoding are represented;

(3) transmit it - i.e. keeping its position in time fixed, move it through space;

(4) manipulate it - i.e. without changing the representation change the actual symbols that are encoded.

It is plain that option (0) is not really an option at all. If we leave the information alone the information will simply disappear, and the only meaningful possibilities are options (1) to (4).

It is also plain that these possibilities are idealisations of what can be achieved in that our abilities in certain cases are limited by laws of nature. We can (as yet) move through time only in a rather uncontrolled manner; a change of representation will almost certainly take time and produce its outputs physically displaced from its inputs; special relativity insists that we cannot move information at a speed greater than that of light; the manipulation of information will again take time and produce its outputs physically displaced from its inputs. None the less, these four operations can be thought of as ideals, and any digital system will be found to contain units whose prime function is to carry out operations of these four kinds. The more common names for these four types of operation are:

(1) STORAGE

(2) INPUT-OUTPUT

(3) DATA TRANSMISSION

(4) PROCESSING

In this book we shall discuss the construction and interconnection of devices for performing these four functions and we shall see how attempts are made to produce economic solutions to the problem of designing an effective information processing system.

1.3 *The 'black box' and 'interface' concepts*

Large digital systems are extremely complex. A modern digital computing system complete with storage and input-output devices will contain many millions of components, which together constitute a number of interpenetrating systems. For example, the power supply system for such a machine may handle a total load of say 200 kVA and will in turn necessitate an elaborate cooling and ventilation system. It is obviously not possible even to start to describe such a system in detail and we must make use of one of man's great intellectual assets, his ability to suppress consideration of detail. In discussing the operations of a large system of any sort it is frequently possible to consider only the interactions between quite large assemblies rather than the detailed activities within each unit. We can discuss this interaction purely in terms of the external properties of each unit and even then we do not need to consider all its properties but only those relevant to the interaction. Thus we are led to consider a unit as a 'black box' whose contents we choose to ignore, concentrating only on those of its external properties which are involved in its interaction with other black boxes; we refer to these as the 'black box properties'.

The black box properties of a unit are determined by its contents, and by the application in which we wish to use it. Indeed the problem of designing a particular unit from the available simpler elements may be regarded as assembling these simple elements in such a way as to satisfy the interface requirements and simultaneously to achieve the required behaviour if this is possible (it may not be!). We can sometimes set quite sharp bounds on the black box properties which *must* apply regardless of the internal details of construction.

The black box properties of a given functional unit will to some extent depend on the task the particular unit is to perform. However, some black box properties are common to all black boxes. Particularly important amongst these are:

COST - the cost of a black box has two components:

(1) the CAPITAL cost of acquiring the unit in the first instance

(2) the RECURRENT cost of keeping the unit serviced and operated.

We can frequently convert between costs to a limited extent by rental or hire-purchase to convert a capital cost to a recurring form, and by purchasing service or operation on a single-payment system.

PHYSICAL PLANNING - any unit will require floor space, together with services (AC and DC electrical power, signal cables, chilled water or refrigerant for cooling, compressed air, hydraulic fluid). Exceptionally heavy or fragile units may require special provision for moving. As the speed of operation of digital systems continues to increase, it is becoming necessary to consider the placement of one unit with respect to another so as to avoid delays caused by signal propagation. It is always necessary to allow access for maintenance purposes.

RELIABILITY - any unit is always prone to failure and these failures will require detection and subsequent repair. It is important to consider the full implications of a failure both in terms of the cost of spoiled work and the cost of repair work. Annual maintenance charges typically lie between 1% and 10% of the initial capital cost of a unit, and may well be a major item in recurrent costs.

Complementary to the concept of the black box is the notion of an *interface*, a standardised technique for passing information from one black box to another. Each computer manufacturer appears to have his own 'standard interface' which is used within that manufacturer's equipment. The National Physical Laboratory has for a number of years used a standard interface which has gained widespread acceptance and is now covered by a British Standards Institution specification, and we shall take a slightly simplified form of this interface as an example.

For an interface to function it is necessary to provide a data path across which information can flow, together with data paths for signals to indicate in which direction the flow is to occur, when data are ready, when they have been accepted and whether or not an error occurred. For the sake of simplicity we shall consider an interface in which information can pass in one direction only from the *source* S, to the *acceptor* A, figure 1.4. Associated with the source and the acceptor are signals *source operable* (SO) and *acceptor operable* (AO) which indicate whether the corresponding unit is switched on and functioning correctly. Two further signals *source control* (SC) and *acceptor control* (AC) actually govern the transfer, which takes place over a set of *data* (D_i) lines. Each of the signals mentioned above is capable of taking on one of two

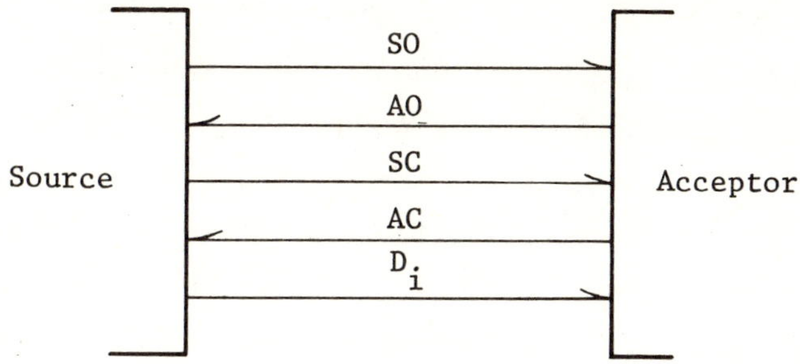

Signal	0 state	1 state
SO	Source inoperable	Source operable
AO	Acceptor inoperable	Acceptor operable
SC	See text	
AC		
D_i	i-th digit is 0	i-th digit is 1

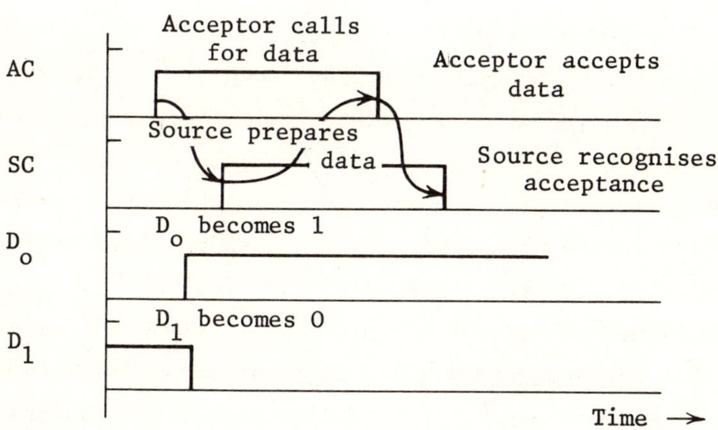

Figure 1.4 Single character transfer over an interface.

values, referred to as the '1' state and the '0' state; exactly how these two values are represented is for the present quite immaterial. We assume only that these states can be recognised and that no others occur. For a transfer to take place at all both the signals SO and AO must be 1, indicating that both source and acceptor are operable. The interface can then transfer a number of 1/0 signals in parallel over the lines D_i, using one line for each signal. The transfer takes place in four stages, each stage being defined by a different combination of the signals SC, AC. Initially AC and SC are both 0, and the sequence starts when AC changes from 0 to 1, indicating that the acceptor is prepared to accept information. The source responds by preparing the data on the D_i lines, and then changing SC from 0 to 1 to indicate that data are available. (On the diagram preparing the data involves setting D_0 to a 1 and D_1 to a 0, their values on this particular occasion.) The acceptor now accepts the data and signals completion of the acceptance by changing AC back to a 0. The source recognises this change of status and in turn changes the value of SC from 1 to 0 thus terminating the transfer. This complete cycle of changes transfers a single character, encoded as the digits D_i from the source to the acceptor. A practical interface might have extra signals between the source and the acceptor which would indicate various kinds of error condition detected either by the source or the acceptor. It is also commonly the case that an interface will be designed to transfer many associated characters in a single group or block, and that there will be special arrangements to deal with initiation and termination of the block. In the NPL standard interface this is achieved by introducing an extra signal line *Source Terminates* (ST) from source to acceptor; this is normally 0 but becomes 1 as the last character of a block is transferred, enabling the acceptor to detect the end of the block. A transfer now operates as indicated in figure 1.5. This shows the

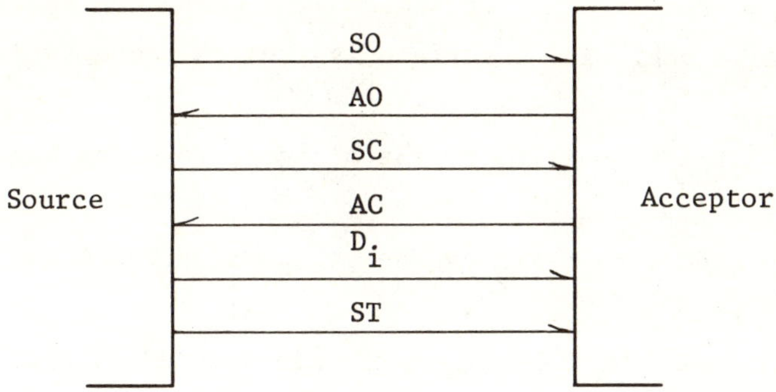

Signal	0 state	1 state
ST	Not last character	Last character

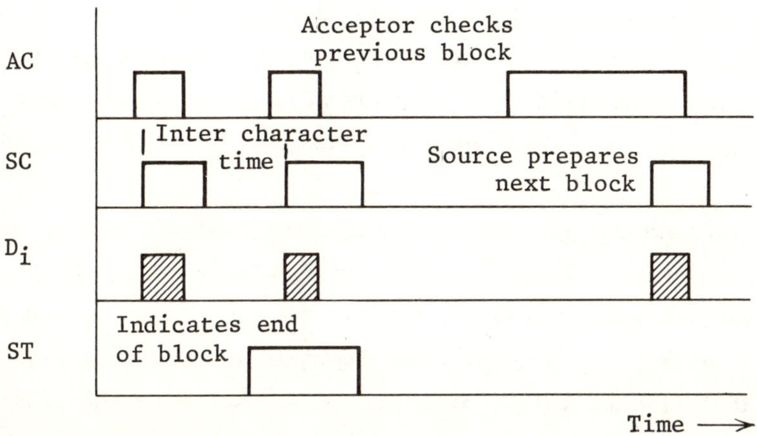

Figure 1.5 Multi-character transfer over a block transfer interface.

last two characters of a block appearing (the shaded areas on the D_i axis indicate the times during which the contents of the D_i lines are valid); the occurrence of the last character is indicated by the fact that ST is a 1. At this point the acceptor may check the block, and then request the next block, by setting AC to 1. Since this is a new block the source will prepare the block, leading to a delay before it sets SC to a 1 indicating that the first character is available. The interface is now free to transfer successive characters up to the next end of block. The interface is thus characterised by three times:

(1) the time taken by the acceptor to check the previous block

(2) the time taken by the source to prepare the next block

(3) the time between characters within a single block.

We shall see these times, occurring under various guises, appearing at several places in the next sections. It is important to grasp that these interface times are governed largely by the behaviour of the black boxes which are acting as the source and acceptor rather than by the interface itself. There are exceptions to this situation when we come to deal with data transmission systems, in which the distinction between the interface and the black box can be rather blurred.

1.4 *Outline description of a computing system*

We conclude this introductory chapter with an outline description of a typical computing system. Figure 1.6 shows such a system, divided into two major areas the 'main frame' and the 'peripherals'. In the terms we have used the peripherals are responsible for input/output operations, data transmission and some forms of storage.

All peripheral operations take place on devices, each attached via a device controller to the input-output controller. The purpose is to free the input-output controller from coping with the details of each individual device, the responsibility for which is delegated to the device controller; each device controller drives a specific type of unit, such as a card reader (an input device), or a magnetic drum (a bulk storage device) and all device controllers present virtually the same interface to the input-output controller. These interfaces will differ principally in handling character or block transfers between the input-output controller and the device controller. The communications controller handles traffic between the system and distant equipment, such as teletypes, remote job entry work stations or even other computing systems.

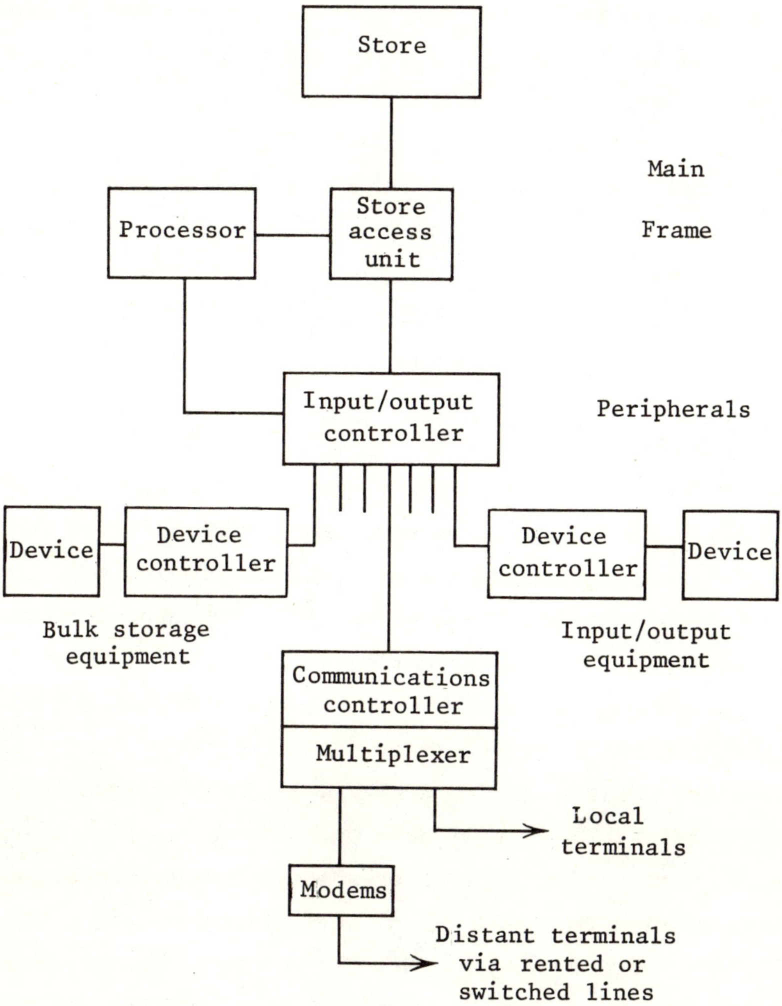

Figure 1.6 Major components of a computing system.

The main frame contains three major units. The store access unit handles all traffic into or out of the main store.

This traffic originates in the input-output controller described above, or the processor; it is the processor which actually handles the processing of information. The processor fetches instructions from the store, and carries out operations on data already in the processor or fetched from the store, finally returning results to the store. The processor also originates transactions on peripheral devices by passing to the input-output controller information about the transaction; when the controller has successfully completed a transaction it in turn informs the processor.

Clearly this is a highly simplified description; the next four chapters describe the principles underlying the operations within such a system, while chapter 6 outlines ways of improving the utilisation of the entire system, and of making it more readily available to its users.

1.5 *Bibliography*

Standard Interface. The British Standard Interface is defined by BS4421; however, a much more accessible description is in an appendix to *Communications Networks for Computers* by D.W. Davies and D.L.A. Barber, Wiley and Sons, 1973. The appendix describes both the logical and electrical construction of an interface, and gives a detailed description of its application.

An interface system widely used in the application of computers to process control and high speed data capture is the 'CAMAC' system. Originally developed for use in high-energy physics, CAMAC defines both a standard interface for signalling between modules (the CAMAC term for a black box) and a large number of standard modules. Details can be found in the CAMAC bulletin, which is produced regularly by the ESONE committee (JRC Euratom, I-21020 Ispra, Italy) and distributed by the Commission of the European Communities, 29 rue Aldringen, Luxembourg.

2 · Storage

2.1 *Black box properties*

The purpose of a storage device is to retain information written into it without altering the information in any way and to allow it to be read back later. It is almost always necessary to change the physical representation in order to achieve this, but this change of representation is quite secondary to the process. However, the particular change of representation does have important effects on the black box properties of the storage device, and in that respect the internal details of storage devices are important.

We have already seen that any black box has the following properties

(1) Costs

(2) Physical Planning

(3) Reliability

(4) Operating Speeds.

For a storage device the operating speeds are normally quoted as the *access time*, the *cycle time* and the *transfer rate*. The access time applies to reading only and is the time between first requesting information, that is when AC* changes from 0 to 1, to the time when the first item of information is present on the D_i lines, that is when SC first changes from 0 to 1. The cycle time applies to a transfer in which only one item of information passes across the interface and is the

* The terms AC, D_i, SC refer to the description of an interface given in section 3 of chapter 1.

minimum time between successive changes from 0 to 1 on SC in response to AC being 1. Obviously this limits the maximum rate at which the device can either yield information when reading or accept information when writing. Notice that the cycle times for reading and writing may differ. The transfer rate applies to transfers in which many characters pass across the interface, and is the reciprocal of the time between successive changes from 0 to 1 on SC.

Storage devices will have further properties which apply only to storage devices and not to other units. An important property is the *CAPACITY* of the store, the amount of information that it can hold. This is usually expressed in units which relate simply to the way in which the store is organised or used, and without enquiring too deeply into the origins of the various measures we may list them as

bit	a single 1/0 digit
character	a group of six bits
byte	a group of eight bits
word	a group of four (or six, eight or even ten) characters or bytes.

For larger stores it is usual to express the capacity in multiples of these; the two common multiples are the kilobit (or byte, word, etc.) and the megabit (byte, word). One might expect these to be one thousand and one million of the appropriate unit respectively. It happens that 2^{10} is equal to 1,024 and 2^{20} is equal to 1,048,576. Since, for engineering reasons, many stores are organised so as to contain a number of bits or words say which is an exact power of two, it is quite common to use Kilobit or Kiloword as meaning 2^{10} bits or words and Mega- as meaning 2^{20}. With so many meanings attached to one name, quoting the capacity of a store may be misleading. Where it matters we shall quote store sizes in bits, indicating how this total is arrived at.

For a store which holds only a single bit (or byte, word, etc.) there can never be any confusion as to which item of information is referred to when using the store. However, where a store holds a multiplicity of items, it is important to know the item we are using. There are several ways in which this can be achieved. The store may be *addressable*, and we can refer to any particular item by quoting its address. This implies an extension to the interface which the store presents to the outside world, for we must now be able to insert addresses into the storage device as we are using it. If the store is not addressable, then we must still be able to discover which item of information we have read from the store, or specify what we are writing into the store. This can be done by including with the information we write to the store extra information which identifies the item with which it is associated. Subsequent reading may be in one of two forms; we may simply be allowed to read the next item from the store and to discover its identity only after we have read it. Alternatively, we may be allowed to specify the identifying part of the information and the store itself will search through all the items in store and retrieve the one with that identification if it is present, or inform us if it is not. A store of this last kind is an *associative* store, and plays a central role in some computing systems.

There are two further possibilities in common use. The first-in-first-out (FIFO) store allows one to write on the end of a stream of items; when the store is read it delivers the *oldest* item in the store and erases it from the store. Clearly a store organised in this way is suitable for storing a queue of items in which the oldest entry in the queue is the first to be serviced. The last-in-first-out (LIFO) store again allows one to write on the end of a stream of items; when the store is read it delivers the *newest* item in the store and

	Device	COSTS				PHYSICAL PLANNING			
		Capital for unit	Capital per bit	Recurrent	Reliability	dimension of unit	weight	power	stand by power/bit
FLIP-FLOP	(1) Discrete	£5	£5	nominal	good	30 × 30 × 10 mm	10 gms	0.1 w	0.1 w
	(2) Integrated circuit	£2	£1	nominal	excellent	3 × 5 × 20 mm	1 gms	0.05 w	0.02 w
	(3) Medium scale integrated circuit	£25	2.0p	nominal	excellent	3 × 5 × 20 mm	1 gms	1.0 w	1 mw
	(4) Large scale integrated circuit	£200	0.2p	nominal	good	5 × 50 × 50 mm	20 gms	50 w	0.4 mw
	(5) Ferrite core	£40,000	0.4p	low	good	0.5 × 0.5 × 1.0 m	100 Kg	2 Kw	
	(6) Plated wire	£30,000	0.3p	low	excellent	0.5 × .05 × 1.0 m	100 Kg	1 Kw	
MOVING MAGNETIC SURFACE	(7) Drum	£20,000	120 mp	low	good	1.0 × 1.0 × 1.5 m	300 Kg	3 Kw	
	(8) Head per track disc	£20,000	6 mp	medium	good	0.8 × 0.8 × 1.2 m	150 Kg	3 Kw	
	(9) Moving head disc	£10,000	0.6 mp	high	fair	0.8 × 0.8 × 1.2 m	150 Kg	3 Kw	
	(10) Magnetic tape	£10,000	4 mp	very high	poor	0.8 × 0.6 × 2.0 m	300 Kg	2 Kw	

access time	PERFORMANCE speed	capacity	organisation
(1) NIL	10^8 bits/sec	1 bit	single bit
(2) NIL	10^8 bits/sec	2 bits	2 bits/DILIC
(3) 50 ns	10^7 bits/sec	1 k bit	10^3 bits/DILIC
(4) 300 ns	1.6×10^7 bits/sec	128 k bits	10^5 bits/unit as 16 k addressable bytes (8 bits)
(5) 300 ns	3.2×10^7 bits/sec	1 M bit	10^6 bits/unit as 32 k addressable words (32 bits)
(6) 150 ns	6.4×10^7 bits/sec	1 M bit	10^6 bits/unit as 32 k addressable words (32 bits)
(7) 8 ms	1.6×10^7 bits/sec	16 M bits	1.6×10^7 bits/unit as 2 M x 8 bit bytes in addressable blocks
(8) 12 ms	3.2×10^6 bits/sec	320 M bits	3.2×10^8 bits/unit as 40 M × 8 bit bytes in addressable blocks
(9) 30-80 ms	2.4×10^6 bits/sec	1.6×10^3 M bits	1.6×10^9 bits/unit as 200 M × 8 bits bytes in addressable blocks
(10) 5 ms-3.00 secs	1.0×10^6 bits/sec	240 M bits	240 M bits as 30 M × bit bytes in serially accessed blocks

Table 2.1 Summary of black box properties of storage devices.

erases it from the store. Stores organised in this way are useful when one is writing a compiler, or designing a processor to handle the output from a compiler. Obviously neither a LIFO nor a FIFO store requires any addressing information to be supplied through the interface or alongside the stored item.

A store is ERASABLE if the contents of any part can be different on different occasions. A store whose contents can never be altered once they are written is a non-erasable or 'read only' store; such stores have particular values when constructing micro-programmed units (see chapter 6). Finally a store is VOLATILE if its contents are lost when the unit is switched off. It is essential to have some non-volatile storage associated with any system in which information is to be stored for long periods of time.

Table 2.1 gives a summary of the black box properties of three major classes of storage device, each major class being further subdivided into separate types in which slightly differing technologies are applied to the same basic physical phenomena to yield devices with different black box properties. The remainder of this chapter discusses in detail the construction of storage based on these devices.

2.2 *Flip-flop storage devices*

The flip-flop forms a basic element in many computing circuits and exists in literally hundreds of variants. As originally conceived by Eccles and Jordan in the nineteen-twenties, this circuit was realised using thermionic valves, but current technology almost invariably replaces these by solid-state (semiconductor) devices.

2.2.1 *Semiconductors.* In an insulator all the electrons are tightly bound to individual atoms, and if an electric field is applied they undergo only a small displacement.

By contrast, in a metal the valence electrons can be

thought of as being totally detached from individual atoms and able to move freely through the crystal lattice. These free electrons give metals their high electrical and thermal conductivity. In a semiconductor nearly all the valence electrons are strictly localised and the number of charged carriers is very much lower. Carriers may be produced in a pure intrinsic semiconductor by thermal excitation of an electron so that it becomes free to move through the lattice. This produces *two* carriers, the free electron, and the 'hole' that it used to occupy. The electron is a negatively charged carrier. The hole can migrate when an electron moves to occupy the hole, leaving a fresh hole where the electron came from; we can think of the hole as a positively charged carrier. Of much greater practical importance are semiconductors in which the carriers are produced by the addition of carefully controlled quantities of impurities, a process referred to as doping. Where the impurity has an excess of valence electrons these will become non-localised and act as negatively charged (n-type) carriers; where the impurity has a deficiency of free electrons a hole is produced and acts as a positively charged (p-type) carrier.

If an electric field is applied to a semiconductor the carriers will tend to drift in the field, n-type carriers towards regions of more positive potential, p-type carriers towards less positive (more negative) regions, and a current will flow through the material.

2.2.2 *The junction diode*. Figure 2.1(a) shows a semiconductor 'junction'. This consists of a slab of material in which one half has been doped so as to contain p-type carriers while the other half contains n-type carriers. When no external voltage is applied the holes will remain mostly in the p-type material, and the electrons in the n-type material, although there will be some diffusion across the boundary between the two types of material.

If the junction is biassed as in figure 2.1(b) so that the p-type material is negative with respect to the n-type material the holes will drift away from the boundary towards the negative voltage and the electrons towards the positive voltage, leaving a large region near the boundary containing no carriers. In these circumstances very little current will flow. If the junction is biassed as in figure 2.1(c) the holes will drift through the boundary towards the negative voltage, while the electrons will also drift through the boundary towards the positive voltage, giving rise to a relatively large current. Thus this junction when connected as in figure 2.1(c) offers a relatively low impedence, that is it behaves as a *diode*. The relation between voltage and current is indicated in figure 2.1(d). A diode is represented schematically as shown in figure 2.1(a); the current will flow readily in the direction indicated by the arrow, and hardly at all in the reverse direction.

2.2.3 *The junction transistor*. Figure 2.2(a) shows a 'junction transistor'. This consists of a slab of p-type semiconductor, with two regions of n-type semiconductor produced on it. The smaller n-type region is the 'emitter', the larger the 'collector' and the large p-type slab forms the 'base'. The junctions between the emitter and the base, and between the base and the collector can each function as diodes as has just been described. The usual mode of operating such a transistor is with the collector more positive than the emitter, and with the voltage on the base varying between these two voltages; for convenience we have shown the emitter as being at earth potential (0 volts), and the collector at a *positive* voltage V_{cc} (usually about +4.5 volts).

If the potential at the base is less than about +0.5 volts the emitter/base junction is either reverse biassed or so weakly

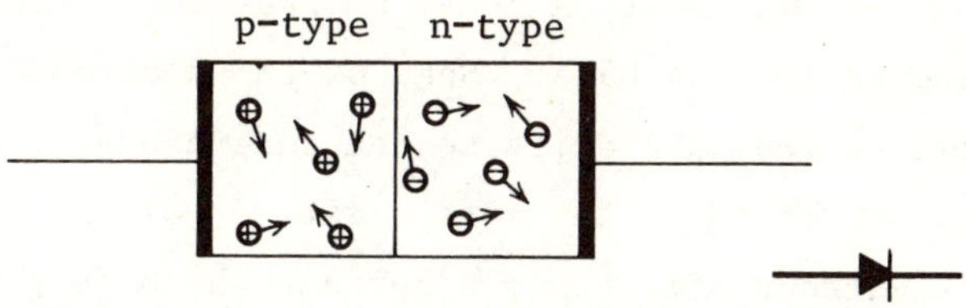

(a) A semi-conductor junction and its symbol

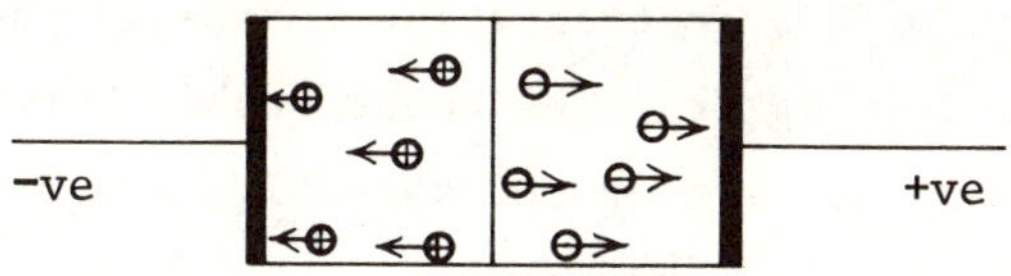

(b) A reverse biassed junction
p-type carriers migrate to the left, n-type carriers to the right leaving a depletion layer and no current flows

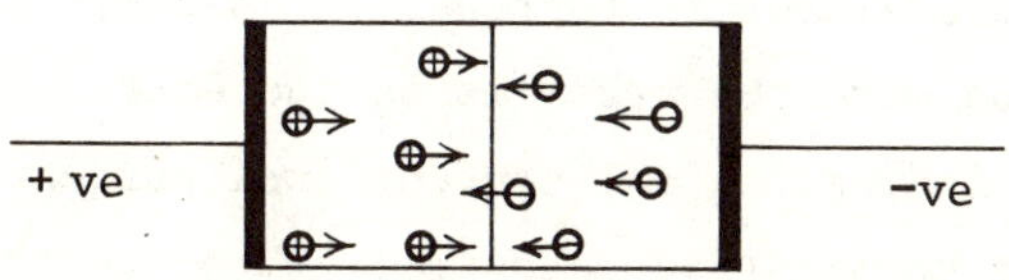

(c) A forward biassed junction
p-type carriers migrate to the right, n-type carriers to the left and a heavy current flows

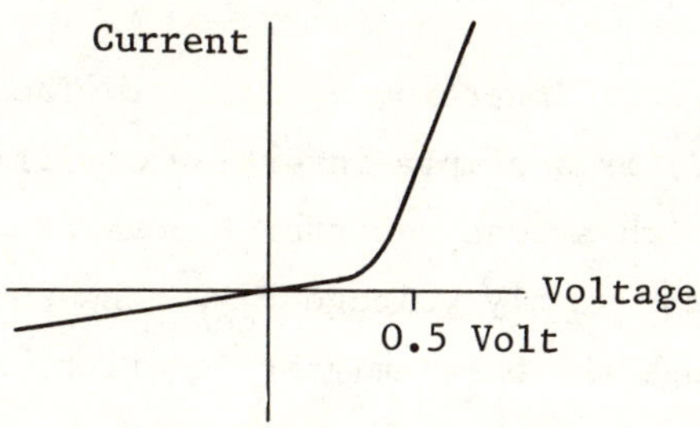

(d) Voltage current relation

Figure 2.1 The semi-conductor diode.

forward biassed that virtually no current flows across the emitter/base junction. However, as the voltage on the base rises above +0.5 volts a heavy current begins to flow between the emitter and the base. Some of the electrons moving into the base region will drift to the base contact; however, others will be attracted to the more positive voltage at the collector. These electrons will carry a current which is greater than that flowing into the base. This current is greater not only because there are more carriers supporting it, but because each carrier drifts with a greater velocity due to the higher voltage gradient driving it. The relationship between the current flowing between the emitter and base, I_b, and between emitter and collector, I_c, is *approximately*

$$I_c = \beta I_b$$

where β is for obvious reasons known as the 'current amplification'. A transistor is represented as shown in figure 2.2(a); the connection with the arrow is on the emitter, the direction of the arrow indicating the conventional current flow (i.e. from positive to negative potential) when the transistor is conducting. The transistor described is an n-p-n transistor; it is also possible to fabricate p-n-p transistors which function in much the same way, but in which all voltages are reversed.

2.2.4 *Transistor inverting amplifier.* The circuit shown in figure 2.2(b) is a simple inverting amplifier, consisting of a transistor with a load resistor R connected between the collector and the supply voltage V_{cc}. The input voltage V_{in} is applied across the base/emitter junction, and the output voltage V_{out} developed between the emitter and the junction of the collector and the collector-load, L. When V_{in} is zero virtually no current flows in the transistor, and V_{out} will be very nearly equal to V_{cc}. As we increase V_{in} current will

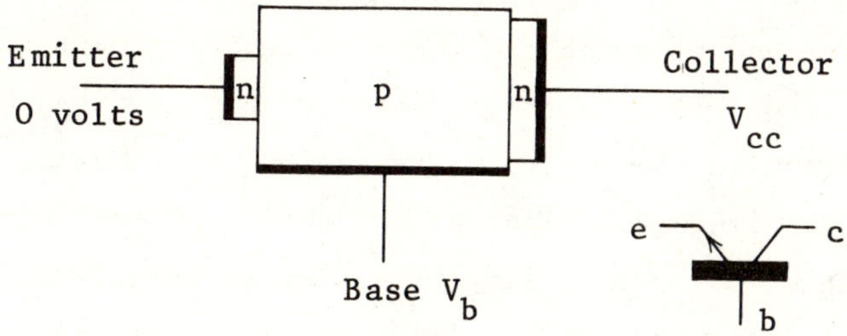

(a) An n-p-n junction transistor and its symbol

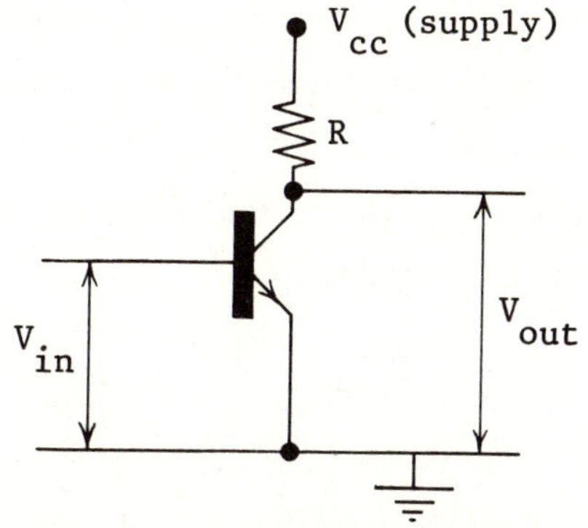

(b) A simple inverting amplifier

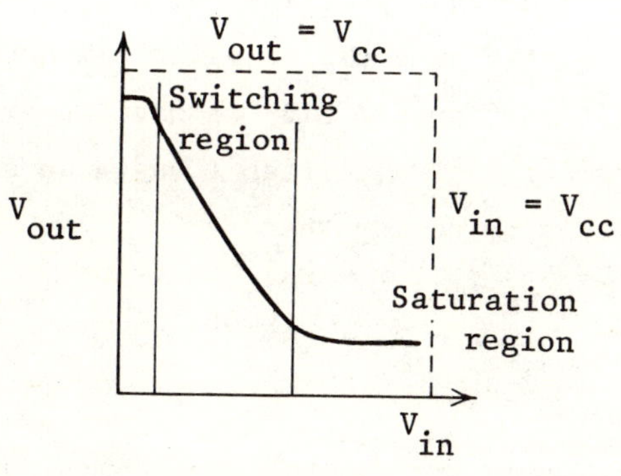

(c) Transfer characteristics of the amplifier

Figure 2.2 The transistor amplifier.

start to flow in the transistor, and the increasing current will cause the voltage drop across the collector load to increase and the output voltage to decrease. Finally a point will be reached at which the input voltage is so great that the transistor can pass no greater current, and V_{out} will remain constant at about 1 volt even as V_{in} is increased right up to V_{cc}. Figure 2.2(c) shows how the output voltage varies as a function of input voltage for such an amplifier. Where the circuit is to be used as a linear amplifier the circuit characteristics are chosen so as to make as wide as possible the region in which $\partial V_{out}/\partial V_{in}$ is nearly constant. However in switching circuits the aim is to make this region as narrow as possible and to make $\partial V_{out}/\partial V_{in}$ have its maximum numerical value; this region is known as the 'switching region' and the reason for making it occur within the smallest V_{in} range will become clear in the next section.

2.2.5 *The flip-flop circuit.* Figure 2.3(a) shows a typical flip-flop circuit. It consists of two similar transistor amplifiers Q_1,L_1 and Q_2,L_2 whose output points are connected via potential dividers F_1,R_2 and F_2,R_1 to the input point (base) of the other amplifier. We can determine the stable states of this configuration by considering the transfer characteristics of the two amplifiers. In figure 2.3(b) we have superimposed the transfer characteristics of amplifier 1 on those of amplifier 2; we can do this by noting that

$$V_1^{in} = V_2^{out} \frac{R_1}{R_1+F_2} = \lambda V_2^{out}$$

$$\text{and } V_2^{in} = V_1^{out} \frac{R_2}{R_2+F_1} = \lambda V_1^{out}$$

where $\lambda = \dfrac{R_1}{R_1+F_2} = \dfrac{R_2}{R_2+F_1} \leq 1$ as the two amplifiers

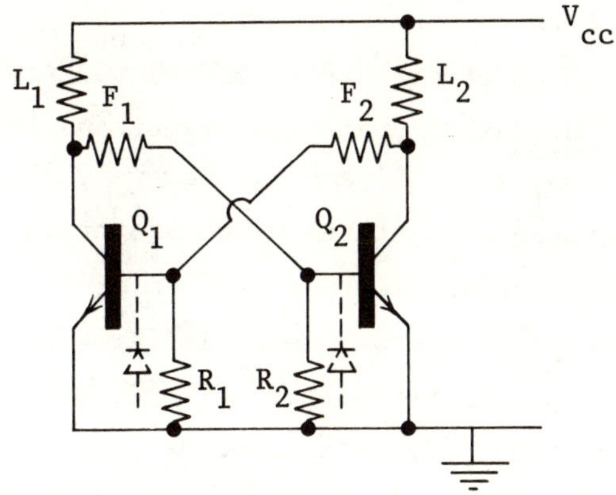

(a) A simple flip-flop circuit

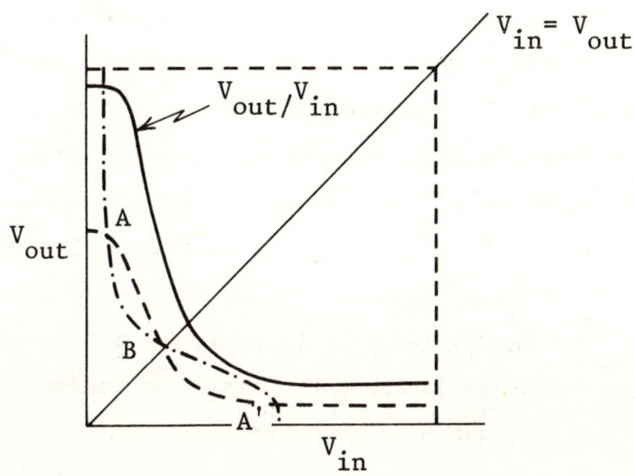

(b) Operating points for a flip-flop

Figure 2.3 The flip-flop.

have similar component values. We have ignored the base current drawn by the two transistors. The curves in figure 2.3(b) are thus V_{out} vs V_{in} for either amplifier (measured at the base and collector) shown as a solid line, and a pair of dashed curves representing λV_{out} vs V_{in} for one amplifier and the reflection of this curve on the line $V_{out} = V_{in}$ for the other amplifier. The stable states of the two amplifiers occur where the two dashed curves intersect and there are three intersections, at A, A' and B. However, whereas the states A, A' correspond to states which are truly stable, state B is in fact metastable. In state A or A' a small increase in the input voltage at one amplifier will produce an even smaller decrease in its output voltage; this slightly decreased output voltage will be applied as input to the second amplifier where it will again produce a very slightly increased output voltage. Thus a small change (due for example to noise) will have very little effect on the circuit which will quickly settle back to its stable state as current is drawn through the feedback resistors F. However in state B the situation is very different. Here a small increase in input voltage at one amplifier will produce a large decrease in output voltage, and this will again be amplified by the second amplifier to produce now a very large increase in input voltage at the first amplifier; B is thus a metastable state, and the circuit can never remain in state B but will always revert to one of the two stable states A or A'. The immunity of states A, A' to noise depends on the extent to which the outputs of the two amplifiers are insensitive to the inputs in states A, A'. The speed with which the circuit will move from the metastable state B to the stable states A, A' depends on the steepness of the V_{out}/V_{in} curve in the switching region. It is for this reason that transistors for use in digital circuits are designed to have a narrow switching region.

We have described one form of transistor flip-flop in outline only. A much more detailed treatment can be found in 'Circuit Design of Digital Computers' by Joseph K. Hawkins (Wiley 1968) which pays special attention to considerations of noise immunity, stability and switching speed. For a flip-flop to be used as a storage device in a computing circuit we require the ability to write fresh information into it, and to read its contents. The reading is quite straightforward, as the output points swing between a voltage near to V_{cc}, and near to ground according as the corresponding transistors is either not conducting (off) or conducting heavily (on). Writing fresh information can be achieved via a connection to the base of each transistor which allows that base to be forced either near to ground (to switch the corresponding transistor off) or near to V_{cc} (to switch it on). It is only necessary to apply this voltage for a short time so as to bring the corresponding input beyond the point B on figure 2.3(b), at which stage the regenerative switching action of the circuit will take over and complete the operation and ensure that the state remains undisturbed even after the input voltage is allowed to return to ground. The application of these voltages is conveniently achieved via diodes connected to the base of the transistor, as indicated by the dotted lines in figure 2.3(a).

2.2.6 *Present technologies*. Present day technology almost invariably realises transistors using 'integrated circuit' techniques. The circuits we have discussed use transistors, diodes and resistors connected together with low-resistance connections. It is possible to fabricate all of these components on a single piece of suitable semi-conductor. The material normally used is silicon, a group 4 element, into which are diffused carefully controlled amounts of group 5 elements (e.g. arsenic or phosphorus) or group 3 elements (e.g. boron) to produce n-type and p-type regions. Before each diffusion is carried out the whole surface is coated with a photo-resist, placed behind a mask which defines which areas are to have impurity added, and the whole assembly exposed to ultra-violet light which hardens the photo-resist where the mask is transparent. The unhardened resist is then washed off and diffusion of impurity only takes place into the areas thus exposed. This whole process may be repeated several times, so as to build up transistors and diodes (as junctions), resistors (as narrow strips of high conductivity n-type material), and metallic connectors (usually as strips of aluminium).

Circuits assembled in this way are very small, a complete flip-flop occupying an area about 0.1 mm square. However, although this small size is an advantage it is not the principal reason for using this form of construction. The attractions are the reliability of the integrated circuit device which has all its connections made by a virtually fool-proof mechanical technique; the fact that all the components are in extremely good thermal contact with one another which frees the designer from the need to concern himself with changes in relative component values caused by temperature difference; and the low unit cost achievable by an almost entirely automated manufacturing process.

Integrated circuit flip-flops are packaged in three quite distinct styles so as to allow them to be assembled. The simplest form offers a very small number of flip-flops, one or two, in a single package; a typical package is illustrated in figure 2.4(a), and is known as a dual-in-line integrated circuit, or 'DILIC'. Two further forms are referred to as 'MSI', medium scale integration, and 'LSI' large scale integration respectively. The border-line between these is somewhat indistinct, but MSI can be thought of as offering a rather larger number of separately addressable flip-flops in a package very similar to a standard DILIC, while LSI uses an *ad hoc* packaging system and offers a very large number of separately

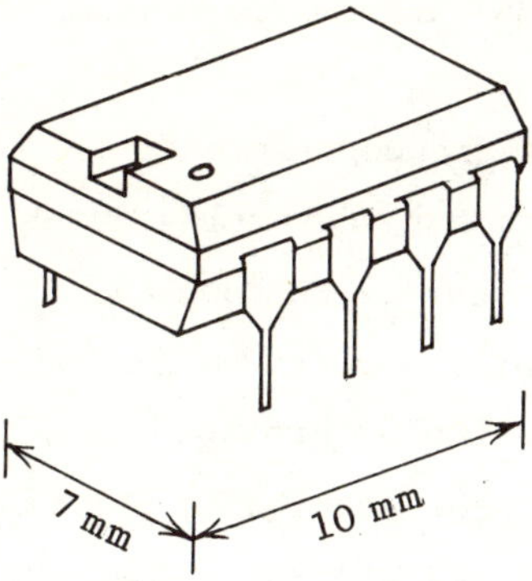

(a) Single flip-flop DILIC

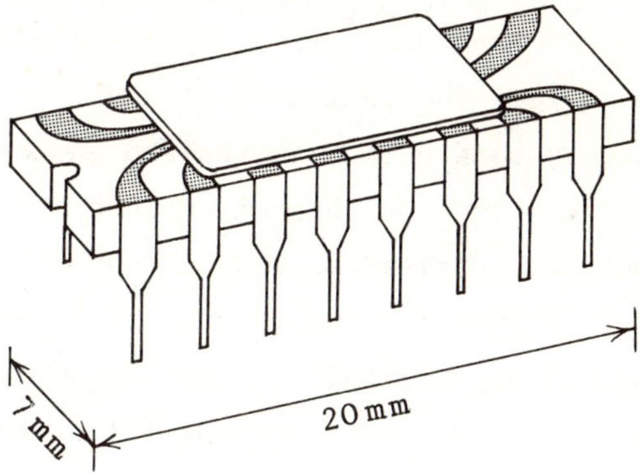

(b) MSI package containing 16 flip-flops

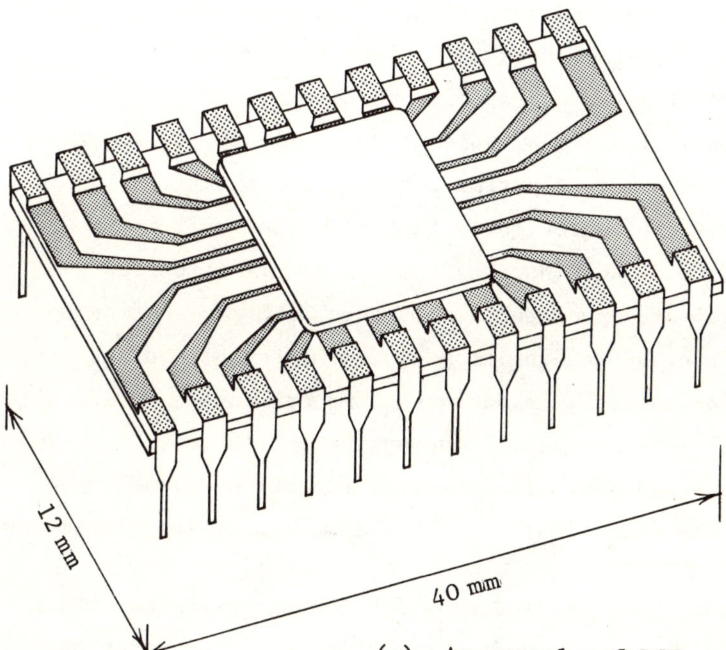

(c) An example of LSI packaging

Figure 2.4

addressable flip-flops. Examples of MSI and LSI packaging are shown in figure 2.4(b) and (c).

Where only one to two flip-flops are contained in a single DILIC there will be no provision for addressing, each flip-flop being regarded as a one bit store. MSI and LSI flip-flop packages storing many bits will require extra inputs to the package to specify the particular bit to be addressed. Equally important of course, the package itself will require suitable circuitry to decode these address digits and to select the indicated element. The details of the techniques used will be discussed in the section on processor design, they can be achieved entirely using the constructional methods outlined earlier.

Flip-flops are used in three principal applications. Within any digital system there will be a small number of working *registers* which hold information actually being processed. Such registers are invariably made up of flip-flop storage, where the relatively high cost of individual flip-flops is justified by their very high speeds. For a single flip-flop the access time is effectively zero, since the output is always available at the collector-load. The cycle time is simply the time required for the flip-flop to change its state, which for a fast flip-flop will be in the order of 2 to 3 ns. (Note that for a single flip-flop the 'interfaces' are in effect always open both for writing to the flip-flop and reading from it.) The second application, of MSI flip-flops, is in various forms of storage intermediate between the main storage of the system and the very high-speed register storage just discussed. These may be associative stores or the 'cache'* store of some models of IBM system 360.

---

* The 'cache' store is interposed between a processor and a store and is used to buffer transfers of information between the very fast processor and the relatively slow store.

MSI flip-flops have somewhat slower access times in the order of 30-150 ns due largely to the delays in the address decoding and selection logic. Their cycle time will be only slightly greater, as much of the delay is due to the addressing delay rather than to the action of the flip-flop itself.

The third application, which has only very recently become feasible, is as the main system storage. Until recently main storage was virtually synonymous with core storage. However, using LSI technology it is now possible to construct flip-flop storage which is economically competitive with core storage. The technique used is invariably based on field effect devices so as to allow the high yield of functioning units necessary for the reliable production of single circuits containing perhaps 2^{13} flip-flops. LSI elements on this scale are slower still, with access and cycle times in the range 250-500 ns, still however faster than any except the highest performance core stores or plated wire stores.

We shall discuss the details of circuit technology further in chapter 5.

2.3 *Ferrite core and plated wire storage devices*

The flip-flop is a storage device which depends entirely on the non-linear electrical properties of semi-conducting materials. Plated wire and ferrite core storage devices depend on the non-linear magnetic properties of ferromagnetic materials. Since the information is stored as a state of magnetisation it is necessary to introduce techniques for changing from a purely electrical representation into a magnetic representation when writing into the storage element, and for converting from a magnetic to an electrical representation when reading from the storage element. These changes of physical representation are necessary to this form of storage, but are carried out entirely within the black box which constitutes the complete storage unit.

2.3.1 *Ferromagnetism.* The basis of these two forms of storage is 'Ferromagnetic hysteresis'. Most materials when placed in a magnetic field become slightly magnetised; when removed from the magnetic field they show no resulting magnetic moment. However, some materials when placed in a magnetic field show an extremely high magnetic moment, which persists even when the material is removed from the magnetic field. If one plots a curve of the total internal magnetic field B as a function of the applied

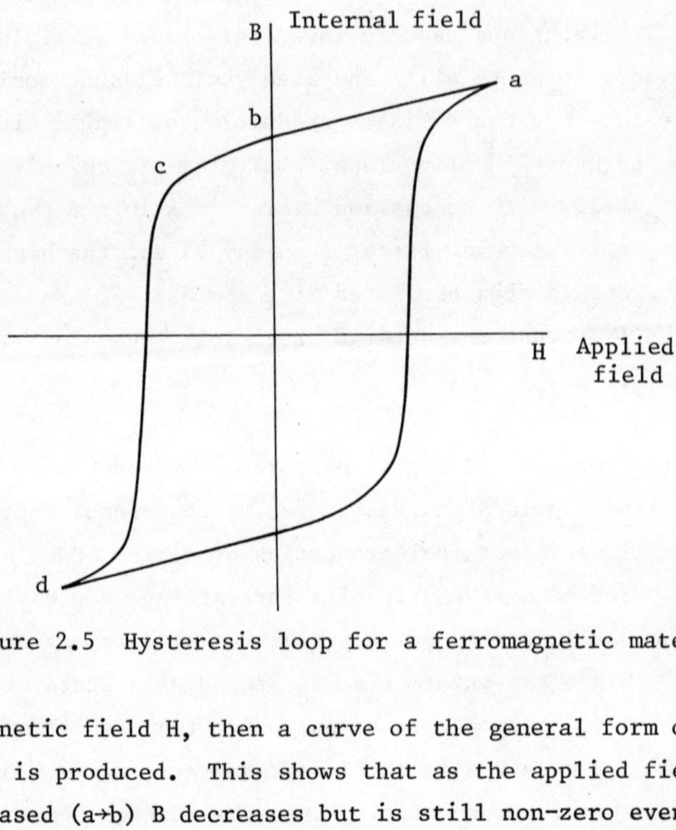

Figure 2.5 Hysteresis loop for a ferromagnetic material.

magnetic field H, then a curve of the general form of figure 2.5 is produced. This shows that as the applied field is decreased ($a \to b$) B decreases but is still non-zero even in the absence of an applied field, H = 0. Application of a field in the opposite direction ($b \to c$) reduces the internal field until at some point the internal field abruptly collapses and reverses its direction ($c \to d$). Removal of the external field at this stage leaves the material magnetised but in the opposite direction. Thus a piece of ferromagnetic material can be left magnetised even in the absence of an external field, and so can be used to store information. We wish to make the different possible states in which the piece of material can be left readily distinguishable, and as we saw in chapter 1 this can be best achieved by making the number of states as small as possible. For material in the form of a thin rod, the only stable states in the absence of an external field are with the internal field aligned along the length of the rod, giving only two possible directions of magnetisation. However, a magnetised rod is rather easily demagnetised, and it is preferable to use a toroid, whose inside diameter is greater than half its outside diameter. Such a toroid can only be left magnetised with the internal field running one way or the other around the circumference and because the flux path is totally closed the toroid is less easily demagnetised.

2.3.2 *Electro-magnetism*. A toroid of ferromagnetic material can be magnetised and left in one of two stable states by applying and removing a suitable external magnetic field; we now consider how to apply this field and how to determine the magnetic state of the toroid.

The external field can be applied by making use of the magnetic field generated around an electric current. This field persists only as long as the current flow and is proportional to the current flowing, so it is trivially simple in principle to apply a magnetic field of the direction and intensity necessary to magnetise the toroid as required. In practice of course one wishes to carry out this magnetisation in the shortest possible time and a circuit capable of generating the required current/time waveform is difficult to construct and is consequently expensive.

Information is written to the toroid by magnetising it in one direction or the other, corresponding in an arbitrary way to a '0' or '1'. To read the information it is necessary to determine the direction of magnetisation, and this is achieved by making use of the EMF generated in a conductor when a magnetic field near the conductor changes. This EMF is given by Lenz's Law, which states that the EMF is equal to the rate of change of flux, i.e. $E = -\frac{dN}{dt}$ where E is the EMF generated around a closed circuit and N is the total flux threading this circuit. We can sense the direction of the magnetisation within the toroid by applying to it a magnetic field; this magnetic field will alter the value of the field in the toroid, and this in turn will generate an EMF in any circuit which threads the toroid. We now describe how these techniques are applied in two commercially important storage systems.

2.3.3 *Ferrite core stores.* A toroid of ferromagnetic material can be used to store one bit of information, represented as a clockwise or anticlockwise magnetisation of the toroid. These toroids are usually referred to as 'cores' and are invariably made of a 'ferrite' such as $FeMnO_4$. These materials are chosen for their high remanence (that is the high value of B when $H = 0$), low electrical conductivity (which minimises eddy current losses in the core) and the fact that they can be arranged to have a very 'square' hysteresis loop as shown in figure 2.6(a). For a material with a square hysteresis loop there is a quite sharply defined value of H at which B will abruptly reverse - this is shown as H_c on figure 2.6(a). If we apply a field of $\sim\frac{1}{2}H_c$ there is very little effect on the value of B, and use is made of this when constructing a core store.

Every core is threaded by two 'drive' wires, (figure 2.6(b)), each of which may carry a current of $\frac{1}{2}I_c$, where I_c is the current necessary to achieve the critical field H_c which can reverse B. Two more wires thread each core. The 'inhibit' wire may carry a current of $\frac{1}{2}I_c$ in a direction which

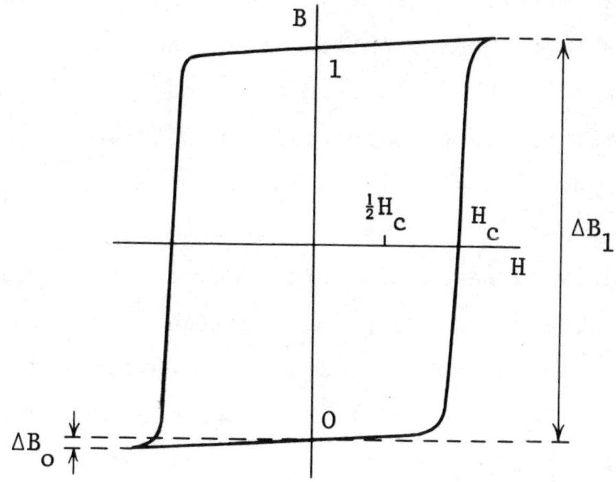

(a) Hysteresis loop for a ferrite core

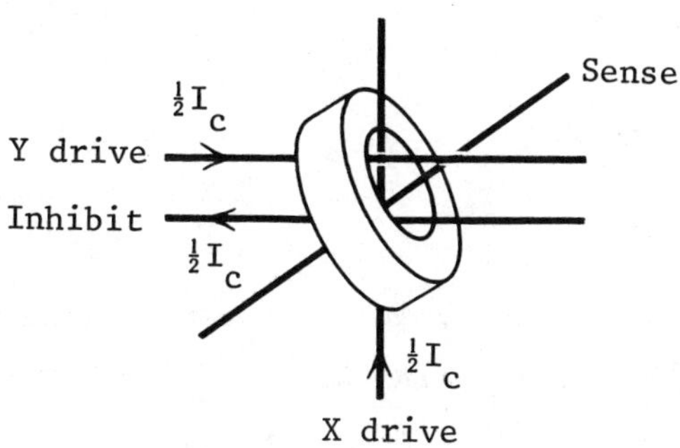

(b) A single core showing writing currents

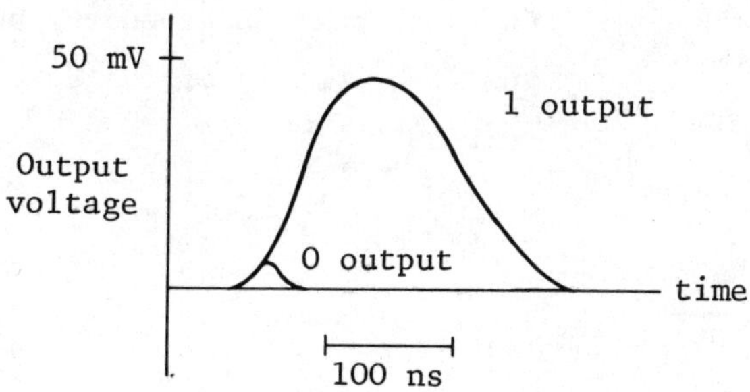

(c) Outputs from a single core

Figure 2.6 A ferrite core.

opposes one of the drive currents. The 'sense' wire is connected to an amplifier which detects the small voltages generated by changes in the field within the core.

Assume that the core is initially magnetised as shown, and that this corresponds to the point labelled '0' on the hysteresis curve in figure 2.6(a). Currents of $\frac{1}{2}I_c$ in both the X- and Y- drive wires would force the core to reverse its magnetisation and move to the point labelled '1' on the figure 2.6(a). However, a current of $-\frac{1}{2}I_c$ (opposing the X drive) in the inhibit wire would prevent this switch-over occurring. Thus we can write 1 or 0 into a core by first forcing it to the 0 state, then passing currents of $\frac{1}{2}I_c$ along the X and Y drive lines, and $-\frac{1}{2}I_c$ along the inhibit lines of those cores where we wish to retain the 0, allowing other cores to switch to the 1 state. We shall see that the act of reading always leaves the core in the 0 state.

Reading is achieved by forcing the core to the 0 state by passing currents of $-\frac{1}{2}I_c$ along the X and Y drive lines, with no current in the inhibit line. When we do this, the core will either already be in the 0 state, in which case B will change only slightly by ΔB_o, or will be in the 1 state and will switch to the 0 state giving a much larger change ΔB_1. Since both these changes occur in approximately the same time Δt we shall observe either a small EMF

$$E_o = \frac{K\Delta B_o}{\Delta t}$$

(K is a constant depending primarily on the geometry of the core and the wires)

or a much larger EMF

$$E_1 = \frac{K\Delta B_1}{\Delta t}$$

and a suitable discriminating amplifier will allow us to determine which of these is actually seen and so decide whether or not a 1 was stored. Notice that after reading the core is always left in the 0 state and so its contents must be re-written if they are required again later.

We have so far discussed a single isolated core. In practice cores are assembled into core-stacks, a complete stack consisting of a number of core-planes; the stack will have one plane for each bit position in the word; each plane will have on it as many bits as there are words in the entire stack.

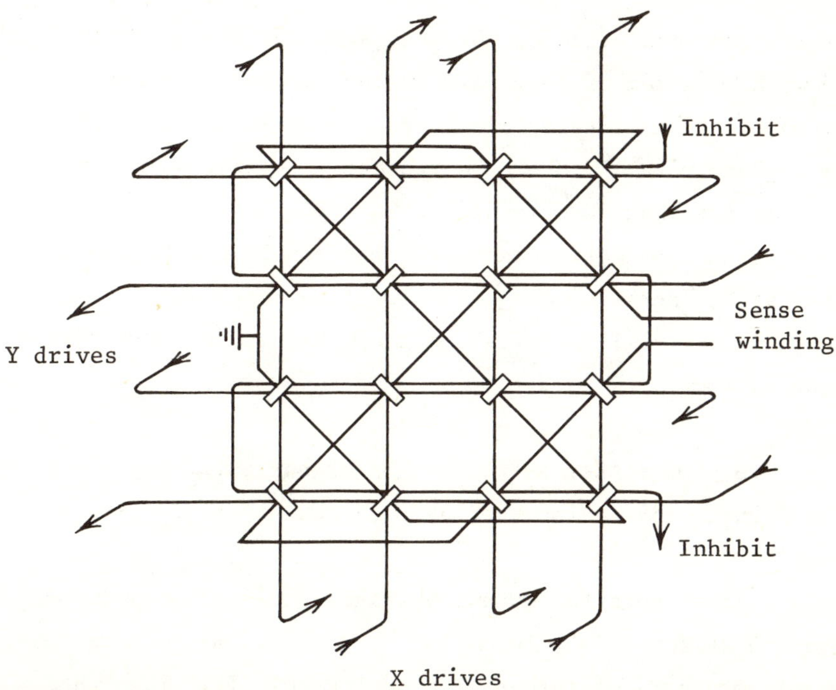

Figure 2.7(a) A 4 x 4 core plane.

Figure 2.7(a) shows a plane, and figure 2.7(b) a stack, for a core store holding 16 words each of six bits. Each plane contains a 4 x 4 array of cores, threaded by X and Y drive wires and by inhibit and sense wires. The currents of $\frac{1}{2}I_c$ in adjacent X drive wires run in opposite directions, and so too do the currents in adjacent Y drive wires. The single inhibit wire threads the entire plane parallel to the Y drive wires. The sense wire also threads the entire plane. It is apparent from the figure that when a single X drive wire and Y drive wire are driven by currents of $\frac{1}{2}I_c$ opposite to those indicated there will be

one core receiving two currents of $\frac{1}{2}I_c$
seven cores receiving one current of $\frac{1}{2}I_c$
eight cores receiving no current at all

and only the one selected core can actually change state. This allows the number of logic and current switching elements required to select a particular core to be reduced from 16 to 8; for a plane with n^2 cores the reduction is from n^2 to 2n. When n^2 is as large as 4096 (= 64^2) this reduction in number offers a significant reduction in cost. The penalty is increased noise in the sense winding. For a plane containing n^2 cores the sense wire will produce a signal which is the sum of the outputs from

one core either switching (1) or not switching (0)
(2n-1) cores disturbed by a current of $\frac{1}{2}I_c$.

For a typical core the output voltages one might expect are about 50 mV for a '1', 10 mV for a '0' and 5 mV for the outputs from a core disturbed by a current of $\frac{1}{2}I_c$. Thus when n is greater than five say the noise produced by the cores disturbed by currents of $\frac{1}{2}I_c$ can exceed the signal produced by a core switching. This noise can be reduced to some extent by winding the cores as shown in figure 2.7 where the sense winding receives noise of approximately equal magnitude but opposing sign from successive cores. In fact the noise is in any case somewhat incoherent and grows approximately like $\sqrt{n}$. A more important technique of noise rejection is to make use of the fact that the 1 output appears much later than the noise, because the core takes a relatively long time to switch, and also that for the noise or a 0 the time integral of the EMF is virtually zero, whereas for a 1 the time integral of the EMF is large. To detect the output from the core a 'gated sense amplifier' is used, which has two inputs, the output from the sense winding and a 'strobe' pulse. The strobe pulse is timed to appear after the noise has died away (say 75 ns after the currents have reached 90% full value), and to extend over the period for which the 1 output is still high (say up to 150 ns after currents have reached 90% of full value). During this period the noise is at a very low level, and in any case is purely oscillatory; the output from a switching core is at a high value (~50 mV) and is unidirectional. This allows the construction of an amplifier with a very high degree of noise rejection which is used to steer the strobe pulse either to the output if a 1 is sensed, or to ground if a 0 is sensed. In practice the output from this amplifier is almost invariably used to control the state of a flip-flop, and the strobe pulse is steered to one or other input of a flip-flop so as to set it to the 1 state or the 0 state.

The complete core stack consists of an assembly of core planes, as shown in figure 2.7(b). Each core plane has associated with it a gated sense amplifier, controlling an inhibit driver. There is a single current source, whose output passes via a row of current switches, controlled by the X-address decoder and along *one* of the X drive wires. The X drive wires in successive planes are linked together in a zig-zag fashion, and at the far end all the X drive wires are returned to a common busbar, and then via a busbar into all the Y drive wires which are again linked in successive planes. The returning current is again controlled by a column of current switches controlled by the Y-address decoder and passes along only one Y drive wire and so back to the current source. During a read operation the address is supplied to the X and Y address se-

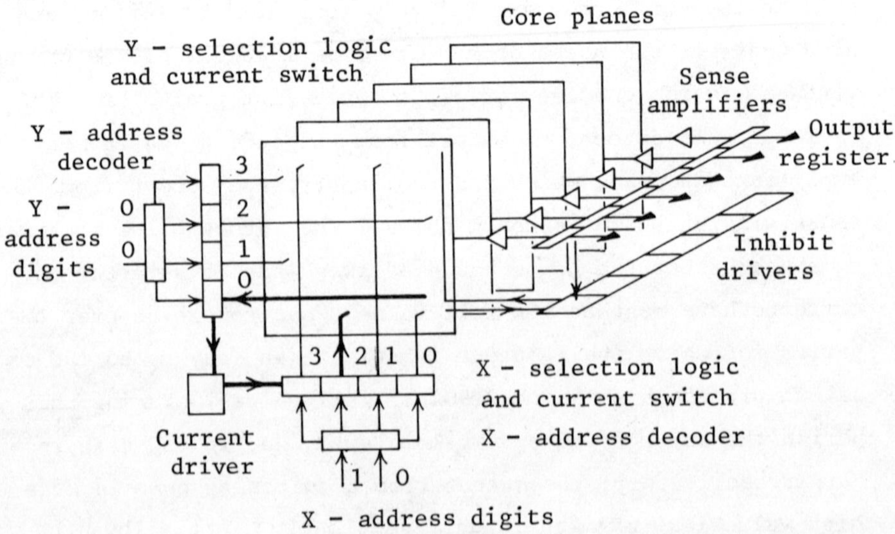

Figure 2.7(b) A core stack containing 16 words each of 6 digits.

lection, and when this has stabilised the current source is stimulated, driving the selected core in each plane into the 0 state - those cores which were in the 1 state will produce a large output which is detected by the gated sense amplifier and staticised in the output register. It is now necessary to rewrite the information. Where a 0 was read, the inhibit current is turned on; this current is equal to $\frac{1}{2}I_C$, and threads every core in those planes from which a 0 was read. When the inhibit current is stabilised, the X and Y drive current is again applied in the opposite sense. Where no inhibit current is present, that is where a 1 was read, a 1 will be rewritten. Where an inhibit current is present there will be *three* currents each of $\frac{1}{2}I_C$ threading the plane; at no point will the net current exceed $\frac{1}{2}I_C$, and so a 0 will remain in the selected core and all others will remain undisturbed. It is essential that the inhibit current should start before, and finish after, the drive currents. If it does not spurious 1's may be rewritten.

If a completely fresh word is to be written into the store, the store executes a read sequence leaving 0's in the selected word, but without supplying a strobe pulse to the sense amplifier. The new word is then written into the output register, and the store executes a write sequence, writing into the store the new contents of the output register.

The arrangement of cores just described is economic in the amount of selection logic associated with the store, but the actual core planes are expensive to construct. Each core in the plane is threaded by four wires, and this calls for considerable refinement of technique. There are also increasing difficulties in constructing very large core stacks, partly mechanical in the assembly of the system and partly electrical in the design and construction of suitable current driving circuits and sense amplifiers.

To overcome these problems, alternative forms of construction are in use, each with its peculiar advantages and disadvantages. One variant is to replace the two drive windings each carrying one half the critical current by a single winding carrying the full current; the inhibit winding and the sense winding are retained. This results in the saving of a wire threading the core and so eases construction, but leads to the number of selection circuits for n^2 words being increased from 2n to n^2, so that overall such a store is more expensive to build. However, when reading from the store there is only one current through the selected word, resulting in a much lower noise level allowing a simpler (i.e. cheaper) sense amplifier. Further since only one word is selected, it can be driven by a current much in excess of the critical current, which allows for a faster access time when reading. Such a system is sometimes referred to as a 2D (two dimensional) arrangement in contrast to the 3D (three dimensional) arrangement shown in figure 2.7.

It is possible to compromise between the simplicity of stack construction and expensive selection logic of the 2D system, and the expensive stack construction and reduced selection logic of the 3D system, by using what is obviously referred to as a '2½D' system. This again uses only three wires per core, with each plane containing the corresponding digits of all the words in the store. Selection is achieved by passing simultaneous currents of $\frac{1}{2}I_c$ through the two windings threading a core during reading, and by controlling the currents $\frac{1}{2}I_c$ appropriately when writing. One current $\frac{1}{2}I_c$ will pass through the entire stack for both reading and writing, but the other current in each plane will be controlled by the inhibit drive for that particular plane to be $\frac{1}{2}I_c$ when reading and conditionally to $\frac{1}{2}I_c$ or 0 to rewrite a 1 or a 0.

Such a system currently seems to offer the best compromise between the various aspects of the design and is in widespread use. However, all core store systems suffer from an inherent difficulty whose resolution is described in the next section.

2.3.4 *Plated wire storage.* In all forms of ferrite core storage information is recorded as the direction of magnetisation of a ferrite toroid. The reading and writing of this information involves the reversal of the direction of magnetisation. This reversal takes place slowly and requires large amounts of energy to accomplish. (By 'slow' here we understand a time measured as a few hundred nano-seconds at most; the 'large' amount of energy is in the order of 10^5 ergs/cc. in a volume of about 5×10^{-6} cc.) Both the slow speed and the high power requirement arise from the way in which the reversal of direction takes place, by the movement of Bloch Walls separating domains of the ferromagnetic material in which the direction of magnetisation is fixed.

An alternative form of storage avoids this total reversal of the direction of magnetisation while retaining much of the basic geometry of the 2D core store; further it achieves this within the context of a production technique which is very highly automated and so ultimately cheaper and less error prone.

This form makes use of the magnetic anisotropy of ferromagnetic materials. If we manufacture a single crystal of ferromagnetic material and plot hysteresis loops (i.e. B - H curves) in which the applied field is aligned along certain directions in relationship to the internal lattice structure of the single crystal, then as we might expect the B - H curves produced depend on this alignment. As a consequence, it is found that if we plot a curve showing the energy stored in the internal magnetic field as a function of the direction of the applied external field there are maxima and minima; the maxima occur when the external field is aligned along a 'hard' direction of magnetisation and the minima along an 'easy' direction of magnetisation. If we magnetise a single crystal, (or a multi-crystal slab in which all the crystallites are aligned parallel) of such a material then when we remove the external field the internal field will always align along an easy direction, as this represents a minimum energy configuration. We can control which particular easy direction will be selected by a relatively small external biassing field which will 'topple' the internal field into the easy direction we wish.

Figure 2.8(a) shows a wire, sections of which have been electroplated with a thin layer of ferromagnetic material, typically an iron nickel alloy so as to form thin walled toroids. During the plating a heavy current is passed along the wire and this ensures that the easy direction of magnetisation runs around the circumference of the toroids. Writing information into the toroids is achieved by passing a current through the word wires (running horizontally in figure 2.8(a)) sufficient to magnetise the plating along the hard direction, while simultaneously passing a small biassing current along the bit wires (i.e. the plated wire running diagonally across figure 2.8(a)). The biassing current produces a small field either clock-wise or anticlock-wise around the circumference of the wire, and is maintained as the current in the word wire is switched off. This biassing field controls the final direction of magnetisation in the toroid when all currents are withdrawn.

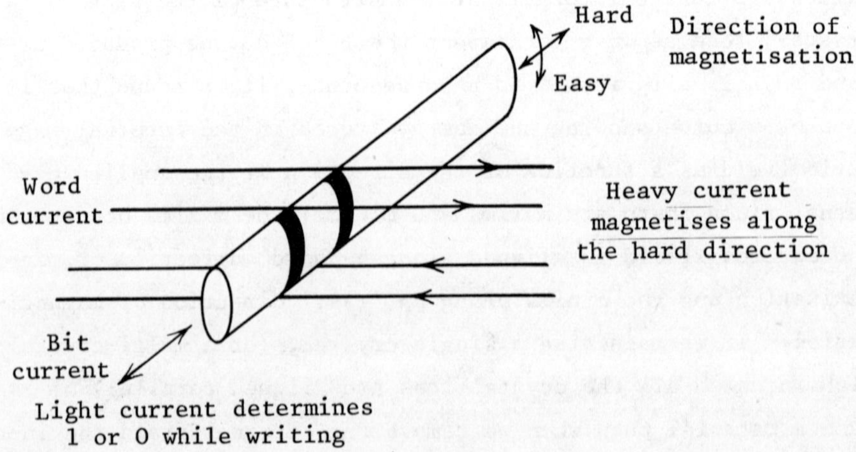

(a) A plated wire element, showing word and bit lines

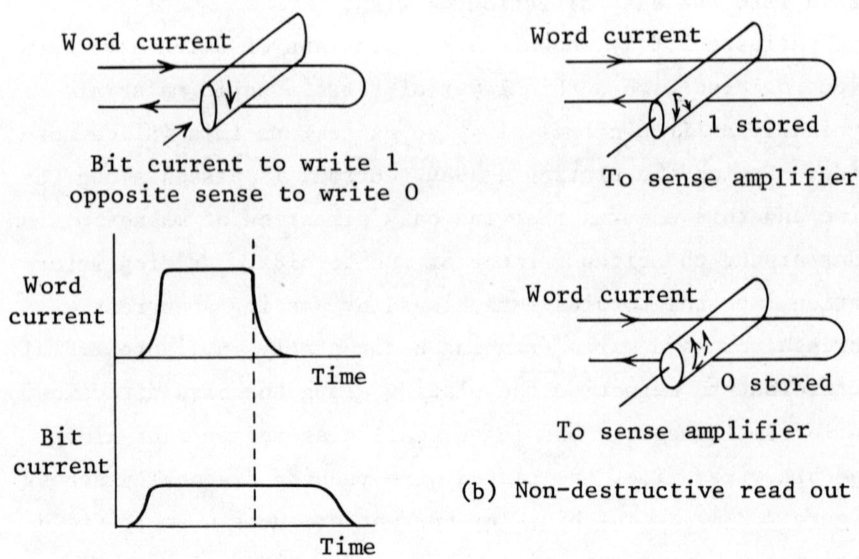

(b) Non-destructive read out

Figure 2.8 The plated wire store.

When reading, a current is again passed through the word wire. This current forces the direction of magnetisation towards the hard axis, and so generates an EMF in the bit wire, which now acts as the sense winding. The sign of the EMF depends on whether a 1 or 0 was stored. The current may be so great as to align completely the direction of magnetisation along the hard axis, in which case the bit must be rewritten, as in a core store. An alternative mode of working uses a 'non-destructive read out' in which the word current does not align the direction of magnetisation along the length of the bit wire, but swings it towards this direction; when the word current is removed the internal field will return to its original direction. Obviously non-destructive read out is faster as no rewrite cycle is involved. However, it requires a more sensitive sense amplifier as the output signal is lower, and a more complicated word current driver to deliver different currents for writing and reading.

Plated wire stores are substantially faster than ferrite core stores of the same capacity. For example commercially available store modules may contain 32,768 words each of 26 bits, have access times of 120 ns and cycle times of 300 ns and are cheaper than core store modules of the same capacity, with 300 ns access time and 750 ns cycle time. It is likely that ferrite core stores will ultimately be displaced by plated wire for higher performance applications, and that core stores will be retained for very large capacity, lower performance applications where they are still very competitive.

Core stores and plated wire stores present very similar interfaces to the devices with which they communicate. They are almost invariably used as 'random access' devices, in which each transfer is to an arbitrary word of the store, and only one word is moved during one transfer. So as to obtain the maximum speed it is usual to operate two or three quite separate interfaces into the store. One is used for addresses, and here the store always functions as the acceptor. There may then be either a single bi-directional interface which carries information to be written to or that has been read from the store, or two uni-directional interfaces, one for incoming, one for outgoing, information. In both cases there will be an interlock between the address interface and the other interfaces to ensure that no attempt is made to transfer into or out of the store on the word interfaces until the address interface signals that the address has been accepted.

2.4 *Moving magnetic surface devices*

The third class of storage devices we consider also uses the hysteresis properties of a ferromagnetic material as the basic physical phenomenon for storing information. However, whereas ferrite core store and plated wire-stores use a static array of magnetisable elements, writing and reading these by steering currents appropriately through the array, and using electromagnetic induction to generate sensing signals, the devices we are about to describe pass currents through fixed assemblies located near to a moving magnetic surface to write the information, and sense the information by detecting the signal produced in a stationary conductor by a moving magnet.

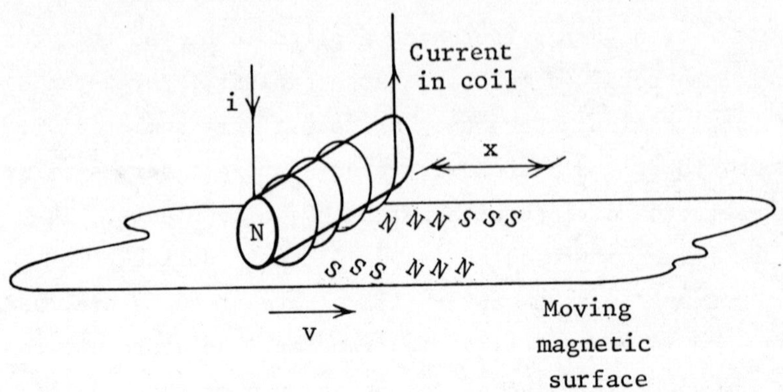

Figure 2.9 Writing on a moving magnetic surface.

2.4.1 *Recording on a moving magnetic surface.* The basis of all these devices is shown in figure 2.9 where a small coil is located immediately above a surface of ferromagnetic material which moves from left to right in the figure. A current in the coil will develop a magnetic field as indicated and this in turn will write a magnetised strip on the surface. Obviously, if v is the velocity of the surface, then at a distance x downstream of the coil the state of the surface will correspond to the current in the coil at time x/v earlier; on the diagram the current in the coil at that time was in the opposite direction. Thus by varying the current in the coil we can arrange to write on to the surface a magnetised strip with the magnetisation at any point running in one of two directions. An alternative geometry lays the coil parallel to the direction of motion rather than at right angles to it - this leaves strips magnetised either parallel or anti-parallel to the direction of movement, rather than pointing left or right across it. In practice the coil would be wound on a high permeability former which has a small gap cut into it, and there will be a number of such coils mounted in a row at right angles to the direction of movement of the surface.

It is important to realise that unlike cores or plated wire, the magnetic surface is not inherently stable in only two configurations. The surface can be magnetised in any direction, and this magnetisation may be partial or saturated depending on the strength of the applied field, i.e. on the current in the writing head. It is also important to consider the signal produced in the reading head when the surface passes by. The reading head is again a coil held close to the surface, wound on a high permeability former (in many systems the same head is used for both purposes). As the surface passes the head, any *change* in magnetisation of the surface will induce an EMF. The magnetic state of the surface at x, H_x, is given by $H_x = k_1 H_t$ (vt) where x = vt and H_t is the field in the writing head at time t and $H_t = k_2 I_t$. It follows that the output from the reading head

$$E_t = k_3 \frac{dH_x}{dt} = k_3 k_2 \frac{d}{dt} \cdot H_t = k_3 k_2 k_1 \frac{dI_t}{dt}$$

and is thus approximately the time derivative of the current waveform in the writing head. The approximations arise primarily from the fact that the gaps in the writing head and the reading head are not infinitely narrow.

2.4.2 *Recording techniques*. Consider now the most straightforward recording technique which writes a 1 on the surface by applying to the head a current sufficiently strong to saturate the magnetisation, and a 0 by switching off the writing current. For obvious reasons this is known as a 'return-to-zero' representation. Figure 2.10(a) shows the current in the writing head as a function of time; the magnetic state of the surface as a function of position; and the output from the reading head as a function of time when writing the pattern 1 0 1 1 0 0 with this representation. This technique suffers from the fact that when no current flows in the writing head it is possible for information already recorded on the surface to remain unaltered, and then to be spuriously read on a subsequent occasion. For this reason the 'non-return-to-zero' method shown in figure 2.10(b) is used. This represents 1 by saturation in one direction and 0 by saturation in the other, thus completely overwriting any earlier information on the surface. The output waveform is still the same shape as for the return to zero representation (although the actual outputs will be about twice as great). For this technique recovery of the original pattern is achieved by the use of an extra clock track, arranged as shown in figure 2.10(b). The clock track produces outputs in its read head at a rate corresponding to

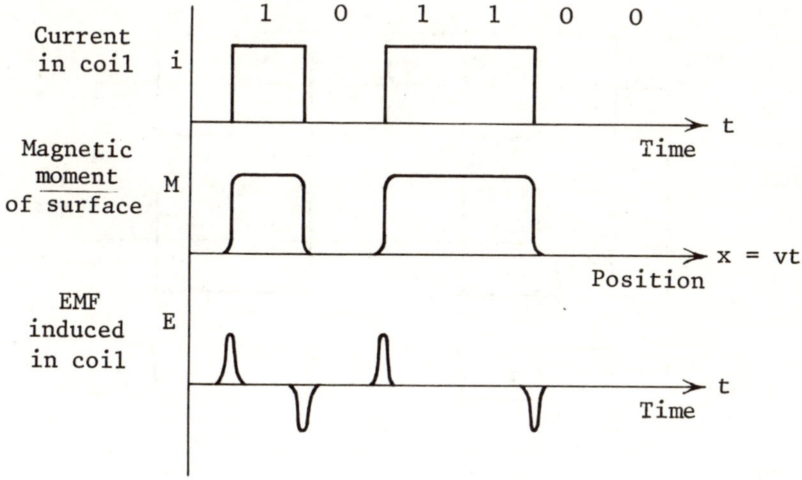

(a) Return-to-zero recording

Figure 2.10 Writing and reading on a magnetic surface.

the recording rate. Where there is an output of *either sign* on the head reading the recorded information, then the value of the recorded digit has changed from its previous value.

An alternative form of non-return-to-zero recording uses a system in which an output of either sign from the head reading the recorded information at the clock time indicates a 1, while no output indicates a 0. The corresponding waveforms are indicated in figure 2.10(c). This technique is sometimes referred to as NRZI recording. Both it and normal NRZ recording suffer from a very serious defect, in that they may yield long regions of the surface in which no signals appear at the reading head (i.e. all 1's or all 0's in NRZ or all 0's in NRZI) or regions in which signals appear at a frequency corresponding to the maximum recording rate (alternate 1010.. in NRZ or all 1's in NRZI). Thus the reading head and its associated amplifier must cope with a very wide frequency range from nearly DC up to a few hundred KHz. To over-

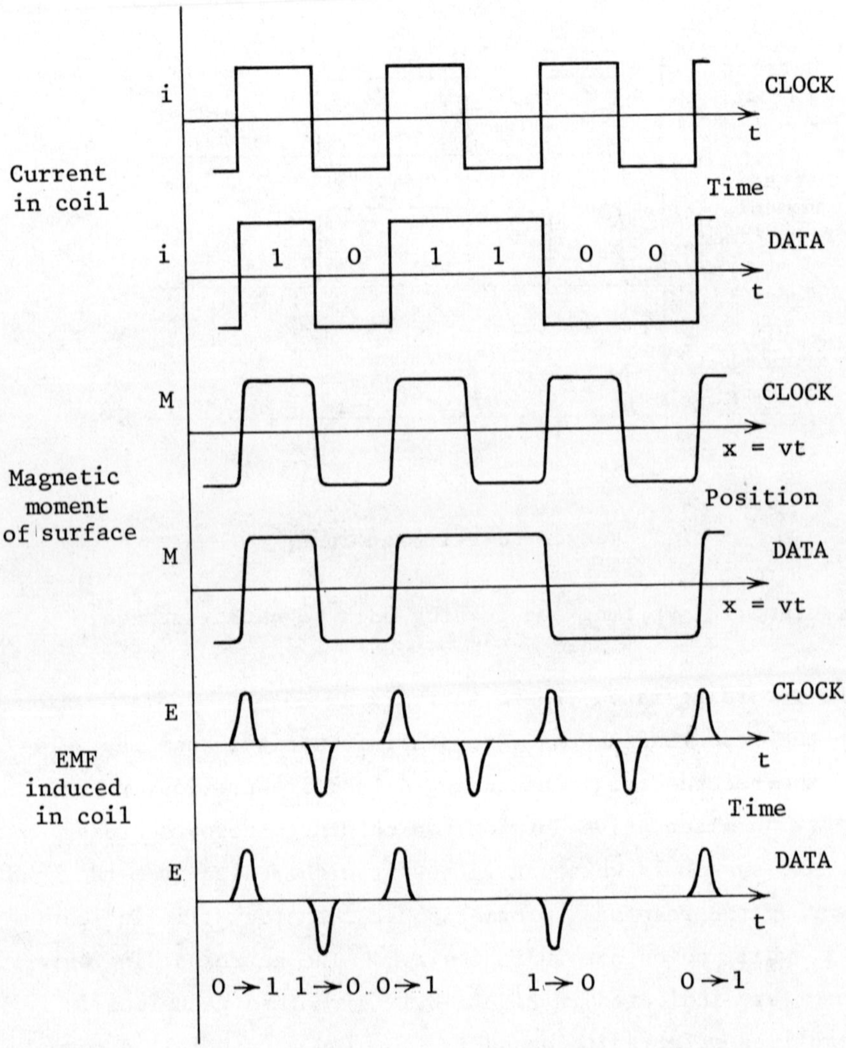

(b) Non-return-to-zero recording with a clock signal

Figure 2.10 Writing and reading on a magnetic surface.

come this an alternative NRZ technique known as 'phase encoding'* is used in very high performance systems.

* Notice that in our terms of chapter 1 we would describe this as 'phase representation'.

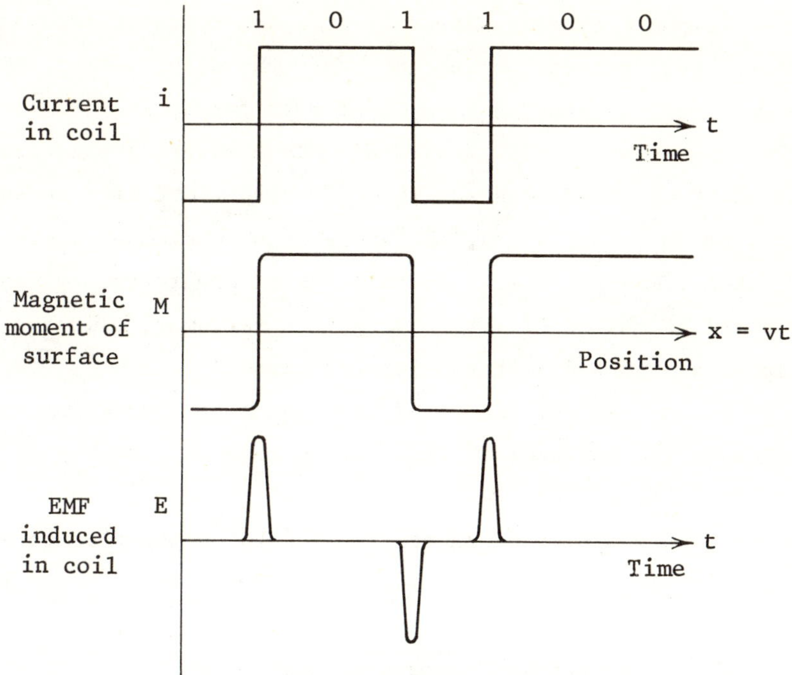

(c) NRZI recording

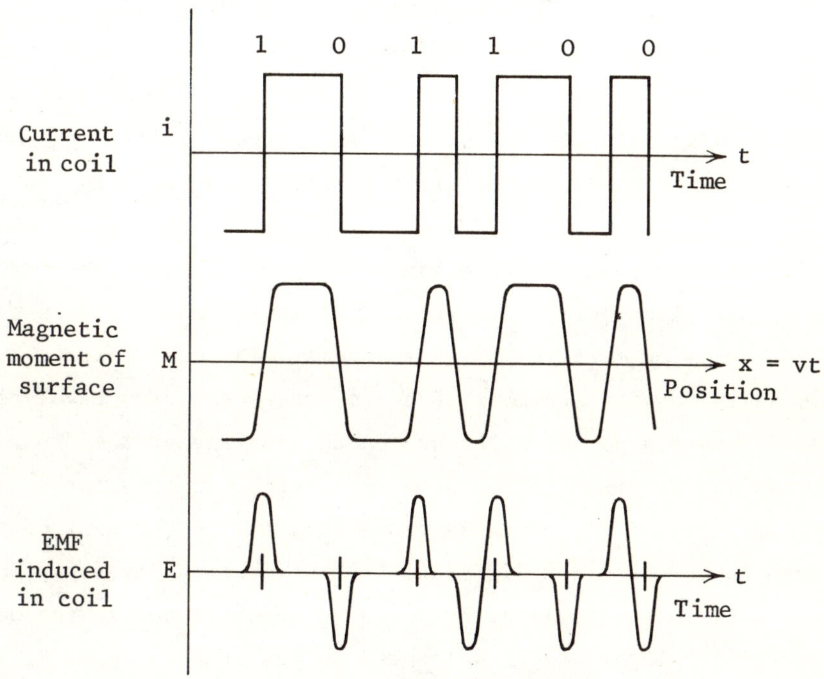

(d) Phase encoding

Figure 2.10 Writing and reading on a magnetic surface.

In phase encoding digits 1 or 0 are represented by a current reversal in the writing head, the direction of this reversal being opposite for a 1 to that for a 0. The waveforms are shown in figure 2.10(d). Each reversal produces an output at the reading head, which is coincident with an output from the clock track, and whose sign determines whether a 1 or a 0 was recorded. In this system the frequency range required of the amplifier is very much narrower, allowing a simpler design and better noise rejection.

We have so far discussed techniques for recording information on the surface; we turn now to consider how the surface itself can be moved. We shall see that the different techniques give a very wide range of black box properties to what are basically rather similar devices. Three methods are in common use to move the surface:

(1) the surface forms a revolving *drum*

(2) the surface forms a revolving *disc*

(3) the surface is a *tape* which is spooled past the heads.

The arrangements are illustrated in figures 2.11(a), (b) and (c) and in more detail in figures 2.12, 2.13 and 2.14.

2.4.3 *Magnetic drums.* The magnetic drum is one of the earliest forms of large scale storage, and indeed formed the main storage device on early computing systems. The drum (figure 2.12) is equipped with a number of heads and as the drum revolves each head sweeps out a 'track' on the surface of the drum. The heads may be fixed, or on some very large capacity rather slow drums, some of the heads may move parallel to the axis of the drum so as to select different tracks (drums of this type have virtually been displaced by discs as we shall see in the next section). Information is located on the drum in terms of its track, selected either by switching among the fixed heads or by moving an adjustable head, and then by selecting a particular

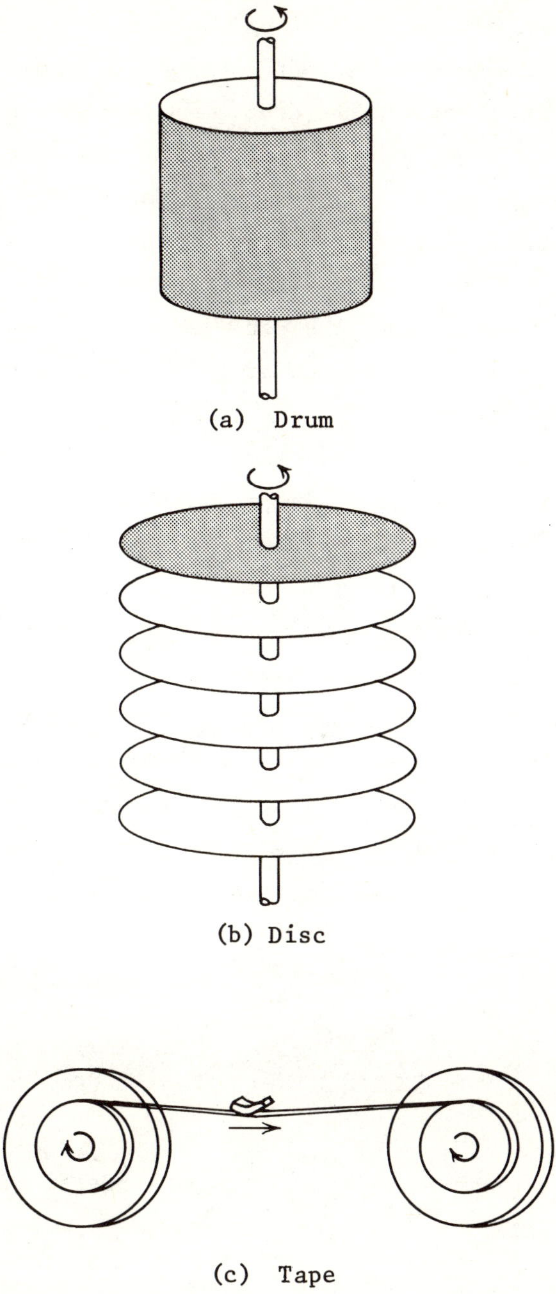

Figure 2.11 Three basic methods of arranging a moving magnetic surface.

part of the track. This is achieved either by writing 'header blocks' in front of each 'block' of characters in each track and reading these from the selected track, or by writing completely separate tracks on the drum which contain only information about the block number, i.e. angular position of the drum. The second method is invariably used on high performance drums, which will have several tracks giving angular position and clocking signals, this frees space that would otherwise be occupied under the data heads.

The access time to a block of information is dominated by the time for the required block to appear under the read/write heads (the time for head selection will be very small, a few microseconds) and this time is usually referred to as the 'latency' of the drum. Assuming that blocks are requested at random, when a block is requested it will be necessary to wait any time up to a full revolution time of the drum for the block to appear, and the latency time is usually quoted as being half the revolution time. Since revolution times are typically of the order of 20 ms (3000 rpm) it is in principle possible to manage a queue of transfers in such a way that requests are drawn from the queue so as to make the average waiting time less than half the revolution time. Once the block

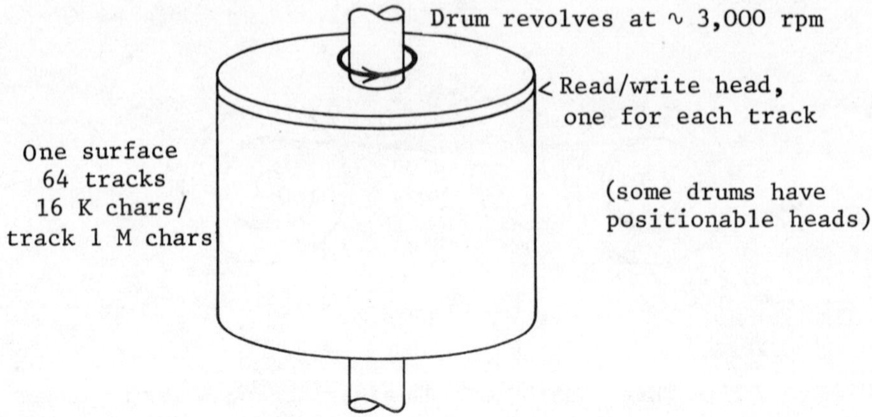

Figure 2.12 Magnetic drum.

of information is located drums are capable of processing the actual transfer at very high data rates, up to several hundred thousand characters per second per head. Even higher rates can be achieved by running a number of heads simultaneously, and such a drum may approach the effective speed of a core store, during the transfer. The overall average rate for a drum will be much lower, due to the latency associated with each transfer.

Performance figures for a typical high speed drum are quoted in table 2.1.

2.4.4 *Magnetic disc.* A drum stores information only on the outer surface of a cylindrical drum; thus the actual packing density of information in terms of numbers of bits stored per cubic metre is rather poor. Looked at the other way on, the equipment needed to store a very large volume of information is very bulky and expensive. The magnetic disc attempts to overcome these defects. Information is recorded on the flat surfaces of revolving discs, usually arranged as a 'stack' of discs mounted on a common spindle. The read/write heads again sweep out a circular track as the disc revolves. It is usual to provide a small number of heads for each disc and to position them radially so as to select tracks, although there are units with one head for every track (head-per-track) or at the other extreme units with only one head which serves every track

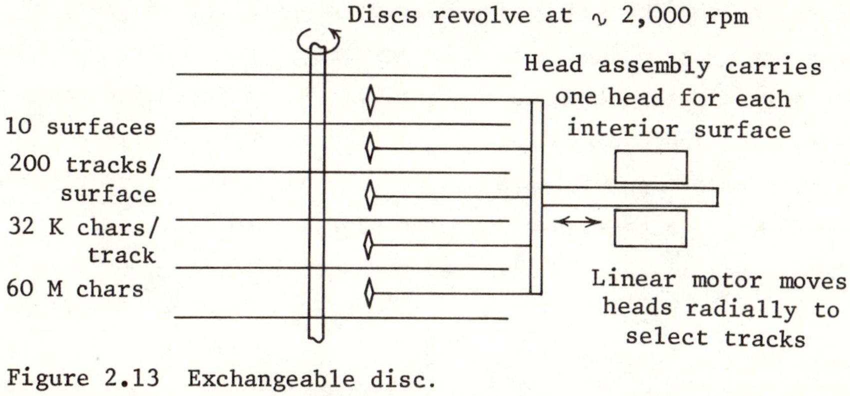

Figure 2.13 Exchangeable disc.

on every disc. Those discs with a head for each track are in some respects much like drums, although their packing density along each track and their rate of rotation both tend to be smaller than for drums and as a consequence their transfer rates are lower; they compensate by their larger capacity and/or cheaper price.

Discs with positionable heads have access times which are made up of two major elements *seek time* and *latency*. The latency is exactly equivalent to that on a drum, although the rather lower rate of rotation leads to a correspondingly larger latency. The seek time is the time needed to move the heads from their present track to the required track. The seek time typically has a minimum value of say 20 ms and a maximum value of 100 ms, depending on the number of tracks between the initial and final positions. The rather long time needed for even a small movement is accounted for by the need to allow mechanical oscillations to die away and by the need to check that the heads have in fact moved to the selected track rather than to some other track, and to ensure that the head is located directly above that track. Checking is achieved by recording in the 'header' of each block of information the track number and block number; the final positioning may be achieved either by mechanical location, or by moving the head under servo control so as to ensure the maximum output from the reading head.

When using a moving magnetic surface the maximum packing density along the track is achieved by operating the read/write heads as near to the surface as possible. For tapes, which are flexible, it is common to run the head in contact with the surface. The subsequent wear on the head is considerable and on heavily used magnetic tape systems the heads require a rigorous schedule of inspection and replacement. With discs and drums the surface is not flexible and mechanical limitations make it impossible to achieve the necessary head clearance by rigidly mounting the heads and the heads are arranged to 'fly'. As the surface revolves a layer of air is dragged round and the head is designed as an aerofoil which flies in this layer of air, and is urged towards the disc by pressure on a piston supporting the head. If the head gap is too great the resultant lift on the aerofoil is less than the thrust from the piston; if it is too small the aerodynamic force is greater than that from the piston, and the head will come to a dynamic equilibrium at the correct spacing, typically .003 mm.

2.4.5 *Magnetic tape*. Magnetic tape systems use a surface in the form of a flexible plastic tape coated on one side with magnetisable material. Typically tape is 12 mm wide, and a full reel 750 m in length; the tape has a clock channel and six or eight data channels written across its width (on many tape systems there are one or more extra channels for error control). Thus each clock pulse allows a single character (six bits) or byte (eight bits) to transfer to or from the tape. Tape speeds are nominally 2 metre/sec., and the nominal packing density along each track of the tape 50 bits/mm, giving an instantaneous transfer rate in the region of 100 K chars/sec.

Information on tapes is recorded in blocks; whereas on discs or drums the blocks are of a fixed size (usually a simple submultiple of the amount of information that can be written in a single revolution) on magnetic tape the size of the block is usually not fixed in advance. In the inactive state the tape is at rest, and before a block of information is transferred the tape must be accelerated from rest up to its nominal operating speed and after the transfer must be again brought to rest. No useful information can be written on the tape during this acceleration or retardation, indeed any signals in this part of the tape will yield spurious information on reading. Thus the inter-block gaps, within which the tape accelerates and retards, reduce the total amount of information

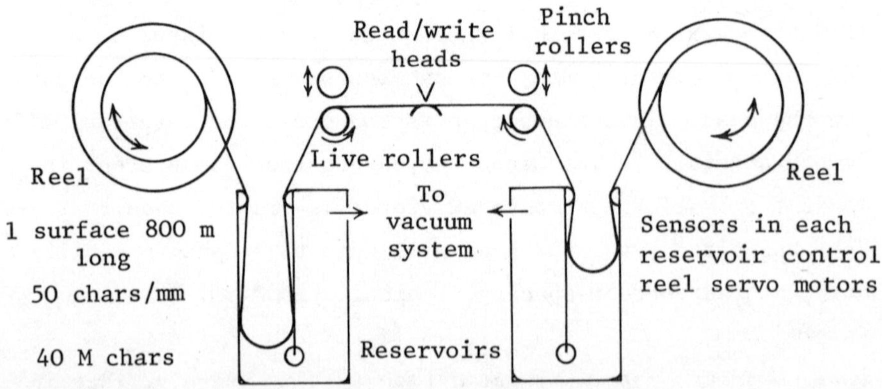

Figure 2.14 Magnetic tape.

that can be stored on the tape. This reduction is obviously minimised by accelerating and retarding the tape as fiercely as possible; this has another benefit of minimising the time that elapses before a transfer to the tape can be started. On a high performance deck the time from rest to full speed may be as low as 2 ms, an acceleration of 1000 m sec^{-2} or 100 g. Since a full reel of tape can weigh about 2 Kg any attempt to accelerate the whole reel by tension in the tape leads to quite impossible engineering requirements. These accelerations are achieved by dynamically isolating the rather short length of tape currently involved in transfers from the two heavy take-up reels on which the tape is stored. The mechanical system which accelerates the tape currently involved in the transfers consists of a pair of live capstans continuously revolving in opposite directions, and pinch rollers which trap the tape against the capstans; there is also a brake, consisting of a pair of opposed pads (figure 2.14). The capstan drives and brakes are arranged as near as possible to the read/write heads, and draw tape from a reservoir at one side and deliver it to a second reservoir. The heavy reels drive tape to and from the reservoirs, controlled by some form of servo sensing mechanism which maintains the amount of tape in the reservoir between fixed limits.

Because of variations in tape speeds the blocks written to a tape are of variable length, even when they contain the same number of characters. It is thus not always possible to rewrite any particular block, and in practice magnetic tapes are almost invariably written block by block from the start of the tape. When writing to the tape, the tape is accelerated up to speed by operating the appropriate pinch roller, during which time a suitable erase current is passed through the write head so as to obliterate any information already on the tape. Once the tape is up to speed a preamble which indicates the start of a block is written. The block of characters is transferred, and then the tape braked to rest, again with the erase current in the write head, so as to obliterate any residual signals on the tape. (On some very high performance decks a separate head erases all information on the tape as it approaches the read/write head when writing.) When reading from the tape, the tape is accelerated and as soon as clock signals start to appear, information is read at each clock time from the read heads on the data tracks; the preamble is used to check that the system is performing correctly and then the information originally written is transferred from the tape. Note that there is no addressing information written by the system and that information must be identified either from its context on the tape, or by including within the block the identity of that block. This simplifies the interface to the tape system which no longer has the addressing inputs found in drums or discs, but of course makes programming the use of magnetic tapes more complex.

2.5 *Summary*

We have examined three types of storage device, and seen how the different physical phenomena on which they are based give rise to a very wide range of black box properties. These are summarised in table 2.1 which shows typical values for a range of properties for devices currently available. In point of fact there is a much wider spread in the values of the various properties than the table would suggest, and figure 2.15 attempts to bring out this spread of values. Figure 2.15(a) shows the range of capacities and costs per bit associated with currently available devices; two points emerge. The first is the enormous spread of storage capacity, from 1 bit up to 10^{10} bits or even higher, and of prices per bit stored, from a few pounds for a single bit of storage on a high performance flip-flop down to small fractions of a millipenny for information on disc or magnetic tape. The second point to note is the almost total overlap as between LSI flip-flops, ferrite core and plated wire, to an extent that can hardly be resolved on the scales of figure 2.15(a). It is almost inevitable that in time the balance will tip in favour of LSI flip-flop storage for stores holding a few megabits except where special con-

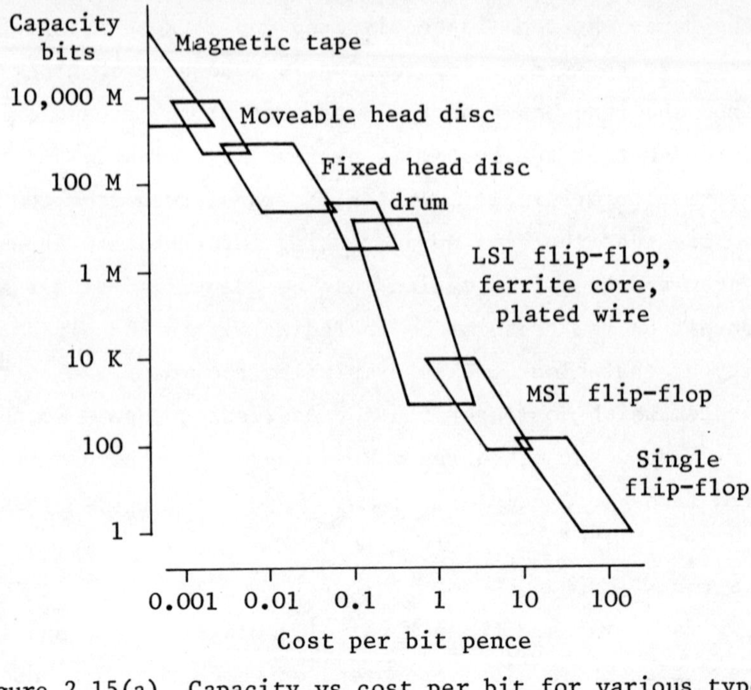

Figure 2.15(a) Capacity vs cost per bit for various types of storage device.

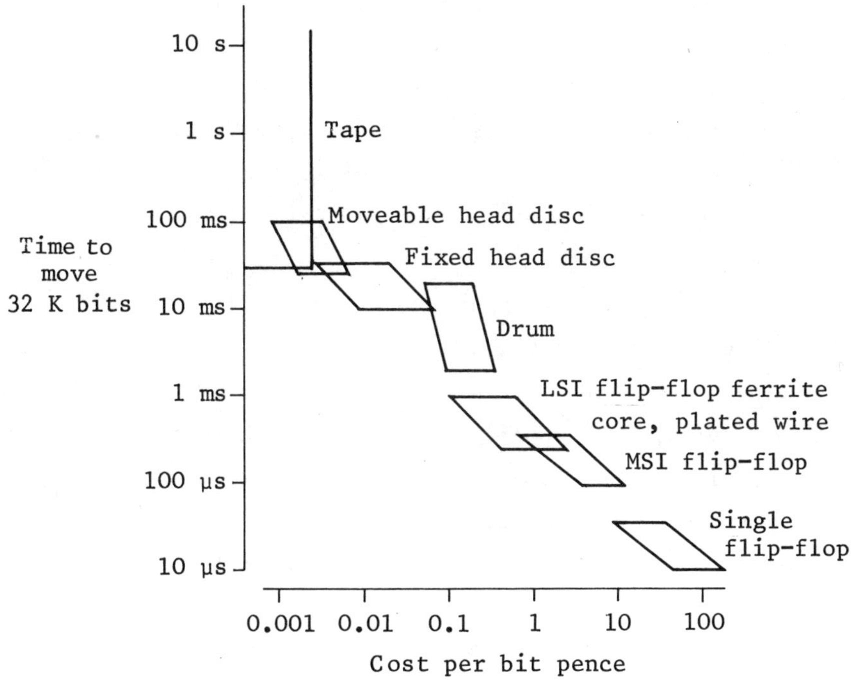

Figure 2.15(b) Speed vs cost per bit for various types of storage device.

siderations apply.

Figure 2.15(b) compares 'speeds' of various storage devices with per bit costs. The 'speed' quoted is the time to move 32 K bits, including access time to the relevant block, and allowing for different forms of organisation, as a 4 K byte block on a magnetic surface store, and as 1 K words on ferrite core, plated wire or flip-flop store. Again there is a very wide range of values, and almost perfect overlap between LSI flip-flops, ferrite core and plated wire.

Figure 2.15 illustrates very clearly that high performance in terms of speed implies smaller total storage capacity and that to a large extent the ability to acquire both high speed and large capacity by simply paying more money is restricted by engineering considerations.

2.6 *Bibliography*

Digital Electronics, by F. Dokter and J. Steinhauer, Macmillan 1973.

Gives a non-mathematical account of many aspects of the design and construction of digital circuits. This book also contains material which is related to the subject matter of chapter 6.

Circuit Design of Digital Computers, by Joseph K. Hawkins, Wiley and Sons 1968.

Gives very detailed mathematical treatments of transistor circuits, with applications to digital circuitry. There is also a detailed account of ferrite core storage and magnetic surface recording.

Digital Storage Systems, by W. Renwick and A.J. Cole, Chapman and Hall 1971.

Describes a wide variety of storage systems in an informal way, and includes a number of devices not treated in chapter 2 which have applications in specialised areas.

Semi-Conductor Memories, by Jerry Eimbinder, Wiley-Interscience, 1971.

Contains a number of separate articles covering aspects of the construction and application of semi-conductor memories. The treatment is for the most part non-mathematical, and assumes a rather high level of knowledge of circuit technology. The article by Robert Norman entitled 'Semiconductor Memories: Make or Buy' is well worth reading as a summary of the many factors influencing a system designer.

2.7 *Examples*

(1) What is meant by the following terms used in connection with storage devices?

(a) access time (c) random access

(b) transfer rate (d) serial access.

Why are computers commonly equipped with a variety of storage devices having widely differing performance in terms of the above characteristics? Illustrate your answer by indicating typical applications of a selection of storage devices.
(University of Leeds, 1971)

(2) What hardware devices would be used to store:

(a) a 3 bit number indicating which of eight programmes is currently running in a multi-programming machine;

(b) a group of 64 numbers of 24 bits each, to be used as modifier registers,

(c) a copy of the text of a programme, amounting to fifteen thousand words in all?

Give reasons for the choice in each case.
(University of Leeds, 1968)

(3) What are the principal requirements for a device which will store one binary digit? Describe how the requirements are satisfied by:

(i) an R-S flip-flop

(ii) a ferrite core

(iii) an element of the surface of magnetic tape.

Give a brief indication of the way in which these three storage media are utilised in a modern computing system.
(University of Leeds, 1974)

(4) Describe in detail one form of coincident current core store. Discuss the factors which limit the speed of this form of storage, and outline techniques which give higher performance.
(University of Leeds, 1974)

(5) Draw a schematic representation of a $2\frac{1}{2}$D core memory of 16 words, each of 3 bits. Show how the contents of any particular word are fetched and restored in a single memory cycle, and state why this structure is superior to the more obvious word-organised memory.
(University of St Andrews, 1973)

(6) The material presented in table 2.1 which was compiled in 1974 dates very rapidly. Reconstruct its contents, estimate the range of performance and prices for present day devices, and re-draw figure 2.15.

3 · Input/output devices

3.1 *Character sets*

In this chapter we study devices which transform the physical representation of a character, without changing the character itself. In the previous chapter on storage devices a character was a group of say six binary digits, and no mention was made of the origin of these digits. In this chapter the word character acquires a second meaning, as 'a graphic symbol standing for a sound, syllable or notion used in writing or printing' (the definition in the Shorter Oxford English Dictionary). The purpose of an input or output device is to transform either from a graphic symbol to an internal representation within the digital system as a group of binary digits (input) or to carry out the converse transformation (output). We can conveniently classify devices into three main groups:

(1) those in which the character remains encoded as a group of binary digits and only the physical representation of 0 or 1 changes

(2) those which transform from a graphic symbol to binary digits (or vice versa)

(3) those in which a quantity is measured and the measure presented as an encoded representation of a number.

Obviously all input/output devices have black box properties which are common to all three of these major groupings; equally obviously there will be some properties which are different in kind for the three groups. The properties which are common to all groups are basically concerned with speeds of operations across the interface between the input or output device and the rest of the system: as for storage devices these will be a measure of the time for an action to start (i.e. an access time) and a measure of the transfer rate at which characters pass across the interface once the access time has elapsed. Obviously there is no question of the capacity of an input or output device, which can supply or absorb an unlimited number of characters if sufficient time is allowed. In fact, most of the input/output devices we shall discuss are slower by several orders of magnitude than the storage devices of chapter 2 and we shall see later that this has important consequences.

The next three sections give short descriptions of currently available input-output devices. Before doing so we examine in slightly more detail the concept of a 'character'. In computing terms 'character' is used to refer to the graphic symbol which is used to represent the character externally in terms of ink on paper or as bright lines on the face of a visual display, and to the internal representation as a group of binary digits. For obvious reasons one generally uses a character set which includes

letters of the alphabet
decimal digits
a variety of punctuation marks
page control characters.

The necessity for the first three groups is obvious; these are the marks one actually makes on paper when writing or printing. Equally important are the characters in the last group which define not what is printed but where. Their presence is required by the fact that the characters will pass across the interface as a single stream and if we are to control the layout of the printed page we must give instructions when to start a new line or new page, how far to move across for column headings and so on.

We have also supposed the existence of *an* alphabet, rather than *many* alphabets each being a different graphic representation of the same basic alphabet. In practice even a very simple device such as a typewriter is equipped with two alphabets corresponding to upper and lower case letters. A quite modest jobbing printer might expect to have twenty different alphabets (i.e. founts) available. The total number of characters to be represented will thus be quite large; upper and lower case letters, digits and an adequate collection of punctuation marks will give eighty or more characters. A dilemma immediately arises, as to whether we represent each graphic character as a single group of binary digits, or reserve a small number of groups of binary digits as 'case definition' characters which define within which of several sets of graphic characters a particular group of binary digits is to be interpreted. There are arguments, none particularly overwhelming, in favour of either choice. The case-free method of working is simple to use, but leads either to a limited character set or to an unacceptably large number of bits per character; the method of using case definition characters allows very large character sets, but may be difficult to work with on occasions. At present both methods are in use, often simultaneously on the same system, a compromise which is undoubtedly much worse than exclusive acceptance of one or the other technique!

However, there is an increasing move towards acceptance of the A.S.C.I.I. (American Standard Code for Information Interchange) character set for many purposes. This is a seven bit code which offers encodings of upper and lower case letters, decimal digits, the more common punctuation marks, commonly used characters such as %, *, and a number of characters reserved for the control of equipment involved in data transmission. Although like all other standards, the A.S.C.I.I. system is a compromise, it has the advantage of wide acceptance and is likely to remain in use for some long time. The A.S.C.I.I. character set is summarised in figure 3.1.

Numeric \ Zone	0(000)		1(001)		2(010)	
0000	TC_o	(NULL)	TC	Data Link Escape	space	
0001	TC_1	Start of Heading	DC_1	Device Control	!	(exclamation)
0010	TC_2	Start of Text	DC_2		"	(quotes)
0011	TC_3	End of Text	DC_3		#	(number)
0100	TC_4	End of Transmission	DC_4	(STOP)	$	(dollar)
0101	TC_5	Enquiry	TC_8	Negative Acknowledge	%	(per cent)
0110	TC_6	Acknowledge	TC_9	Synchronous Idle	&	(ampersand)
0111	BEL	BELL, alarm	TC_{10}	End of Transmission Block	'	(apostrophe)
1000	FE_o	Backspace	CNCL	Cancel	(	(l.pareth.)
1001	FE_1	Horizontal Tabulation	EM	End of Medium	)	(r.pareth.)
1010	FE_2	New Line	SB	Substitute	*	(asterisk)
1011	FE_3	Line Feed	ESC	Escape (Start new line)	+	(plus)
1100	FE_4	Form Feed	IS_4	File Separator	,	(comma)
1101	FE_5	Carriage Return	IS_3	Group Separator	-	(hyphen/minus)
1110	SO	Shift Out	IS_2	Record Separator	.	(period)
1111	SI	Shift In	IS_1	Unit Separator	/	(solidus)

3(011)	4(100)	5(101)	6(110)	7(111)	Zone / Numeric
0	@ (at)	P	_ (underline)	p	0000
1	A	Q	a	q	0001
2	B	R	b	r	0010
3	C	S	c	s	0011
4	D	T	d	t	0100
5	E	U	e	u	0101
6	F	V	f	v	0110
7	G	W	g	w	0111
8	H	X	h	x	1000
9	I	Y	i	y	1001
: (colon)	J	Z	j	z	1010
; (semi colon)	K	[(l.h. brkt)	k	N_1 } Reserved for National Characters	1011
< (less than)	L	£ (pound)	l	N_2	1100
= (equals)	M	] (r.h. brkt)	m	N_3	1101
> (greater than)	N	↑	n	N_4	1110
? (question)	O	_ (underline)	o	\\\\ (delete)	1111

Figure 3.1

3.2 *Encoded character devices*

The first group of devices is that in which the graphic characters have already been converted to digital form (for input) or are produced in digital form which is subsequently printed (for output). Two basic techniques exist for the external representation of the binary digits, holes punched in *paper tape*, or holes punched in *cards*. Punched paper tape commonly uses a flexible paper ribbon about 20 mm wide and up to 250 m in length; the holes, about 2 mm in diameter, are punched at intervals across the width of the tape, and a smaller hole, the sprocket hole about 1 mm in diameter performs the function of the clock track on a magnetic tape. Paper tape comes in various widths, which determine how many rows of holes can be present across the tape, any number between five and eight having been used from time to time. The spacing between successive rows is typically about 2.5 mm.

Punched cards are made of a much more nearly rigid card, about 80 mm by 180 mm; the holes are rectangular 3 mm by 1.5 mm with twelve *rows* for holes each row containing eighty *columns*. (Cards in other sizes and formats are available, but the 80 × 12 card described constitutes the great majority of cards in use.) On the card, each column (containing 12 hole-positions) represents a single character, usually in an extremely redundant form so that of the 2^{12} possible combinations very few (about 50 or so) will actually represent characters. It is obviously sensible to use one card to represent one line of characters; less obviously this again leads to redundancy for now each line is deemed to hold eighty characters, regardless of the position along the line of the rightmost printing character.

The argument as between punched paper tape and punched cards as an input medium is possibly even more bitter than that between case-free and case-defined encodings. In general paper tape equipment offers a wider character set and the net effective transfer rate of paper tape is probably higher than that of cards; however, paper tape is difficult to edit and handle. Punched cards are easy to edit (one simply removes the incorrect card and inserts a new one) and to handle; when dropped they become shuffled! It is again common practice to offer both cards and tape simultaneously on the same system. Provided that the origin of the characters is not visible to the user of the system this is a very definite advantage.

3.2.1 *Punched tape and punched card input.* The basic mechanism of a reader for punched paper tape is illustrated in figure 3.2. As for magnetic tape systems, extremely short start/stop times are required, in the order of one or two milliseconds, and it is common to have some form of motorised spooling when large reels of tape are handled. The mechanism comprises a live roller and a pinch roller to move the tape, and a brake mechanism to stop it. The reading station is between the drive and brake. An optical system illuminates a single row of the tape (corresponding to a single character), and shines through the holes onto a row of photosensitive devices containing a detector for each possible hole plus one for the sprocket hole. The character sensed by the detectors is read via an interface when the sprocket hole is sensed. The output from the sprocket

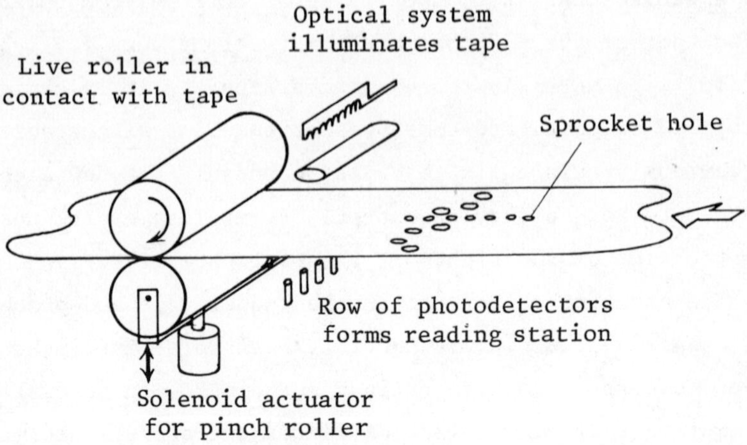

Figure 3.2 Punched paper tape reader.

hole serves as the S signal on the interface, and the outputs from the other detectors will drive the D_i lines.

A punched card reader is essentially rather similar. However, the requirements for very rapid start/stop movements of cards are less stringent, and there is no need for any spooling mechanism for the complete deck, as individual cards pass separately through the reading station. Cards are picked up one by one and passed along a card track, commonly by a system of live rollers. There are no holes on a card corresponding to sprocket holes, and it is necessary to infer the position of successive rows by sensing the edge of a card and then driving it at a uniform predetermined speed past the sensing station. It is thus not possible to read only part of a card - once the card starts to move past the sensing station it must be read in its entirety - and its interface is that of a block transfer device rather than the character-by-character interface of the paper tape reader.

Card readers and paper tape readers can reach surprisingly high transfer rates, up to 2000 cards per minute (about 2500 characters per second) for cards and about 1000 characters per second for paper tape.

3.2.2 *Punched tape and punched card output.* The corresponding output devices are an order of magnitude slower, this drop in speed being largely attributable to the fact that forming holes in the card or tape requires the exertion of quite high forces and the corresponding mechanical system is very heavy. Both tape punches and card punches form the hole by driving a servo-controlled punch pin into a die, across which the tape or card passes in steps corresponding to the distance between successive characters (or columns). Again this requires the tape or card to be moved and then brought completely to rest between successive characters, which still further reduces the overall transfer rate. The very low overall transfer rate, about 100-150 characters per second, coupled with the fact that the resulting output still requires interpreting to give a printed record, has led to the virtual disappearance of tape or cards as an output device in many systems. However, they are still valuable for transferring digital data from a computing system to a piece of digitally controlled equipment (for example a semi-automatic machine tool) or for exchanging small amounts of information between computers.

3.3 *Graphic symbol to binary representation devices*

The devices in this category transform directly between a character represented as a graphic symbol (i.e. a mark on paper) and a group of binary digits or vice versa. Obviously a conversion from a graphic symbol to a group of digits is an input, and from a group of digits to a graphic symbol is an output.

3.3.1 *Keyboard input devices*. The most straightforward input device in this class is the keyboard, operated by a human operator. On reflection, one may be convinced that in fact the keyboard does not truly belong in this class, since the conversion it performs is from one digital encoding, corresponding to which key on the device is depressed, to another, corresponding to the encoded character; the conversion from the original graphic symbol to the particular key is of course carried out by the human operator. (The precise way in which this is achieved is not too well understood!)

When the selected key is depressed, it can operate either mechanically or electronically. In a mechanical system each key is supported by a keylever and is positioned above a row of codebars, figure 3.3. Depressing the key will press it against the codebars; those bars that have a cut-out in this position will be undisturbed, but those that are not cut out will in turn be depressed, and will operate switches associated

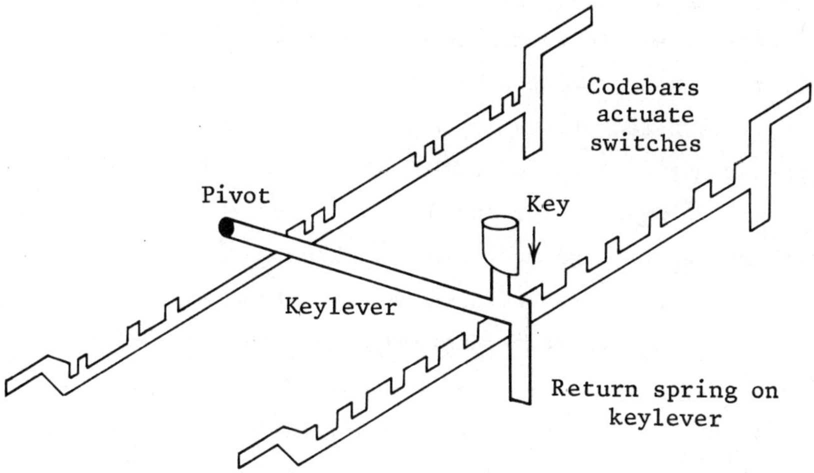

Figure 3.3 Keyboard mechanism using mechanical encoding.

with each code bar, thus completing the encoding. Obviously the presence or absence of a cut out defines whether or not the switch will be operated when the selected key is depressed and so will define the code generated. Depressing any key operates a further switch which generates the control signals for the interface. On some keyboards the absence of a Source Operable signal, or an Acceptor Ready signal, will cause a bar to raise which prevents any key from operating.

On an electronic keyboard, each key has a switch directly beneath it; depressing the key will activate circuitry which generates the encoded form of the corresponding character and produces the signals to drive the interface. The switch drives current into a 'diode matrix' (figure 3.4), in which each horizontal line is driven from a switch on the keyboard. Operating the switch applies a positive voltage to one, and only one, of the horizontal connectors, and this in turn produces positive voltages only on those vertical lines where a diode connects to the horizontal line. Thus the presence or absence of diodes determines whether the output for a given key will be positive or earth. Such a matrix is easily produced and *changed*, thus allowing relatively easy changing of the coding.

It is possible to connect the output from the keyboard either to a paper tape punch or card punch, so as to generate a tape or card deck for subsequent input to a computer. Equally the output may be attached via a multiplexer* directly into a computer for immediate processing. In fact, the price of computers has now reached the point at which it is economic to operate a number of keyboards directly into a small computer, which writes the characters onto a magnetic tape ready for subsequent processing by a large computer. It is possible for the small computer to carry out checks on the format of all data keyed in, and this, combined with the greater transfer rates

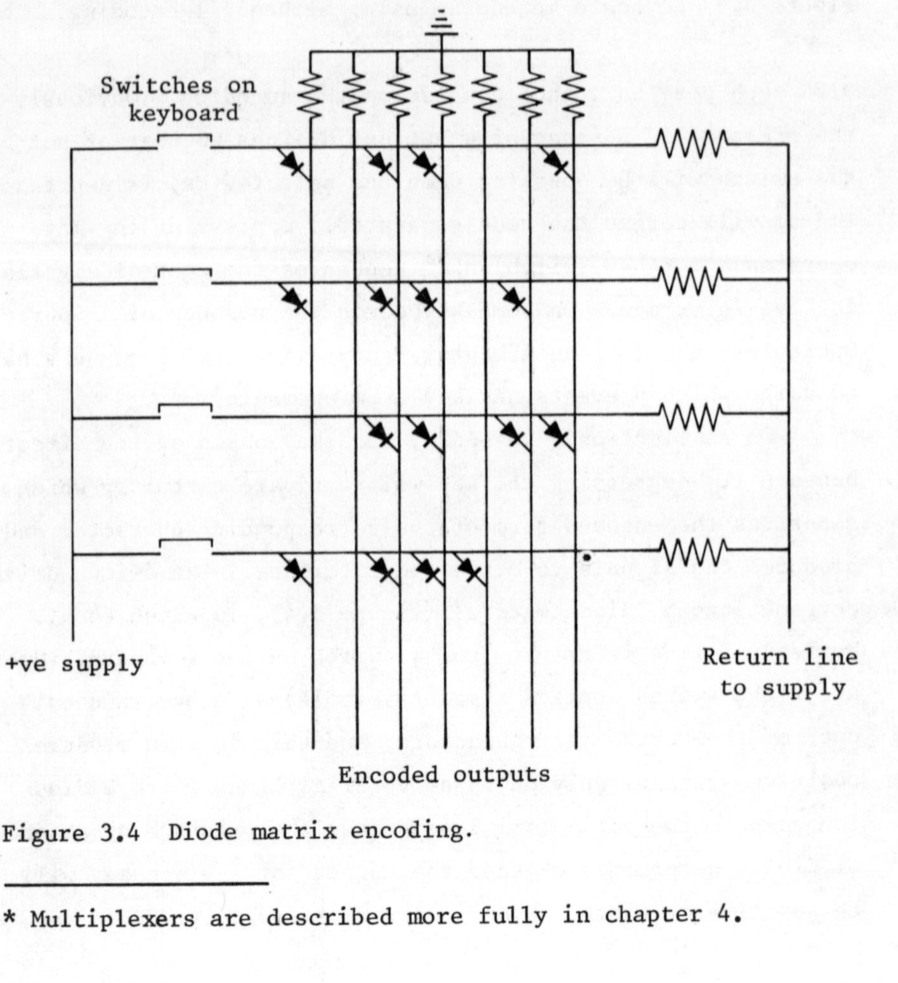

Figure 3.4 Diode matrix encoding.

* Multiplexers are described more fully in chapter 4.

possible with magnetic tape, makes such a system very attractive.

3.3.2 *Other input devices.* Keyboard devices are relatively simple, as the character recognition is performed by the human operating the keyboard. The devices which operate directly from a written or printed document are much more elaborate. They can be subdivided into

(a) mark sensing devices - which convert marks on a document to an internal representation, but do not effect any recognition of characters, and

(b) character recognition devices - which recognise characters on a document, and produce an internally coded representation.

Mark sensing devices generally operate with a document which is in effect a blank punch card. Marks are written by hand on the document, using either an ordinary pen or pencil, the marks being optically detected, or using a 'pencil' which incorporates a ferromagnetic material in its 'lead', the mark being detected via its magnetic properties. The marks are either used to produce punchings in the card, which is subsequently handled as a standard punched card, or may be passed directly into a digital system for further processing. Such systems rely on the human user of the pen or pencil to position his marks appropriately; by and large systems of this sort are of limited appeal.

The character recognition devices rely on the recognition of characters printed in the normal way and read optically (OCR) or printed in a magnetic ink and read via their magnetic properties (MICR). In each case the characters are printed in a manner which is chosen so as to facilitate recognition by the device; the resulting characters would not be acceptable for use as a standard type face, but can be read by a human reader. These techniques are used to encode information directly onto documents which will remain unchanged throughout

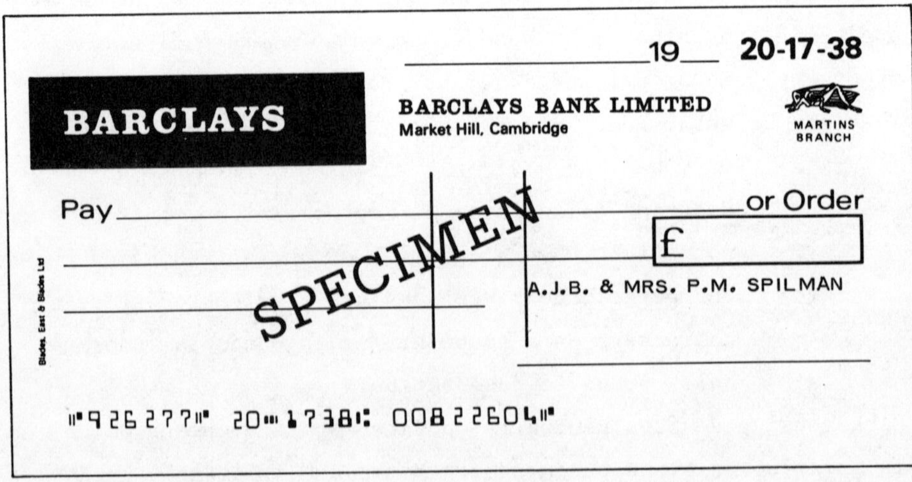

Figure 3.5 An example of MICR characters.

the working life of the document, a common application being in banking where items such as the account identification are printed on the cheque in MICR characters (figure 3.5). Both OCR and MICR operate by using a type face which is itself an encoding of the character, arranged so as to resemble the character of which it is an encoding. As the character is scanned the thick areas can be sensed as 1's and the thin lines as 0's, and the resulting binary pattern can be re-encoded as the internal encoding of the character.

3.3.3 *Output devices producing hard copy*. All the output devices to be described transform from an internal character, encoded as a group of binary digits, to an external graphic symbol recognisable directly by a human reader. These devices handle a major part of the output from computers. We deal first with those which produce a 'hard copy', that is a printed version on paper, and then deal with devices which produce the output as a transient image, generally on a cathode ray tube.

The devices producing hard copy fall under three headings

(a) slow character-by-character devices, similar to a typewriter

(b) medium speed line-by-line printers, using a single copy of the available character set

(c) high speed line-by-line printers, using multiple copies of the available character set.

As always such a classification is slightly arbitrary in that some devices are not used in the way one might expect.

The character-by-character devices operate at fairly low speeds, between about 10 and 40 characters per second, and form the natural complement to keyboard input devices. The most commonly used is the Teletype, figure 3.6. (Teletype is actually a trade-marked description of a particular manufacturer's unit, in this case Westrex Corporation. However, just as 'Hoover' has passed into common use as a word for a vacuum

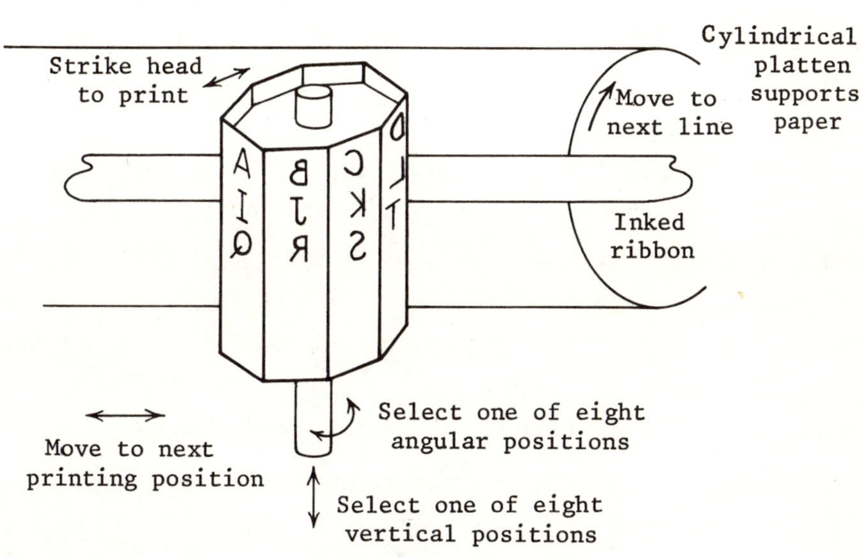

Figure 3.6 Character-by-character printer.

cleaner, so has 'Teletype' for a character-by-character printer/keyboard set.) The printing on a Teletype is achieved by striking characters against the paper with an inked ribbon trapped between the two. All the available characters are mounted on a cylinder whose cross-section is a regular octagon; the characters are typically arranged in eight rows, eight characters to a row, on the surface of this octagonal cylinder. The digits of the incoming character are used to control the angular and vertical positions of the head, which is then struck on to the ribbon and paper. The whole assembly then moves one character's width to the right and the sequence repeats. Those characters which control page layout simply move the printing mechanism or advance the paper to the next line as appropriate; paper movement is achieved as on a normal typewriter by advancing the cylindrical roller which supports the paper during printing. Teletypes are very cheap, about £600 largely because they form the basis of the telegraph systems operated by postal services, and this brings the benefits of a very large market. However, their speed is limited to little better than 10 characters per second, and for some applications high speeds are necessary. A slightly faster alternative is the 'matrix printer'. Here each character is formed by selecting pins on a matrix, typically with seven rows and five columns, which when struck against a ribbon will print a recognisable representation of a character. Since the individual pins are much lighter than the printing head, higher speeds up to about 100 characters per second are possible. The character set is very flexible, requiring only a change as to which pins are selected for each character. Matrix printers are very quiet in operation, which is an added attraction in certain applications.

For higher speeds, up to a few hundred characters per second, a chain* printer is used. Here the characters are arranged on a chain which runs continuously over a pair of drive

* The term 'train printer' is sometimes used.

Figure 3.7 Chain printer.

gears, in front of a ribbon and paper supported by a platten. The characters are attached by flexible strips to the chain and a separate hammer serves each print position across a line. A chain printer may print each character as it is received; as the character to be printed at a given position passes by on the chain control circuitry drives the hammer and traps the ribbon between the paper and the type head, each character requiring one revolution of the chain. In an alternative system a buffer store holds a complete line of print; as the chain revolves control circuitry determines which print positions have opposite them the characters required in those positions and actuates the appropriate hammers. Such a printer will print the entire line in the time for one revolution of the chain, but requires more elaborate control circuitry.

For still higher speeds a barrel printer is used. Complete sets of characters for each print position are arranged in rings on the circumference of a revolving barrel; print hammers below the paper trap the paper and ribbon against the corresponding character. A buffer store holds the line of characters awaiting printing, the entire line being printed in one revolution of the barrel. Both chain and barrel printers control paper movement by a sprocket drive engaging perforations on the edges of the paper, which is supplied as a continuous sheet folded in a zig-zag for ease of handling. A fast printer may print one sheet per second and an automatic stacker

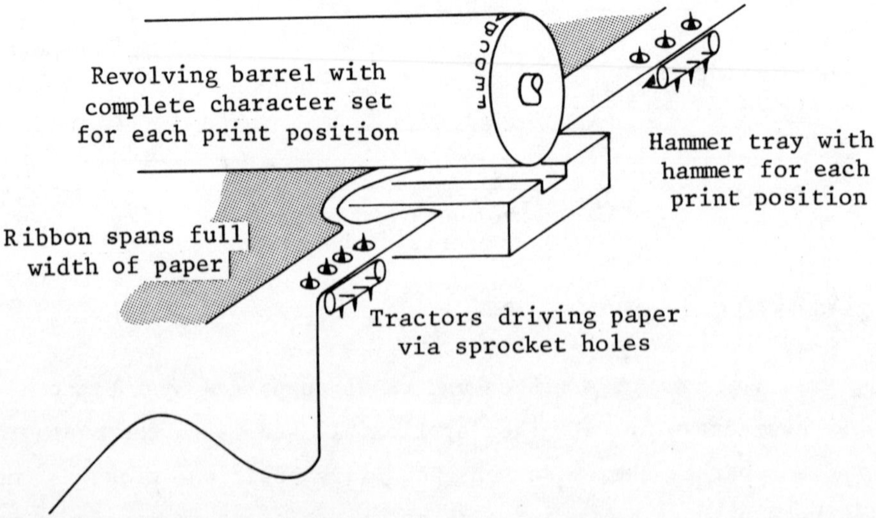

Figure 3.8 Barrel printer.

handles the sheets as they come off the printer.

The transition from Teletype, to unbuffered chain printer, to buffered chain printer to barrel printer is an illustration of the way in which increased speed of overall operation can be achieved by introducing steadily higher degrees of parallelism into the operation of a system. Each change implies that some part of the activity which was previously achieved by using one item of equipment repeatedly in time, has now been replaced by an operation in which replicated sets of equipment simultaneously carry out the activity.

3.3.4 *Output devices based on character displays.* We turn now to devices which produce a transient output on the screen of a cathode ray tube (CRT). Figure 3.9 shows a simplified CRT; it contains an electron gun, which produces a variable intensity stream of high velocity electrons by accelerating electrons emitted from a heated rare earth oxide cathode and focusing these using suitably shaped electrodes; X- and Y-deflector systems, which control the direction of travel of the emerging electron beam; and a flat surface coated with a phosphor, a material which emits light where the electron beam strikes the surface. The tube shown in figure 3.9 uses electrostatic deflection of the electron beam; a voltage difference between the left- and right-hand X deflector plates, or between the upper and lower Y deflector plates will deflect the negatively charged

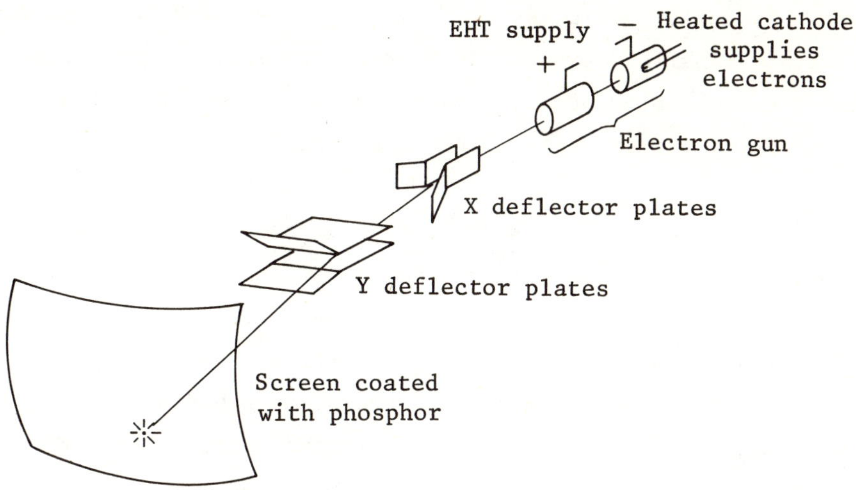

Figure 3.9 Cathode ray tube.

beam towards the more positive plate. The deflection may also be achieved by producing a magnetic field; a magnetic field whose lines of force run horizontally across the tube will deflect the electron beam upwards or downwards; similarly a magnetic field whose lines of force run vertically will deflect the beam to the left or the right. Since the only moving parts are electrons, the CRT is capable of very high speed operation, and it interfaces readily to electronic devices in general. As an output device the CRT may be used either to draw lines or to display characters and it is in this mode that we consider it first. The characters are generated rather as in the matrix printer, by displaying a pattern of dots which give a recognisable representation. To allow such a display to be used without flicker it must either be presented on a screen in which the phosphor has a long persistence (i.e. glows for a long time after being stimulated by the electron beam) or the display must be refreshed many times per second. Since the use of long persistence phosphors leads to other complications, it is usual to refresh the screen. The characters to be displayed are stored in a first-in-first-out store, usually fabricated as a suitably organised integrated circuit flip-flop memory. This store contains one character for each possible position on the screen. The characters are continually withdrawn from the store, processed, and then returned to store, so that in effect they circulate within the store, and each character's position on the screen is determined from its position in the store. A second, read-only store, defines the transformation from the binary representation of a character to its representations as a dot pattern on the face of the CRT. As each character emerges from the circulating store, the X- and Y-deflectors position the beam at the position of the character on the screen. The deflectors then scan over the dot matrix, and the electron beam is turned on or off as indicated by the contents of the read-only memory, building up the character. Devices of this form are very attractive in certain applications. They are totally electronic, which means that in comparison with electromechanical devices they are quiet and reliable. They can also accept information at very high speeds, up to several thousand characters per second, which means that the contents of the entire screen, amounting to perhaps 25 lines each of 80 characters can be changed in a few seconds or less. Because of the high degree of automation which their construction allows they are cheap and may well become cheaper. It is possible to attach a keyboard as an input to such a unit, and to extend the logic to allow the keyboard operator to edit the contents of the store (i.e. what is displayed) in a very flexible manner. It is also possible to attach several slave displays to a single master unit. They do not, of course, produce a printed hard copy, although some units on the market allow the attachment of a hard copy device to overcome this deficiency.

3.4 *Analog-digital and digital-analog devices*

The devices in this group transform a quantity of some sort into a digital representation of a measure of that quantity (for input to a digital system) or the converse transformation. For obvious reasons these are referred to as analog-digital (A-D) or digital-analog (D-A) conversions.

3.4.1 *Operational amplifiers.* Central to both types of converter is the 'operational amplifier', an inverting amplifier with a very high input impedance and a very high voltage gain, gains as high as 10^6 being commonplace.

Consider a circuit in which such an amplifier, with a gain of -M has a feedback loop containing a resistor R_f and has inputs V_1, V_2 applied via two further resistors, R_1, R_2. The three resistors are all of accurately known values (figure 3.10(a)).

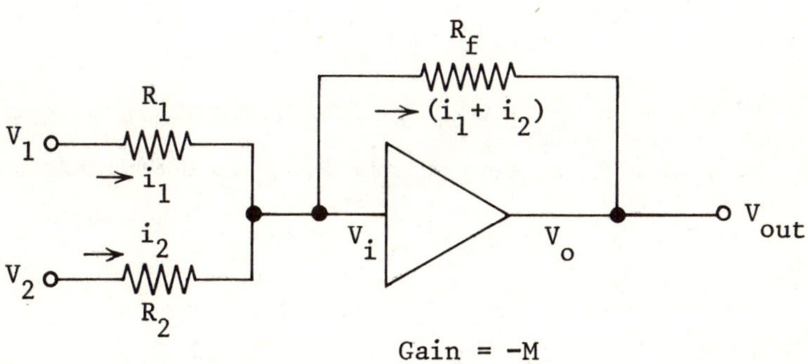

Figure 3.10(a) Operational amplifier used as an analogue adder

If the voltage at the input to the amplifier is V_i we have

$$V_1 - V_i = i_1 R_1$$
$$V_2 - V_i = i_2 R_2$$
and $$V_i - V_0 = (i_1 + i_2) R_f,$$

where V_0 is the output voltage and we have neglected any current into the amplifier. We also know that

$$V_0 = -MV_i$$

for the amplifier. Elimination of i_1, i_2 gives

$$V_i - V_0 = \left\{ \frac{V_1 - V_i}{R_1} + \frac{V_2 - V_i}{R_2} \right\} R_f$$

i.e. $$V_i \left\{ 1 + \frac{R_f}{R_1} + \frac{R_f}{R_2} \right\} - V_0 = V_1 \frac{R_f}{R_1} + V_2 \frac{R_f}{R_2}$$

and equating V_i to $-V_0/M$ gives

$$- V_0 \left\{ 1 + \frac{1}{M} \quad (1 + \frac{R_f}{R_1} + \frac{R_f}{R_2}) \right\} = V_1 \frac{R_f}{R_1} + V_2 \frac{R_f}{R_2}.$$

If $M = -10^6$ and $R_1 \approx R_2 \approx R_f \approx 1$ Megohm say then the term in braces on the left-hand side is very nearly equal to unity and so

$$-V_0 = V_1 \frac{R_f}{R_1} + V_2 \frac{R_f}{R_2}.$$

Obviously we can use the ratios of the input resistors to the (single) feedback resistor to allow scaling of the inputs to the operational amplifier which will then produce as its output the (inverted) sum of their scaled values.

Now consider the circuit of figure 3.10b.

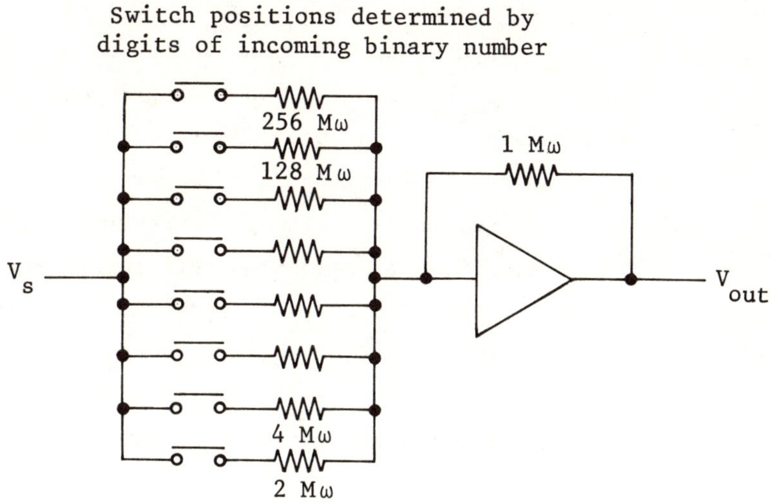

Figure 3.10(b) Operational amplifier used as a digital/analogue converter.

This contains an operational amplifier with a feedback resistor of 1.0 Mω and eight inputs. The inputs come through eight switches and eight input resistors with values 2.0 Mω, etc. up to 256 Mω (=2^8 Mω); closing any switch connects the the relevant input to a stabilised voltage source V_s. The resulting output voltage will be

$$- V_0 = \sum_1^8 V_s x_i \frac{1}{2^i} = X V_s,$$

where x_i is 0 or 1 according as the relevant switch is open or closed, V_s is the output voltage of the stabilised supply and X is the number

$$X = \sum_1^8 x_i 2^{-i} \quad \text{and} \quad 0 \leq X < 1.$$

Thus this circuit converts directly from a digital internal representation to a voltage in the range 0 to V_s and can form the basis of a digital to analog converter.

Analog to digital conversion can be achieved by the use of a digital to analog converter and a 'comparator'; the comparator has two analog inputs and yields a digital output which is 1 or 0 according as to which of the two analog inputs is more positive. Associated with the D/A converter is a flip-flop register which holds the result of the conversion, and which is initially cleared, and a multiposition switch which sweeps from the most significant end of the register to the least significant end. The switch is set to the most significant position, a 1 injected into the register and the output of the D/A converter compared with the input; if the input is more positive the 1 is left in the register, otherwise it is removed, and in either case the switch advances to the next less significant position, until the end of the register is reached. The result of the conversion is of course left in the register.

A/D and D/A converters can be extremely fast and accurate. A 12 bit D/A converter will cost a few pounds and will produce its results, accurate to about 1 part in 4000 in a few microseconds (in general of course the cost increases as the speed and accuracy increase). A/D converters are slower, because of their repetitive mode of operation, but can again produce 12 bit precision in about 20 microseconds for only a few pounds. Both A/D and D/A converters are available as integrated circuit units.

3.4.2 *Applications of A/D and D/A.* An obvious application of A/D and D/A converters as input devices is in 'process control'; this is a general term applied to any context in which a computing system is used to control a piece of equipment. For this to take place, the digital system must be able to sense the state of the equipment, and to supply to the system controlling signals. Where the state of the system is defined by some continuous quantity (for example pressure or temperature of a chemical reactor) it will be convenient to supply its value to the digital system via an A/D converter. A less satisfactory alternative is to convert the continuous quantity to a discrete one (for example 'pressure too high'). Similarly, the outputs from the digital system to the process may either be given as continuous quantities, via a D/A converter, ('open the inlet valve to this setting') or as simple two-state values ('open/close the inlet valve').

A particularly important application of D/A conversion is in the CRT graphics systems, often referred to as 'vector plotters'. The coordinates of the end points of linear vectors are presented in digital form, and used to control the drawing of the corresponding vectors on the face of a CRT. Extra signals are needed to control whether the vector is drawn with an intense electron beam, giving a bright vector, or with the electron beam current shut off. This system allows vectors to be drawn at very high speeds, up to several thousand vectors per second. Obviously curves can be represented by an appropriate set of line segments. Equally, it is possible to assemble collections of vectors so as to give representations of letters, allowing the production of annotated diagrams.

The input associated with such diagrams may be achieved with a 'tracker ball'. A pair of variable resistors are used to control the X- and Y-deflections of the electron beam, and the values of the corresponding deflecting voltages can be read via an analogue/digital converter so as to give a digital representation of the spots position. An alternative technique uses a 'light pen'. A fast response photo sensitive device is placed very near to the face of the CRT, and the CRT is programmed to display a tracking cross, a pair of lines intersecting at right angles. The cross is always displayed at the last known position of the light pen, and when the pen picks up light emitted by the cross it signals this fact to the processor. From the time at which this signal is generated it is possible to deduce the new position of the pen, and so to display a fresh cross at this new position, so tracking the motion of the light pen.

3.5 *Miscellaneous devices*

There are numerous other devices which have from time to time served as input or output devices for digital systems.

3.5.1 *The Rand tablet.* This is a form of graphical input, consisting of a tablet a few centimetres square, with a slightly flexible surface. Behind the surface is a grid of pressure sensitive transducers, which typically allow the surface to be divided into say 32 × 32 areas. When the user writes on the surface the tablet generates a sequence of 5-bit coordinate pairs, which define the order in which the writing instrument passes through the small areas on the tablet.

3.5.2 *The incremental plotter.* The incremental plotter produces output directly in graphical form. A pen, which can be raised or lowered, is traversed on a slide and writes on a paper wrapped on the surface of a drum which can rotate. Pen traversal and drum rotation are achieved by stepping motors, which produce an accurately reproducible step at each input. The step may be of 1 or 0 in traverse or rotation, allowing the generation of eight vectors (on some plotters steps of 2, 1, 0 in each direction may be possible, allowing the generation of 24 vectors). Each increment will be in the order of 0.2 mm, and obviously the production of even a simple picture with dimensions of say 300 mm square will require many thousands of incremental steps, a task which could not be contemplated other than with a computer. Despite their apparent limitations, incremental plotters are very widely used for the production of graphical output, especially where accuracy of the drawing is important.

3.5.3 *Plasma displays.* The plasma display can be used as a substitute for the CRT in some applications. The display consists of a mesh of fine wires, one set running horizontally the other set vertically, in an inert gas atmosphere. The two sets of wires are maintained at equal and opposite potentials sufficient to maintain a plasma discharge, but not high enough to initiate the discharge. The discharge can be initiated at any selected intersection by raising the potentials on the wires which define the intersection to half the voltage required to initiate the discharge, which will then remain even when the voltage is lowered. Similarly, the discharge can be erased at any point by lowering the potentials to below half of that required to maintain the discharge, when it will quench and not restart as the voltage is again raised. Notice that initiating or erasing the discharge at one intersection will leave all others undisturbed. Plasma displays provide a relatively cheap, stable and bright display, but are rather slow for some graphics applications.

3.5.4 *Touch sensitive screen.* A touch sensitive screen consists of a rectangular glass plate, with piezo-electric drivers fastened along two adjacent edges. The transducers are used to initiate plane mechanical waves which propagate across the plate; touching the plate, even lightly, with any object causes scattering of the waves, and the scattered wave can be detected and used to determine the position at which the plate is touched.

It is possible to locate a plasma display as output, behind a touch sensitive screen as input, and to use back projection techniques to show a computer selected slide on the same screen. A combination such as this provides a very flexible data path between a computer system and a human user, and such systems are finding application in enabling communication between a computer and a user in educational systems.

3.6 *Summary*

This rather rambling chapter has covered a wide range of devices; we have attempted to produce a systematisation of the various types of unit, although in some cases the divisions made have been somewhat arbitrary. As for storage devices we now attempt to summarise the black box properties of the various input and output devices. While doing so one important distinction between storage devices and input/output devices must be borne in mind. Storage devices all perform inherently the same function, and it is possible to a quite considerable extent to substitute one type of storage for another. Such substitution forms a major part of some operating systems. With input/output devices this is not possible; if there is a requirement to read cards, then a card reader *must* be used and it is not possible to use some other input device. However, it may be possible to arrange that the program which requires the cards to be read can be supplied with a virtual card reader, which to the program has all the properties of a card reader, but for which the physical act of reading the cards takes place in advance of the program calling for the cards to be read. The card images are retained in storage until such time as the program calls for the card images, when they are supplied as if they had been read via the reader. This concept is explored more fully in chapter 6.

The summary table 3.1 shows the major black box properties of the various input devices. There is a very wide range of equipment available and all the data here are to be regarded as indicative of what is available, much of table 3.1 is self-evident. The column headed 'media' gives an indication of the charges for consumable supplies, such as paper tape or punched cards. Some devices do not consume any supplies of this nature;

DEVICE		COSTS			RELIABILITY	PHYSICAL PLANNING			PERFORMANCE	
		capital	recurrent	media		dimension of unit	weight	power	start time	speed bits/sec
ENCODED SYMBOL DEVICES	paper tape reader	£2,000	high	low	good	0.5×0.5×1.0 m	100 kg	1 kW	1 ms	10^4
	paper tape punch	£1,000	high	low	poor	0.5×0.5×1.0 m	100 kg	1 kW	10 ms	10^3
	card reader	£5,000	high	medium	good	0.5×1.5×1.5 m	200 kg	1 kW	50 ms	2.10^4
	card punch	£5,000	high	medium	poor	0.5×1.5×1.0 m	200 kg	1 kW	50 ms	3.10^3
GRAPHIC SYMBOL DEVICES	OCR	£10,000	high	-	good	0.5×1.5×1.5 m	200 kg	2 kW	50 ms	5.10^3
	MICR	£10,000	high	-	good	0.5×1.5×1.5 m	200 kg	2 kW	50 ms	5.10^3
	teletype	£500	medium	low	good	0.5×0.5×0.3 m	20 kg	100 W	100 ms	100
	slow chain printer	£2,000	medium	low	good	0.5×0.5×0.3 m	20 kg	1 kW	-	500
	fast chain printer	£5,000	medium	low	good	0.7×1.0×1.5 m	100 kg	2 kW	-	5.10^3
	barrel printer	£10,000	medium	low	good	1.0×1.5×1.5 m	200 kg	3 kW	-	2.10^4
ANALOG DIGITAL and MISCELLANEOUS	A/D converter	£500	nominal	-	excellent	30×30×100 mm	100 g	nominal	$\sim\mu s$	10^6
	D/A converter	£500	nominal	-	excellent	30×30×100 mm	100 g	nominal	$\sim\mu s$	10^6
	CRT character display	£1,000	low	-	excellent	0.5×0.5×0.5 m	20 kg	500 W	$\sim\mu s$	3.10^3
	CRT vector display	£4,000	low	-	excellent	0.5×0.5×1.0 m	30 kg	1 kW	$\sim\mu s$	3.10^3
	incremental plotter	£5,000	medium	high	good	0.7×0.7×1.0 m	50 kg	1 kW	100 ms	2.10^3

Table 3.1 Summary of black box properties of input/output devices.

it is assumed that for OCR and MICR the relevant documents which carry the characters would exist in any case and so represent no extra cost.

3.7 *Bibliography*

There are very few texts which deal solely with input and output devices. Many of the books referred to in chapter 2 and 5 contain sections which describe various input and output devices, though usually in no more detail than the present chapter.

In addition, many manufacturers of computers produce publicity material which describes their peripheral devices in considerable detail.

4 · Data transmission

4.1 *Basic components*

The function of a data transmission system is to transfer information from one location to another. In general it is necessary for the physical representation of the individual digits which form the encoding of the information to be changed but this change is quite incidental. It is also quite common for a data transmission system to add redundant information to that to be transmitted, for error detection and correction, and to remove this information at the receiving end.

Any data transmission system can be envisaged as containing three major components, a transmitter, a channel, and a receiver (figure 4.1). The *transmitter* accepts incoming information and converts this into a physical representation suitable for propagation along the *channel*. The representation passes via the channel to the *receiver*, which reconverts it to an acceptable local representation of the information. Figure 4.1 contains one other major feature which is also always present in a data transmission system, a source of *noise*. The effect of noise is to introduce disturbances on the channel, and it is essential for the design of a data transmission system to allow for the effect of noise in the channel.

Because of the rather difficult nature of some of the mathematics required to describe data transmission systems a detailed treatment of the relevant topics has been deferred to the later sections of this chapter, and we give here a brief informal description of the physics of the electrical transmission of signals over long distances. When an electrical

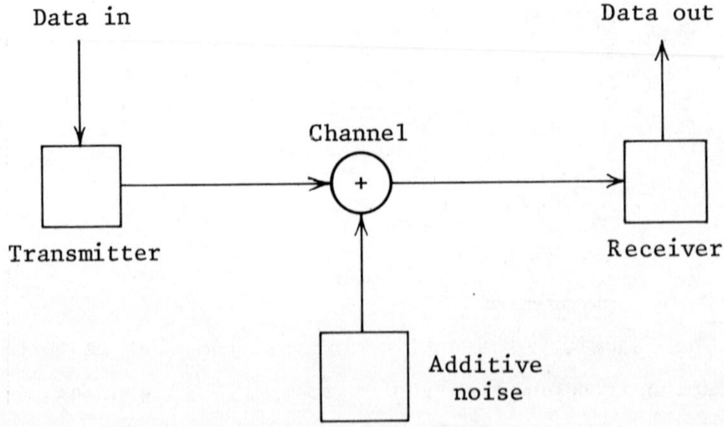

Figure 4.1 Essential elements in a data transmission system.

signal is transmitted either by conduction along a wire or other conductor, or by radiating the signal as in a wireless or TV transmission, the signal suffers distortion; in addition the receiver will always pick up a certain amount of noise, due to electrical signals generated in wires by stray magnetic fields, interference from other transmitters and thermal noise in the receiver itself. The net effect is that the received signal is always a distorted version of the transmitted signal, and is received above a general background of noise, and it is the function of the receiver to recognise the incoming signal even in the presence of distortion and noise. The distortion involves two quite separate phenomena, *attenuation* and *dispersion*. Attenuation arises because as the signal is transmitted it inevitably becomes weaker. In a signal carried on conductors there will always be resistance along the conductor due to the finite resistance of the conducting element, and leakage caused by the fact that the insulation around the conductor is not perfect. Where a signal is transmitted by radiation it falls off in strength as the signal spreads out (the well known 'inverse square law') and there will also be loss of signal strength if any conducting objects lie on the signal

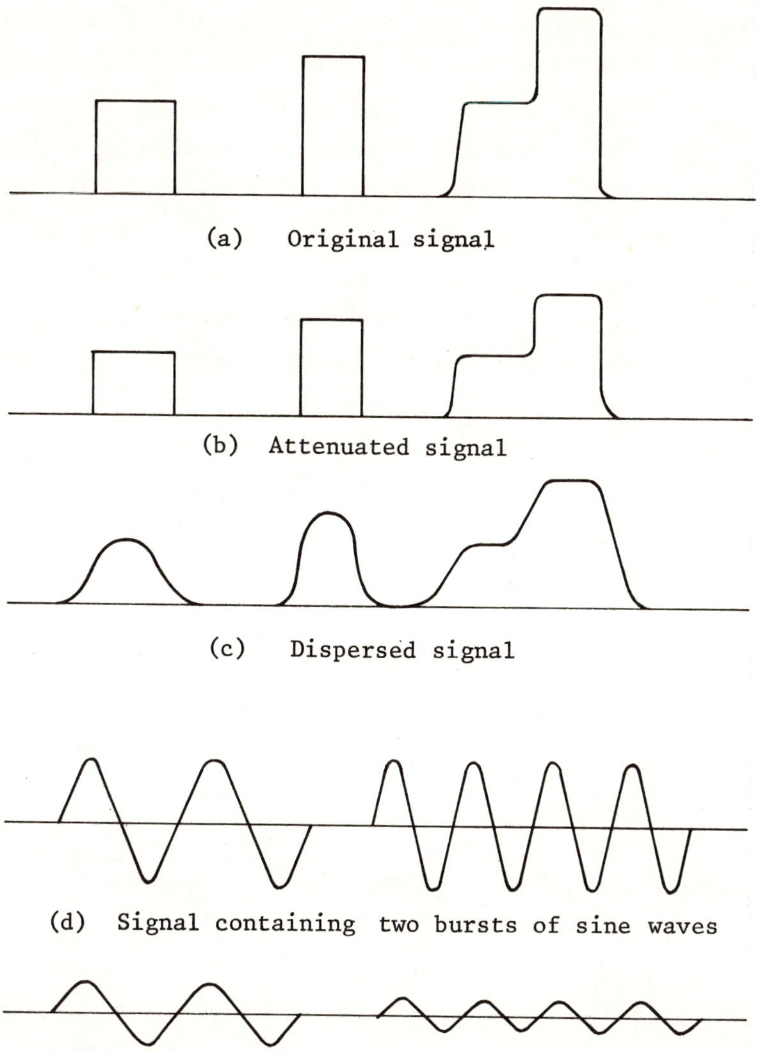

(a) Original signal

(b) Attenuated signal

(c) Dispersed signal

(d) Signal containing two bursts of sine waves

(e) Received signal shows differential attenuation

Figure 4.2

path. Dispersion arises from the fact that different parts of the signal will travel over the transmission path at slightly different speeds; the effect of dispersion generally shows as a tendency to 'smooth' the received signal. For example, if a transmitter sends out square pulses, the received signal may contain pulses with 'smoothed' corners - these effects are illustrated in figure 4.2. Figure 4.2(a) shows the output from a transmitter, and figures 4.2(b) and 4.2(c) show the effect of attenuation on the received waveform. Figures 4.2(d) and 4.2(e) illustrate a special case, the transmission of a pure sine wave at one frequency, followed by a pure sine wave at a different frequency. In this special case it is possible to show that under a wide range of conditions the effects of attenuation and dispersion lead to the received waveform being a pure sine wave of the same frequency, although the sine wave will have undergone different amounts of attenuation and will have undergone different phase shifts. The ability to transmit sinusoidal waves which are received as sinusoidal waves forms the basis of several transmission systems. The process by which this is achieved is referred to as 'modulation'.

4.1.1 *Modulation systems.* As we have just seen, any transmitted signal undergoes attenuation and dispersion between the transmitter and receiver; in addition the received signal will have noise added to it, giving rise to a still more distorted signal. However, attenuation and dispersion while they alter the amplitude and phase of a sine wave, do not alter its frequency. The phase shifts, and amplitude reduction are both functions of the frequency of the transmitted sine wave. However, if we can use a sufficiently narrow group of frequencies to transmit the signal, then to a first approximation all the frequencies transmitted will undergo the same attenuation and dispersion, and we can recover the original transmitted signal by the use of a suitable amplifier. If the phase of the received signal is important then we may be able to transmit a suitable pure sine wave as well as the signal and use the phase of this second signal as a datum from which to determine the phase of the first signal.

A sine wave is characterised by three properties;

(1) amplitude

(2) phase

(3) frequency

We can make variations in any one of these characteristics in order to impress the signal we wish to transmit on to the sine wave. For obvious reasons the wave whose characteristics we vary is referred to as the carrier wave; the process of varying the characteristic is referred to as modulation; and varying the three characteristics gives rise to amplitude modulation, phase modulation and frequency modulation respectively. Much less obviously we shall see in section 9 of this chapter that any one type of modulation inevitably gives rise to some variations in the other characteristics of the carrier wave, although these variations will be small.

The purpose of modulation is to allow us to select as a carrier a frequency for which the attenuation and dispersion introduced by the channel are either minimal, or show the least variation with frequency, or are known functions of frequency. Clearly where the channel distortion is minimal, or shows the least variation with frequency we can ignore its effects. In the last case, where the distortion is a known function of frequency, we can introduce a compensating distortion which removes the effects of channel distortion. This process is often used for transmission over telephone cables and is referred to as 'equalisation'.

4.2 *Practical data transmission systems*

We now examine some of the data transmission systems in practical use; for convenience we shall treat these as

(1) very low speed systems i.e. a few hundred binary digits per second

(2) low speed systems i.e. about 10^4 binary digits per second

(3) medium speed systems i.e. about 10^5 binary digits per second

(4) high speed systems i.e. greater than 10^6 binary digits per second.

These divisions are to some extent arbitrary and there is considerable overlap in technology and application of the various systems.

4.2.1 *Very low speed systems.* These systems are used at rates up to about 200 binary digits per second, for driving Teletypes or similar character by character devices. A Teletype produces characters each encoded on several binary digits which are transmitted serially over a single line; for transmission purposes each character is preceded by a single 0 (the 'start' digit), followed by the digits of the encoding, and then two 1's, as shown in figure 4.3. Thus, a Teletype, running at ten characters per second requires to transmit about one hundred binary digits per second.

Signalling in this form, in which each character is preceded by timing signals announcing the start of a character, and followed by further signals indicating the end of the character is known as 'asynchronous signalling'. Clearly asynchronous signalling makes rather inefficient use of the capacity of the channel since every character involves the transmission of extra timing digits; thus for 8-bit teletypes code, of every eleven bits transmitted only eight carry useful information, the remaining three being used only for timing purposes.

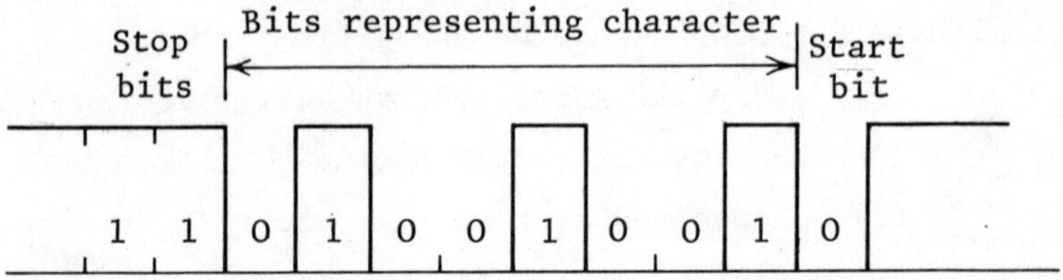

Figure 4.3 A single eight-bit character on an asynchronous line.

Transmission of asynchronous, teletype like signals is handled in one of two ways:

(a) Telegraph signalling. Here the 1's and 0's are encoded as voltages (either +120v and 0v or +80v and -80v) and applied directly to a transmission line. The current in the line is a nominal 20 ma. The transmission line may consist of a single wire, with an earth return, or of a twisted pair, two insulated conductors twisted together. The frequencies involved are very low, less than about 300 Hz and as the capacitance between the single line and earth, or the two conductors of the twisted pair, is very low, and the leakage conductance is also very low, the loss of amplitude of the current waveform is very slight even over very long distances.

(b) Telephone signalling. For transmission over longer distances, or more important for transmission over the switched telephone network, the methods used for telegraph signalling are inappropriate. The switched telephone network operates at much lower voltages and is carefully designed to accommodate frequencies occurring in human speech (nominally 100 Hz to about 4,000 Hz); voltages and/or frequencies outside these limits are not acceptable. In addition, the telephone system represents a formidable capital investment, and the authorities who operate such systems rightly set stringent safeguards on the nature of the devices which can be attached to the network. For transmission of teletype signals it is necessary to use a Modem (MOdulator DEModulator) which acts as an interface between the users equipment and the switched network, and also performs a frequency modulation, representing 1/0 as either 980/1180 Hz or 1650/1850 Hz. The use of two pairs of frequencies allows the modem to deal with incoming and outgoing signals simultaneously. A modem transmitter section contains two free running oscillators; the resonant circuit associated with each oscillator is arranged in such a way that extra capacitance or inductance can be switched in and out of the circuit so as to change the frequency of oscillation, the switching being controlled by the state of the data to be transmitted. Whenever the extra capacitance or inductance is switched in or out there will be abrupt changes in the oscillator output, and these are smoothed to some extent by passing the signal through a filter circuit which allows only frequencies in the range from about 900 to 1300 Hz (or 1500 to 2000 Hz for the higher frequency carrier) to pass through on to the telephone line. The modem also incorporates circuits which prevent unacceptable signals appearing on the telephone line.

The receiver section of the modem handles the incoming signal from the line. The signal is passed through a filter circuit which admits only the range 900 to 1300 Hz or 1500 to 2000 Hz: the signal is then amplified, and applied to tuned circuits which are arranged to respond only when a frequency corresponding to 0 or 1 is applied (i.e. to frequencies very close to 1180 or 1850 Hz); the output from these circuits when rectified and smoothed yield the original data signals.

Modems also contain circuitry which is required to determine whether the modem transmits on 980/1180 or 1650/1850 Hz, and to detect failures by the distant modem, or interruption of the connection. This control circuitry may either be operated manually, or be in turn linked through to the computing system which is to transmit or receive data and which can play some part in the establishing of a call and in handling error conditions.

4.2.2 *Low speed systems.* Low speed systems operate at up to 10,000 binary digits per second, and are used for faster character by character devices, for slow card readers and line printers, or similar speed punched paper tape devices. They operate over twisted pairs, using either phase or frequency modulation, sometimes grouping several binary digits together so as to provide greater effectiveness (e.g. a phase modulation using only one binary digit at a time would require nearly the same bandwidth as one encoding three binary digits - it would probably be less affected by noise however). The carrier frequencies used are in the order of a few KHz, approximately equal to the bit rates.

The systems in this speed range use synchronous rather than asynchronous signalling; the individual characters are no longer preceded by a start digit (always 0) and terminated by stop digits (at least two successive 1's). Instead only the actual digits of successive characters are transmitted. The modems used must therefore be designed to operate at an accurately controlled frequency, either generated within the modem itself or supplied externally. It is also necessary to ensure that not only is the time corresponding to a single bit accurately determined, but also the time corresponding to the start of individual characters (i.e. groups of bits). This is commonly achieved by the use of the 'synch' character; the modems are connected in such a way that when they have no information to transmit they continuously transmit the 'synchronous idle' or synch character. The receiving modem can use this to ensure that it idles in step with the transmitting modem.

At the lower speeds, up to 2,400 binary digits per second

transmission is possible over normal speech quality lines; such lines can be either 'switched' lines, obtained by dialling the call in the normal way (or by operator connection), or 'private' lines. Private lines are leased from the telephone authority (in Britain the Post Office), and form a permanent connection between the transmitting and receiving points. The actual line used at these speeds is still a standard twisted pair, but all intermediate connections are made as soldered joints, rather than via the switching elements found in a telephone exchange. The absence of switched connections in the line reduces noise; there is also a much reduced incidence of the miscellaneous clicks, buzzes, snatches of conversation and so on familiar to any regular users of the telephone system.

For higher speeds up to 9,600 binary digits per second, leased private lines are essential, and it is also necessary to balance the modem, that is to introduce a filter whose characteristics are chosen so as to remove the frequency dependent effects of attenuation. The line may also be conditioned, by introducing extra inductance into the line so as to reduce dispersion by making all waves travel with approximately the same speed.

4.2.3 *Medium speed systems.* Medium speed systems operate at between a few tens of KHz to a few hundred KHz, carrying up to 10^5 or so binary digits per second and using synchronous signalling. At these frequencies twisted pairs start to become impracticable except over short distances at lower speeds as they suffer loss by radiation and by dielectric losses in the insulation. For higher speeds coaxial cables are used or twisted pairs with repeater amplifiers every few kilometres. Coaxial cables cannot readily be switched, and such cables are installed as a separate point-to-point connection. The signal may either be applied directly, or more often may be used to modulate a carrier.

The relatively high cost of coaxial cables means that over very long distances in this speed range microwave links are economically attractive. The bandwidth of a microwave link is very great (12 MHz is common) and it is usual to subdivide this into a number of disjoint bands, each of which carries the traffic of a single coaxial cable (say 750 KHz). Such medium speed systems are as yet relatively uncommon for digital signalling but the advent of 'packet switching' systems described later may make their use increasingly attractive.

4.2.4 *High speed systems.* These are systems used within a single computing system, for example to connect a high speed peripheral unit to the main storage (up to say 1 million binary digits per second) or to connect two parts of a processor at up to 10^8 binary digits per second. The speeds above refer to the data rates on a single line; higher total speeds are achieved by running a number of lines in parallel.

Within a computing system the distances involved are usually quite small, of the order of a few metres at most, and it might be thought that attenuation presents no problems. However, as data rates rise to very high values losses due to radiation begin to occur, and this causes both attenuation of signals and increased noise on neighbouring signal paths. For data rates up to one megabit per second the use of twisted pairs or coaxial cable is satisfactory, but at the very highest data rates it is necessary to consider the signal path as a *wave guide*, that is to treat the path by solving Maxwell's equations for the particular boundaries defined by the conductors which carry the signal. It is possible to fabricate a wave guide on a double-sided etched circuit board by forming a narrow conducting track to carry the signal on one side, and having the other side of the board consist of a conducting sheet, which forms an earthed ground plane. With careful control of the dimensions of the conductors and the distance of the track from the ground plane wave guides can be formed with accurately known properties. In particular it is possible to adjust the value of the 'impedance' of the wave guide, that is the ratio of the amplitudes of the voltage and current waves in the wave guide. It is important to have this control since any discontinuities in the impedance of a wave guide cause reflections and attenuations of the signal in the wave guide. Discontinuities can occur particularly at the input to the wave guide, or at its output and they may be reduced by matching the output impedance and input impedance of the functional units to those of the wave guide. If this matching is not carried out signals may be interjected into the line, undergo a double reflection once at each end, and generate spurious signals at the receiving end.

4.3 *Multiplexing*

A commonly occurring situation is one in which a number of separate sources, physically rather near to each other, wish to transmit to a single distant receiver, or a single source to a number of separate receivers, figure 4.4(a). One can cater for this by supplying individual point-to-point links, between each source and the receiver. However, it may be more economic to install a single channel with a capacity sufficiently great to carry all the traffic, and to arrange to 'multiplex' the signals from each source into this single channel, figure 4.4(b). The multiplexer can be viewed as a multi-position switch which can connect each source in turn to the receiver, sending the outputs from all the sources down the single channel to the receiver. The receiver will need a 'demultiplexer' to unscramble the incoming message stream and reconstruct the output from each separate source.

Multiplexing can be achieved in basically two ways.

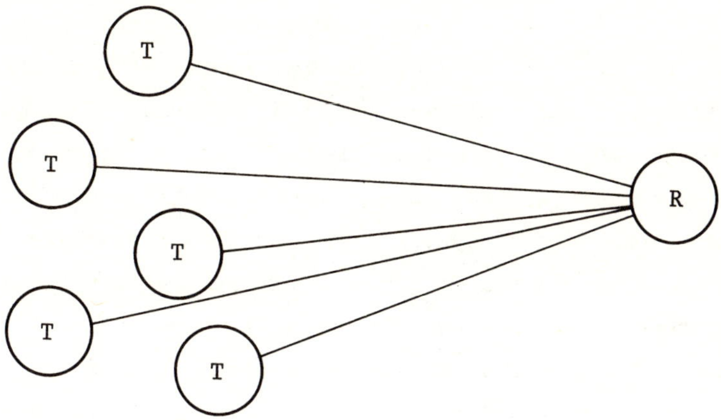

Figure 4.4(a) Five separate transmitters connected to a single distant receiver via separate lines.

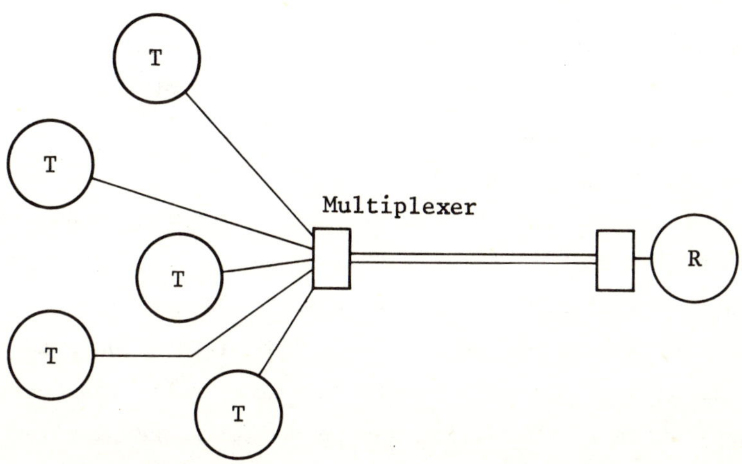

Figure 4.4(b) The same five transmitters connected to a multiplexer and then by a single line to the distant receiver.

4.3.1 *Time division multiplexing* - here each slow speed line is allocated a portion of the *time* of the high speed line. For example, 20 teletypes, each requiring a 110 bits per second line, might share a single 2400 bit per second line. The outputs from the teletypes would be fed to a small store with twenty words of eleven bits capable of holding the eleven binary digits that represent a single character from each teletype and their contents would be transmitted word by word down the 2400 bits per second line to an equivalent store at the receiver. This mode of use requires some form of synchronising between transmitter and receiver to ensure that the time slots on the fast channel are correctly synchronised, i.e. that the two selector switches on each end of the fast channel rotate in step. In this mode of sharing, each transmission channel operating at the slow speed has the use of the high speed channel for a fraction of the time.

4.3.2 *Frequency division multiplexing.* A frequency division multiplexer operates by using a single channel of such a bandwidth that it can simultaneously handle a number of separate carrier frequencies each one of which is modulated to carry a separate signal. For example as we have seen a single teletype normally operates by transmitting a frequency modulated signal of either 980/1180 or 1650/1850 Hz; we may regard these as modulations of ±100 Hz on carriers of 1080 or 1750 Hz. However, it is possible on a channel with a total bandwidth of say 25 Kc/s to transmit twenty carriers, with frequencies 4+n Kc/s, where n = 0,1...19, and to modulate each carrier separately. The receiver will then contain filter circuits, each of which admits a narrow range of frequencies centred on the unmodulated carriers into an appropriate detector which regenerates the modulating signal. In this mode of sharing, each transmission channel operating at the slow speed has the use of a fraction of the bandwidth of the wideband channel for all the time. We shall find repeated examples of the contrast between these two ways of sharing a single large resource to perform several separate tasks.

4.4 *Circuit switching*

In virtually all countries of the world the transmission of data is administered by some form of centralised agency, either a department of Government or a public or private corporation which operates under a licence from Government. Where data are transmitted for use in connection with computers the data may be transmitted either over the existing telephone network, or over specially installed transmission lines, available only for that user. Such a private line would be used either where the normal telephone network could not handle the necessary data rate, or where a private line would be cheaper than using the existing network and using dialled connections.

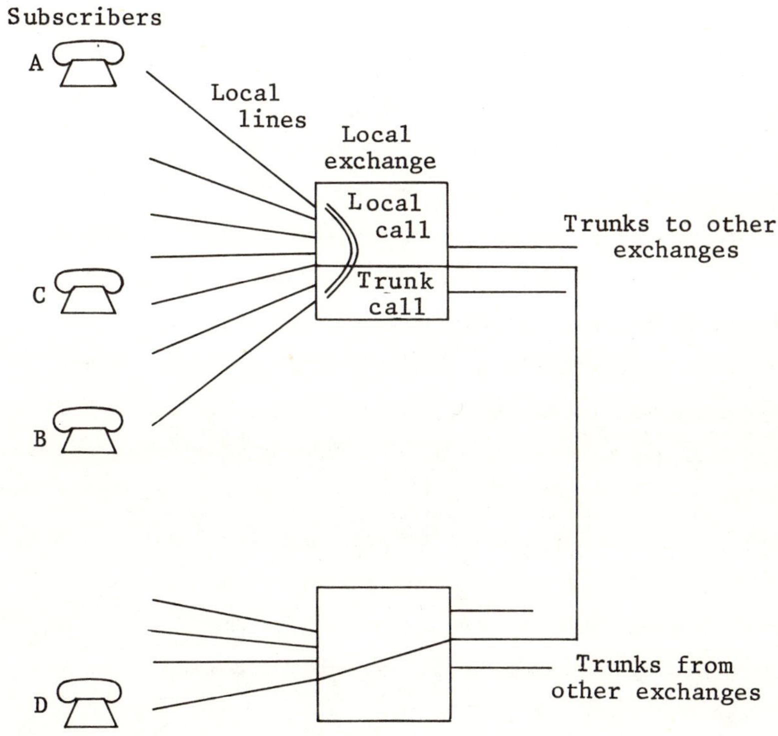

Figure 4.5 Circuit switching system.

The standard telephone system, figure 4.5, operates on a 'circuit switching' basis. Each terminal (i.e. each telephone handset) has a permanently wired connection to a local exchange. A subscriber making a call to a number on the same exchange will have the circuits from his telephone switched on to those of the number he is calling, and for the duration of this call those two subscribers will have the uninterrupted use of the equipment within the exchange necessary to effect the call (subscribers A, B in figure 4.5). If the call is to a subscriber on a different exchange then the call will involve setting up circuits.

(a) within the calling subscribers local exchange between the incoming circuit and the 'trunk' circuit which links the two exchanges,

(b) within the called subscribers local exchange between the incoming trunk circuit and the outgoing circuit to the call destination.

Again for the duration of the call, the two subscribers will have the uninterrupted use of *two* sets of switching, one set in each exchange, and of one of the circuits in the trunk linking the two exchanges (subscribers C, D in figure 4.5). In practice, there will be other exchanges, which deal only with trunks between exchanges, and the individual trunk circuits will be multiplexed in a single wideband channel. The important point to grasp is that in such a *circuit switching* system the network has two major types of resource, *circuits* which link units of equipment, and *switches* which allow any incoming circuit to connect to any outgoing circuit. In general the circuits and switches are supplied so as to cope with the average demand, and cannot deal with the situation in which all subscribers wish to make calls simultaneously.

4.5 *Packet switching*

An alternative to circuit switching which is especially

applicable to digital data is to use 'packet switching'. When using circuit switching the subscriber supplies two distinct sets of information to the data transmission system. He starts by supplying addressing information, which defines with which subscriber he wishes to communicate (e.g. by dialling). The circuit switching system uses this information to establish a circuit between the caller and the receiver. When a successful connection has been established, the caller then supplies information which is simply transmitted via the circuit previously established to the receiver.

In a packet switching system the caller supplies packets of digitally encoded information, and associated *with each packet* is information which defines the subscriber for which the information is destined. This packet is accepted in its entirety and stored at a 'packet switching centre'; each packet is then taken from store and transmitted to the store in the next centre on the route towards the ultimate destination, until the packet switching centre to which the final destination connects is reached. In such a system it is common to provide more than one route between pairs of centres, so as to increase the overall reliability, and it is necessary to provide enough information within the packets to allow multi-packet messages to be reassembled in their correct order, as packets travelling by different routes can become transposed.

Packet switching systems offer substantial advantages in some types of data communications, and it is likely that they will become increasingly widely used, especially for digital data.

The remaining sections of this chapter treat in more detail some of the mathematics associated with data transmission. Section 4.6 deals with measures of the information content of a stream of characters, and with the way in which information is lost during transmission over a noisy channel. Section 4.7 examines the physical properties of electrical transmission lines, and describes how such lines distort the signals they carry. Section 4.8 shows how a signal can be resolved into a set of components each of which is a sine wave, whose behaviour on a transmission line can be determined. Finally, section 4.9 deals with some of the ways in which an arbitrary signal can be superimposed onto a carrier wave, chosen so as to minimise the effects introduced by the transmission line on the Fourier components of the transmitted signal. The material in these sections requires more advanced mathematics than the remainder of the book; it has been included here since most of the references are somewhat inaccessible.

4.6 *Entropy*

In order to discuss the properties of a data transmission system it is necessary to introduce some basic concepts concerning information. We can regard any digital information as being represented as an ordered stream of symbols; when attempting to describe the overall properties of such symbols we find that we are particularly concerned with the relative frequencies with which particular symbols occur. If we have a source of symbols with the property that the relative frequencies with which symbols occur are independent of the length of time for which the source has been running then the source is known as a *stationary* source. If we have a stationary source whose behaviour is always the same whenever we switch it on, then the source is known as an *ergodic* source. (The definition we have given here is obviously arbitrary and over-brief. A full account can be found in any text book on information theory, e.g. 'Information Theory' by J.F. Young, Butterworth, 1971.) An ergodic source is a convenient mathematical device in that any statistic concerning the relative frequency of symbols found by observing one source for a long time can equally well be found by observing many separate sources for a shorter time. It also corresponds quite adequately to the behaviour of real sources of information for the purposes of data transmission.

An ergodic source capable of emitting n distinct symbols, for which the probability (normalised relative frequency) of the i-th symbol is p_i is said to have an entropy H defined by

$$H = -\sum_{i=1}^{n} p_i \log_2 p_i \quad \text{bits per symbol.}$$

The entropy of the source measures the amount of information carried on average by each separate symbol, and can be regarded as the amount of uncertainty about the state of the source that is on average removed by the arrival of one new symbol. Uncertainty here is thought of as the minimum number of yes/no questions required to specify the state of the source, and the state of the source is defined by listing the outputs from the source as they occur. It may be instructive at this point to evaluate from the formula above the entropy of an unbiassed coin (1 bits/symbol), an unbiassed six sided die (2.59 bits/symbol), a biassed coin which comes down heads three times out of four (0.81 bits/symbol) and a biassed die which shows 6 three times out of eight and 1 to 5 each one time in eight (2.25 bits/symbol). Notice the specific examples of the general result that any move from equal distribution over all possible symbols lowers the entropy of the source.

4.6.1 *Channel capacity and noise*. C. E. Shannon stated and proved a theorem which relates the entropy of a source of symbols to the rate at which a given noise-free data transmission channel can accept output from the source. A formal statement is:

'Let a source have entropy H bits per symbol, and a channel have a capacity to transmit C bits per second. Then it is possible to encode the output of the source in such a way as to transmit on the channel at an average rate $C/H - \varepsilon$ symbols per second, where ε is arbitrarily small. It is not possible to transmit at an average rate greater than C/H.'

This theorem sets an upper bound to the average number of symbols that we can transmit per second over the channel, *even if the channel makes no errors*. Now consider a channel which is noisy, and in which a symbol x inserted into the transmitter may be recognised as a symbol y by the receiver, due to noise in the channel. On the assumption that the symbols fed to the transmitter and output from the receiver could come from ergodic sources we can define

$$H(x) \quad = \quad -\Sigma_x p(x) \log_2 p(x)$$

the entropy of the source, and similarly

$$H(y) \quad = \quad -\Sigma_y p(y) \log_2 p(y)$$

the entropy of the receiver, where $p(x)$, $p(y)$ are the probabilities of a symbol in the source (x) or the receiver (y) and the sums are taken over all possible symbols.

We can define the uncertainty associated with transmitting a symbol x and receiving a symbol y

$$H(x,y) \quad = \quad -\Sigma_x \Sigma_y p(x,y) \log_2 p(x,y),$$

where $p(x,y)$ is the probability of transmitting a particular x and receiving a particular y. (Notice that for a noise free channel $p(x,y) = \delta(x,y)$, i.e. $p(x,y)$ is zero unless $x = y$, when its value is unity.) We can also define a 'transmitter conditional entropy'. We transmit a particular symbol x and observe the probability distribution of the receiver outputs $p_x(y)$ and average over all possible x's to give

$$H_x(y) = -\Sigma_x\, p(x)\, \Sigma_y\, p_x(y) \log_2 p_x(y).$$

The 'receiver conditional entropy' is similarly found by observing the probability distribution of transmitter inputs which give a particular receiver output $p_y(x)$ and averaging over all outputs to give

$$H_y(x) = -\Sigma_y\, p(y)\, \Sigma_x p_y(x) \log_2 p_y(x).$$

The receiver conditional entropy $H_y(x)$ gives the uncertainty at the receiver as to precisely which symbol was actually input to the transmitter. It thus forms a convenient measure of channel noise and is known as the *equivocation* of the channel. The *rate* R of the noisy channel, i.e. the number of bits per binary digit transmitted that it can carry, is given by

$$R = (H(x) - H_y(x)).$$

There are two equivalent expressions for R

$$R = (H(y) - H_x(y)) = (H(x) + H(y) - H(x,y)).$$

If the maximum value of R is taken as the channel capacity of a particular noisy channel, then there is a version of Shannon's theorem for such a channel:

'Let a discrete channel have capacity R and a discrete source have entropy per symbol H. If $H < R$ there exists a coding system such that the output of the source can be transmitted over the channel with an arbitrarily small equivocation. If $H > R$ it is possible to encode the source so that the equivocation is $H - R + \varepsilon$, where ε is arbitrarily small. There is no method of encoding which gives an equivocation less than $H - R$.'

Shannon's Theorems are important in that they allow us to establish upper bounds on the performance of a channel, and from this to set upper bounds on the data rates of the devices we wish to attach to the channel. However, they only assert the existence of a suitable coding system, and do not tell us how to discover which particular coding systems are most valuable in any given circumstances. We now turn to consideration of the physical properties of transmission systems currently in use.

4.7 *Transmission lines*

In this section we examine some of the properties of transmission lines carrying an electrical signal, and show how the properties of a transmission line depend on the frequency of the signals being transmitted. In fact, the signals associated with the transmission of digital data are essentially aperiodic, and so the next section, on Fourier Transforms, deals with the way in which any signal can be regarded as a sum of periodic signals. This provides us with an adequate basis for the discussion of transmission lines actually in use.

Consider a pair of conductors as shown in figure 4.6. The two conductors have

resistance R per unit length
capacitance C per unit length
inductance L per unit length
Leakage conductance G per unit length.

An element of the conductors lying between x and $x + \delta x$ will have potentials V and $V + \delta V$ at its ends; this will be balanced by a resistive potential drop of $iR\delta x$* and an inductive drop of $\frac{\partial i}{\partial t} L\delta x$ so we may write

* Note that we are using i to denote an electrical current, and j to denote the imaginary quantity defined by $j^2 = -1$.

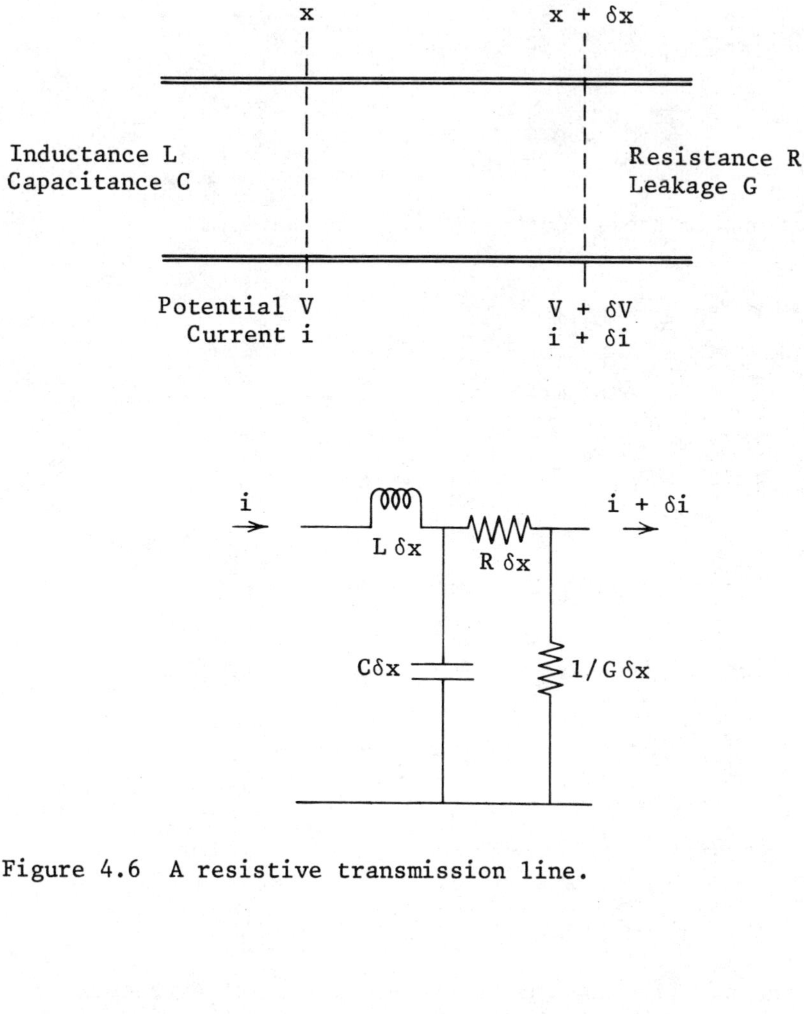

Figure 4.6 A resistive transmission line.

$$V - (V + \delta V) = (iR + \frac{L\partial i}{\partial t})\ \delta x.$$

At the same time there will be a leakage current between the two conductors of $V.G\delta x$ current due to the time change in the potential $\frac{\partial V}{\partial t}.C\delta x$ and the net current flow within the segment will be

$$i - (i + \delta i) = (GV + C\frac{\partial V}{\partial t})\delta x.$$

We may write these equations in the form

$$-\frac{\partial V}{\partial x} = iR + L\frac{\partial i}{\partial t}$$

$$-\frac{\partial i}{\partial x} = GV + C\frac{\partial V}{\partial t}.$$

Solutions to these equations exist in the form

$$V = V_o \exp(j\omega t - hx)$$

$$i = i_o \exp(j\omega t - hx)$$

i.e. $-\frac{\partial V}{\partial x} = hV \qquad -\frac{\partial i}{\partial x} = hi$

$$\frac{\partial V}{\partial t} = j\omega V \qquad \frac{\partial i}{\partial t} = j\omega i.$$

Substitution gives $hV = iR + j\omega ih = i\,(R + j\omega L)$

$$hi = GV + j\omega CV = V\,(G + j\omega C)$$

and elimination of i,V gives

$$-h^2 = L\omega^2 - j\omega\,(RC + GL) - RG.$$

For the special case when R = G = 0 (i.e. for perfect conductors embedded in perfect insulators) h is purely imaginary and has the value

$$j = j\omega\sqrt{LC}$$

and the voltage wave is of the form

$$V = V_o \exp(j\omega t - j\omega\sqrt{LC}x)$$

corresponding to a wave which propagates with constant amplitude with a velocity $\frac{1}{\sqrt{LC}}$ independent of the frequency of oscillation. It is easily shown that for conductors of *any* configuration in a medium of dielectric constant ε and magnetic permeability μ the velocity is given by $\frac{C}{(\varepsilon\mu)^{\frac{1}{2}}}$ where C is the velocity of light. If ε,μ are independent of frequency ω then the wave velocity is independent of ω, and waveforms on such a pair of conductors propagate without attenuation or distortion.

The more interesting situation is where R and G are small in the sense that $R<j\omega L$ while R^2 can be neglected in comparison with $(j\omega L)^2$ and similarly $G<j\omega C$ while G^2 can be neglected in comparison with $(j\omega C)^2$. For such a line the voltage wave velocity is given by

$$V_\omega = \frac{1}{\sqrt{LC}} \left\{ 1 - \frac{1}{8\omega^2} \left(\frac{G}{C} + \frac{R}{L} \right)^2 \right\}$$

so that the wave velocity is now a function of frequency. Thus waves of different frequency will travel with different velocities on such a line - the line is said to be *dispersive*. In addition the quantity h now includes a real component which implies that the amplitude of the voltage wave is an exponentially decaying function of frequency. Thus, waves propagating in the line will suffer an *attenuation* which is not the same for all frequencies, i.e. the relative amplitudes of different frequency signals applied to such a line will be altered.

4.8 *Fourier series*

We have just seen how a transmission line will transmit different frequency sine waves with different velocities and with different attenuations. We now show how any signal can be resolved into a sum of sine waves of different frequencies. We start first by considering a periodic function of time f(t), with period τ, so that

$$f(t) = f(t + n\tau)$$

where n is any integer, positive or negative. We assume that we can express f(t) as a sum of sinusoids whose frequencies are multiples of τ^{-1} i.e. we assume the existence of coefficients α_r such that we may write

$$f(t) = \Sigma_r \alpha_r \exp 2\pi jrt/\tau.$$

The range of r is assumed to be unbounded and in general both f and α are complex. We multiply both sides of this equation by a particular sinusoid $\exp -2\pi jr_o t/\tau$ and integrate over any range τ to give

$$\int_{t_o}^{t_o+\tau} f(t).\exp -2\pi jr_o \frac{t}{\tau}.dt = \int_{t_o}^{t_o+\tau} (\Sigma_r \alpha_r \exp 2\pi jr\frac{t}{\tau}).\exp -2\pi jr_o\frac{t}{\tau}.dt.$$

Under certain conditions we can interchange the order of the two limiting operations on the right-hand side and express the integral of the infinite sum as an infinite sum of integrals. If we assume that these conditions apply then the right-hand side takes the form

$$\Sigma_r \alpha_r \int_{t_o}^{t_o+\tau} \exp 2\pi j(r - r_o)\frac{t}{\tau}\,dt.$$

The integral here is a δ-function, with the value 0 except when $r = r_o$, when its value is τ; in this case the sum of integrals collapses to the value $\tau\alpha_{r_o}$. We thus have the result

$$\alpha_r = \frac{1}{\tau}\int_{t_o}^{t_o+\tau} f(t) \exp -2\pi jr\frac{t}{\tau}\,dt.$$

The set of sinusoids with complex amplitudes α_r is called the Fourier series for f(t) and allows us to resolve f(t) into a sum of sine waves, the Fourier components, whose frequencies are multiples of τ^{-1} and whose amplitudes and phases are determined by the α_r. It is possible to extend this concept to *any* function, whether or not it is periodic. An intuitive approach is to allow the period τ to become indefinitely long, so that the frequencies become indefinitely close together and the sums over discrete frequencies become integrals over continuous frequency ranges.

This ability to resolve any signal into a sum or integral of sine waves is important in that it allows one to consider the effects of the transmission line carrying the signal in terms of its effects on individual Fourier components, and then to recombine these at the far end of the line. Most transmission lines of practical interest are *linear*, that is for a given input displacement (voltage or current) the corresponding output displacement is a linear function of the input. It is easily shown that for such a linear transmission line a pure sine wave applied as input will produce a pure sine wave of the same frequency as output, although the amplitude and phase of the output sine wave will differ from those of the input. We can separate these effects, as we have already seen, into *attenuation* which reduces the amplitude of the output signal and *dispersion* which causes different frequency Fourier components to travel with different velocities. Since both attenuation and dispersion are frequency dependent, the relative amplitudes and phases of different components will become altered and the reconstructed signal will be a distortion of the original signal.

4.9 *Modulation systems*

A signal transmitted over a transmission line undergoes both distortion and attenuation, and these effects are both dependent on the frequencies present in the signal. It is often the case that the frequencies (i.e. Fourier components) of the signal to be transmitted are such that if it were applied directly to the transmission line it would undergo unacceptable distortion, leading to errors of transmission. In such cases the signal may be transformed into one which contains Fourier components which will undergo much less distortion when transmitted, and the received components can then be used to control the reconstruction of the original signal. The transformation of the signal to a new set of frequencies is known as 'modulation' and the recovery of the signal as '*demodulation*'. In this section we examine briefly some aspects of this subject.

4.9.1 *Amplitude modulation*. Suppose we have a signal which is a function of time S(t), and assume that the Fourier components of S(t) all have frequencies that are small compared with some frequency f_c. We start with a pure sine wave $A \sin 2\pi f_c t$, the 'carrier' and use S(t) to control the amplitude of this sine wave to give a wave (k + S(t)).

$$A \exp 2\pi j f_c t$$

where k is chosen so that k+S(t) is always positive. If we express S(t) as a sum of its Fourier components

$$S(t) = \Sigma_r \alpha_r \exp 2\pi j r t/\tau$$

then the modified waveform will be

$$(k+\Sigma_r \alpha_r \exp 2\pi j r \tfrac{t}{\tau}).(A \exp 2\pi j f_c t)$$
$$= Ak \exp 2\pi j f_c t + \Sigma_r A \alpha_r \exp 2\pi j((\tfrac{r}{\tau} + f_c)t).$$

The effect of amplitude modulation is to produce the same Fourier components but with their frequencies shifted so as to be centred around the carrier frequency. We can use as the carrier a frequency chosen so as to best match the properties of the particular transmission line, in the sense that dispersion and attenuation are minimised.

4.9.2 *Phase modulation.* We again start with a signal S(t) and a pure sine wave carrier of frequency f_c. We maintain the amplitude of the carrier at some fixed value, and use S(t) to control the phase of the carrier, so that the signal has a phase given by

$$(2\pi f_c t + \phi S(t))$$

and so can be expressed as

$$A \exp j(2\pi f_c t + \phi S(t)).$$

The Fourier transform of a phase modulated signal is substantially more complicated that the rather simple one for an amplitude modulated signal. However, it can be shown that for many applications the bandwidth of the modulated signal (i.e. the *range* of frequencies involved) is centred on the carrier frequency and has a width slightly greater than $2\phi S_m$ where S_m is the highest frequency present in the signal S(t). Typically $\phi \simeq 5$, so the required bandwidth is ten times that for amplitude modulation.

4.9.3 *Frequency modulation.* In a frequency modulated signal the frequency of the carrier, rather than its phase, is varied in sympathy with the signal S(t). The frequency is then

$$2\pi f_c + \phi' S(t);$$

we regard this as the time derivative of the phase and the resulting signal is

$$A \exp j(2\pi f_c + \phi' S(t))t$$

which is obviously very similar to the expression above for a phase modulated signal. Again analysis of the resulting signal is complicated, but it can be shown that the FM signal requires again a bandwidth of rather more than $2\phi' S_m$.

4.9.4 *Comparison of amplitude, phase and frequency modulation.* It is important to grasp the distinctions between amplitude, phase and frequency modulation. Any *pure* sinusoidal wave is characterised by its amplitude, its phase and its frequency; if any one of these is continuously altered then the resulting wave is no longer a pure sinusoidal wave. We can understand this most simply by considering the Fourier components of the wave. A pure sine wave has only a single Fourier component, whose position on the frequency axis determines the frequency of the waveform and whose complex amplitude determines both the amplitude and phase of the waveform. The three types of modulation all change the single complex amplitude at a discrete frequency into a distribution of complex amplitudes over a range of frequencies but do so in different ways.

Amplitude modulation takes a carrier wave of fixed phase and frequency, and varies the amplitude of the carrier. Phase modulation takes a carrier of fixed amplitude and frequency, and varies the phase of the carrier. Frequency modulation takes a carrier of fixed amplitude and phase and varies the frequency.

In figure 4.7 we attempt to show these differences by showing the resulting signal when a signal shown at figure 4.7(a) is used as the modulating function. Figure 4.7(b) shows the resulting amplitude modulated signal, in which the fre-

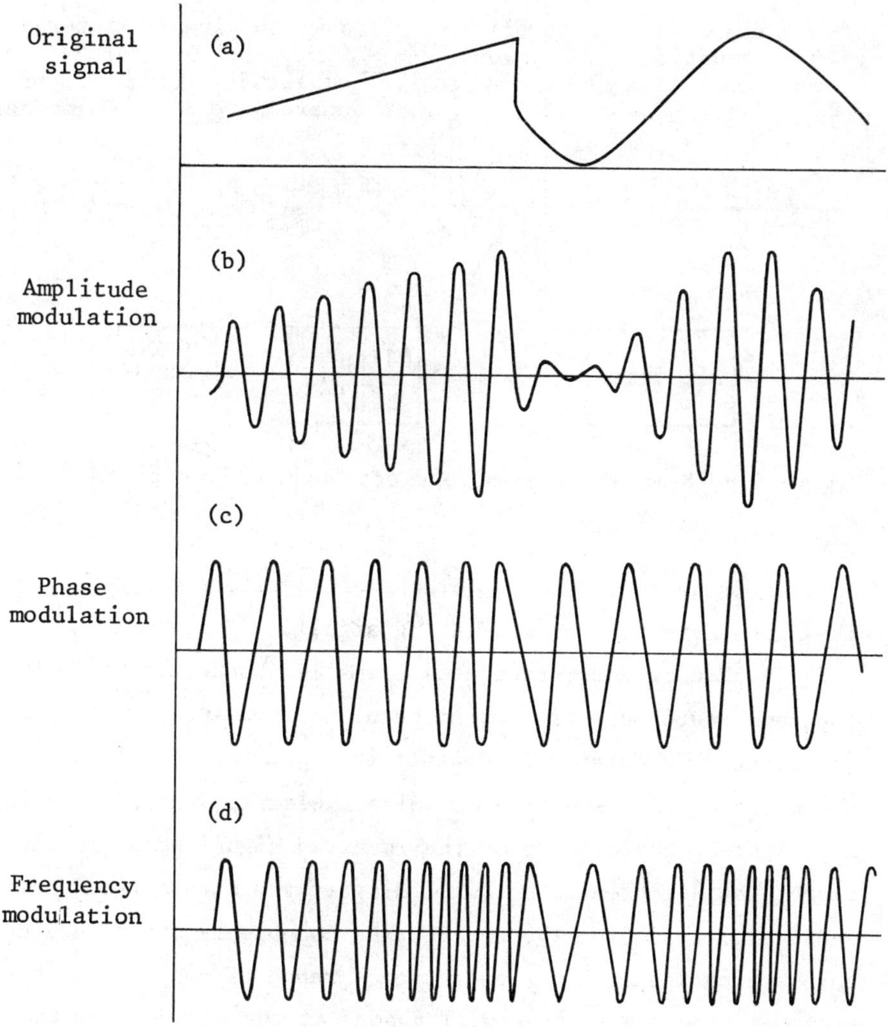

Figure 4.7

quency and phase are effectively unaltered; figure 4.7(c) shows a phase modulated signal, with constant amplitude and nearly constant frequency; and figure 4.7(d) shows a frequency modulated signal with constant amplitude and continuously varying instantaneous frequency. Note that in figure 4.7 the carrier frequency has been deliberately chosen to be very low in comparison with the frequencies in the modulating signal. Normally

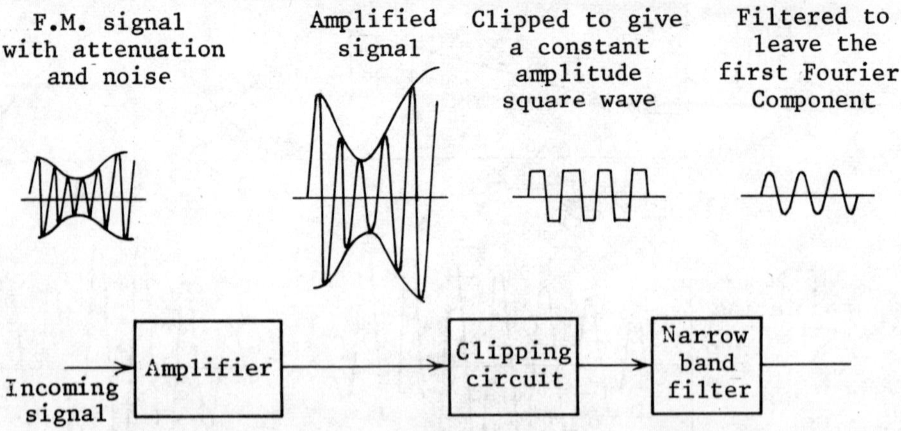

Figure 4.8 Removal of noise and attenuation from an FM or PM signal.

carrier frequencies are two orders of magnitude greater than the frequencies in the modulating signal.

Amplitude modulation uses a smaller bandwidth to carry the same amount of information than is generally used by phase or frequency modulation. However it is much more affected by the presence of distortion or noise. Clearly distortion which may reduce the amplitude of the received signal by different amounts at different times will distort the output from the receiver. Less clearly, any Fourier components of the added noise which lie within the frequency range of the modulating signal at the transmitter will appear at the output from the receiver. Phase and frequency modulation are in general more able to reject the effects of distortion or noise. It is the phase, or frequency, of the incoming signal at the receiver which carries the signal; if the received signal is

(1) amplified very greatly

(2) 'clipped' by limiting the voltage excursions

(3) passed through a narrow band-pass filter

then the output of this filter is a very good reconstruction of the output from the transmitter. This process is nearly always used with phase or frequency modulation techniques.

4.10 *Bibliography*

Data transmission systems, and their interaction with data processing systems, are amongst the most rapidly developing areas of the whole subject. The first two references deal specifically with data transmission as related to computing systems and to digital data.

Data Transmission (McDonald, London 1973), by M.D. Bacon and G.M. Bull, is a non-mathematical treatment of the subject of digital data transmission, and gives an account of some of the software implications which arise when handling teletypes.

Communications Networks for Computers (Wiley, London 1973), by D.W. Davies and D.L.A. Barber, is a very full account of the use of digital data transmission techniques coupled with computer control in the construction of complete data transmission networks.

The three references that follow deal with more general aspects of information theory and data transmission.

Symbols, Signals and Noise (Hutchinson 1962), by J.R. Pierce, is a highly readable introduction to such concepts as entropy and error measures.

Information Theory (Butterworth, London 1971), by J.F. Young, gives a more mathematical and quantitative treatment of the same subject area.

Signals and Information (Butterworth, London 1970), by C.C. Goodyear, is still more mathematical and concentrates particularly on modulation systems for both continuous (analog) and discrete (digital) data.

4.11 *Examples*

(1) A signal

$$a(t) = A \cos 2\pi ft$$

applied as input to a transmission line produces an output

$$b(t) = A\alpha(f) \cos (2\pi ft+\emptyset(f))$$

where $\alpha,\emptyset$ are functions of the frequency f of the input. Explain the effect of this on an arbitrary waveform applied as input to the transmission line.

For a particular line $\alpha(f)$ is known to be very small near to a certain frequency f_c. Explain how such a line can be used to transmit a signal whose spectrum includes frequencies near to f_c.

(University of Leeds, 1972)

(2) Let $F(t) = A \cos 2\pi(f_o+g(t))t$ where $g(t) \ll f_o$ and let a(t) be a slow varying function of t.

Let $S(t) = +1$ if $a(t)F(t) \geq 0$

$S(t) = -1$ if $a(t)F(t) < 0$

and let Z(f) be the Fourier Transform of S(t).

Let $M(f) = 0$ if $|f-f_o| > \delta$

$M(f) = 1$ if $|f-f_o| \leq \delta$ when $\delta \ll f_o$.

What is the relation between the Fourier Transform of M(f) Z(f) and F(t)? Explain the importance of this result when processing frequency modulated signals.

Outline the circuitry necessary to achieve this processing.

(University of Leeds, 1972)

(3) Derive a relationship between the signalling capacity of a channel, its bandwidth, and its signal-to-noise ratio.

A teletype operates at ten characters per second, each character containing effectively eleven binary digits. The binary digits are transmitted as on/off pulses, of 100 volts at 20 milliamps, on a channel with a bandwidth of 330 Hz. Estimate the maximum permissible noise power on the channel, and comment on your result.
(University of Leeds, 1974)

(4) It is required to transmit the successive values of a voltage, sampled at 1 millisecond intervals, with a nominal accuracy of 1 millivolt in the range 0 to +4 volts. Estimate the entropy of the transmitter, and the channel capacity of the signal path. Design a suitable code which would correct single-bit errors, and detect 2 bit errors in any value. If the voltage is initially always exactly zero, and has a maximum rate of change of 15 volts per second, show quantitatively what economies can be made in the system, whilst retaining the error detection and correction capabilities.
(University of Leeds, 1970)

(5) (a) 'Data entering or leaving data-processing machines is normally binary in form, and consist of rectangular pulses. To be able to transmit the data over certain lines the pulses have to be manipulated electronically.'

Describe how data such as that above may be transmitted over long distances giving at least three methods of modulation.

(b) Explain the difference between time-division multiplexing and frequency division multiplexing.

(University of St. Andrews, 1974)

(6) Why is there a need to use modulation techniques when transmitting information over telephone lines? Describe the methods of modulation used and compare the performance of these methods when used to carry binary-coded data transmitted over telephone lines.
(University of Essex, 1971)

(7) Describe the difficulties inherent in communications via long transmission lines and detail techniques which are typically employed in overcoming these difficulties.

A transmission line has the following constants per mile loop; $R = 20\ \Omega$, $L = 3$ mH, $C = 0.06\ \mu F$ and $G = 10\ \mu$mho. Calculate the value of the impedance that would correctly terminate the line at a frequency of 5000/2 Hz.
(University of Essex, 1973)

5 · Processing

The primary function of a processing unit is to operate on a particular physical representation of an encoding of digital information, and without changing the representation, to produce an encoding of fresh information. In current digital systems the particular physical representation used is almost always a voltage measured with respect to a local earth as zero volts, and our description will be confined to this case. Also, as was explained in chapter 1, the encoding is almost always a two valued encoding in which the voltage takes on a value in one of two predetermined ranges to represent either a 0 or a 1, and we shall not consider any other systems. We therefore require firstly physical devices constructed in such a way as to allow us to generate and manipulate the physical representations of 0 and 1, and then we require a convenient algebraic symbolism which allows us to construct larger assemblies of such devices to carry out operations on encodings of information without paying undue attention to the details of the physical representation. Using this symbolism we shall consider the construction of units to carry out some of the more common manipulations encountered in the processors of computing systems.

5.1 *Basic computing elements*

In order to discuss the basic computing circuits that we shall require it is necessary to consider the particular algebraic operations on two valued variables that we wish to implement. Basically two such classes of algebras exist - one deals with arithmetic over fields of two elements and is in fact of very little direct application. The others deal with Boolean algebras, which are applicable to assertions that are either true or false; the two values are usually mapped on to the symbols 1 and 0 respectively. An earlier volume in this series 'Introduction to Logical Design of Digital Circuits' (Reeves 1970) gives a more formal treatment of Boolean algebras.

If x is a variable which can take one of two values 0 or 1, then we can form the following four functions of x

x	f_0	f_1	f_2	f_3
0	0	0	1	1
1	0	1	0	1

Table 5.1

Of these four functions f_0 and f_3 are independent of x (they are in fact the 'functions' 0 and 1 respectively) while f_1 is simply x itself; the remaining function f_2 is 1 when x is 0 and 0 when x is 1. It is known as 'not x' or the inverse of x and is written as either $\bar{x}$ or $\neg x$.

If x, y are two two-state variables there are sixteen possible functions of x,y:

x	y	f_0	f_1	f_2	f_3	f_4	f_5	f_6	f_7	f_8	f_9	f_{10}	f_{11}	f_{12}	f_{13}	f_{14}	f_{15}
0	0	0	0	0	0	0	0	0	0	1	1	1	1	1	1	1	1
0	1	0	0	0	0	1	1	1	1	0	0	0	0	1	1	1	1
1	0	0	0	1	1	0	0	1	1	0	0	1	1	0	0	1	1
1	1	0	1	0	1	0	1	0	1	0	1	0	1	0	1	0	1

Table 5.2

Obviously not all sixteen of these functions are of practical value; as before two of them, f_0 and f_{15} are simply the functions 0 and 1, independent of the values of either x or y. Others of them are independent of one of the variables; for example function f_3 is simply x while f_{10} is $\bar{y}$. Others still are non-commutative, that is $f(x,y) \neq f(y,x)$, and in general non-commutative functions are difficult to manipulate. However, six of the functions are especially important. They fall naturally into three pairs:

f_1, f_{14}	f_1 is 1 if and only if both x and y are 1; this is the AND or *product* of x,y written $x \wedge y$ or $x.y$ f_{14} is the inverse of f_1
f_7, f_8	f_7 is 1 if either of x or y is 1 or if both are 1; this is the OR or *sum* of x,y written $x \vee y$ or $x+y$ f_8 is the inverse of f_7
f_9, f_6	f_9 is 1 if x and y are equal; this is the *equivalence* of x,y, written $x \equiv y$ f_6 is the inverse of f_9 written $x \not\equiv y$.

It is easily seen that these three functions, and their inverses, are commutative. As is explained in detail in Reeves' book they have other properties which make their use particularly attractive. We therefore require units which will compute the inverse of a single variable, or the sum, product or equivalence of two or more variables. In the next section units to perform these functions are described in terms of existing technology.

5.2 *Circuit technology*

5.2.1 *Inverters*. We have already discussed the inverting amplifier as a component of a flip-flop; we now consider its description in terms of Boolean algebra. We can tabulate the inputs and outputs for a single inverter as

INPUT	OUTPUT
0	V_{cc}
V_{cc}	0

Table 5.3(a)

If we assign a voltage near to earth the value 0, and a voltage near to supply voltage the value 1 this table becomes

INPUT	OUTPUT
0	1
1	0

Table 5.3(b)

and we can use such an amplifier as an inverter.

An inverter used in this way will be designed to have a narrow switching range and to bring its outputs as near to ground and to V_{cc} as possible.

5.2.2 *Diode logic*. Units for evaluating the AND or OR function can be constructed using only diodes and resistors. Such units are frequently referred to as 'gates', and we shall see that the typical implementation uses what is in effect a diode gate, followed by an inverter.

Consider the circuit shown in figure 5.1.

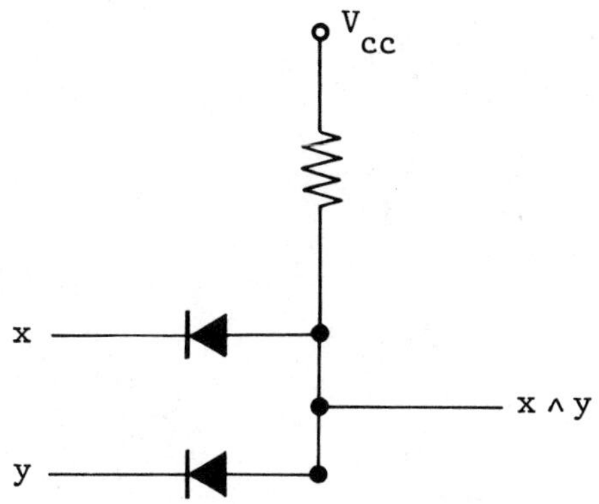

Figure 5.1 Positive logic diode AND gate.

Two diodes are connected via a resistor to the supply voltage. If either of the inputs at x,y is at ground the corresponding diode will conduct heavily and the output will fall nearly to earth. If both x,y are connected to a voltage V_{cc} the output will rise to V_{cc}. We can again draw up a table

INPUT x	INPUT y	OUTPUT
0	0	0
V_{cc}	0	0
0	V_{cc}	0
V_{cc}	V_{cc}	V_{cc}

Table 5.4(a)

or in terms of the assignments of the preceding section

INPUT x	INPUT y	OUTPUT
0	0	0
1	0	0
0	1	0
1	1	1

Table 5.4(b)

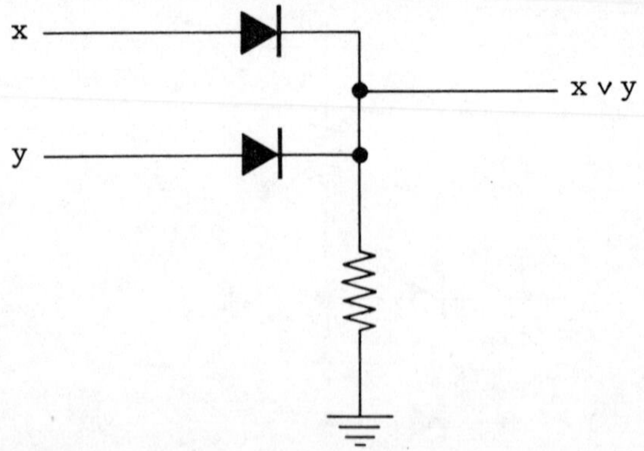

Figure 5.2 Positive logic diode OR gate.

Obviously the circuit of figure 5.1 can function as an AND gate. In a similar way we can construct an OR gate, figure 5.2, in which the output is a 1 (i.e. approximately V_{cc}) if either input is a 1, and is otherwise a 0 (i.e. approximately earth), giving a table 5.5(a) or table 5.5(b). The circuits 5.1, 5.2 suffer from a serious defect. For a typical diode the forward, low resistance may be say 10^3 ohms and the reverse bias, high resistance may be 10^6 ohms. For

INPUT x	INPUT y	OUTPUT
0	0	0
V_{cc}	0	V_{cc}
0	V_{cc}	V_{cc}
V_{cc}	V_{cc}	V_{cc}

Table 5.5(a)

or

INPUT x	INPUT y	OUTPUT
0	0	0
1	0	1
0	1	1
1	1	1

Table 5.5(b)

the AND gate of figure 5.1 we require the load resistor connected to V_{cc} to be of such a value that nearly all the voltage drop occurs across this when either diode conducts i.e. a resistance large compared with 10^3 ohms. In the same way, the resistor to earth in figure 5.2 must have a value high in comparison with 10^3 ohms. However, when either of these gates is driving inputs on other gates, the requirement to draw current from the supply voltage, or to sink current to earth, via this same high resistance will cause the output to move away from V_{cc} or ground, and will ultimately degrade the output to the point where it is impossible to distinguish between a supposed 0 or 1 output. This degradation of output voltage can be reduced by connecting the output of the diode gate as an input to an amplifier, and allowing the amplifier to provide enhanced current driving capability which will reduce the signal degradation caused by loading when driving other inputs. This leads quite naturally to the construction of diode-transistor logic.

5.2.3 *Diode-transistor logic.* The diode gates and inverters described so far were first realised using discrete components. The advent of integrated circuit fabrication techniques in the mid-1960s allows the production of complete circuits containing a multiple input AND or OR diode gate and an inverter on a single integrated circuit. The typical arrangement of such Diode-Transistor Logic (DTL) is shown in figure 5.3(a) and 5.3(b); it consists of a diode logic AND (5.3(a)) or OR (5.3(b)) gate, linked directly to a transistor inverter. The input labelled 'node' allows expansion of the number of inputs, by adding further clusters of suitably connected diodes. Notice that these circuits compute directly the functions f_{14} and f_8. DTL is still very widely used. It is rather slow, but is very cheap, uses relatively little power and has excellent noise immunity.

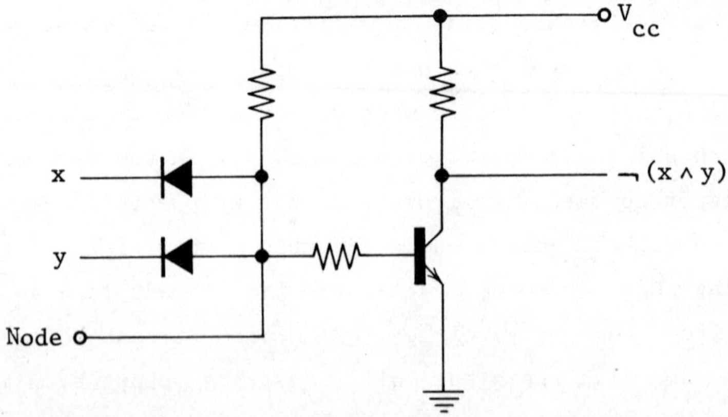

(a) A diode-transistor logic NAND gate

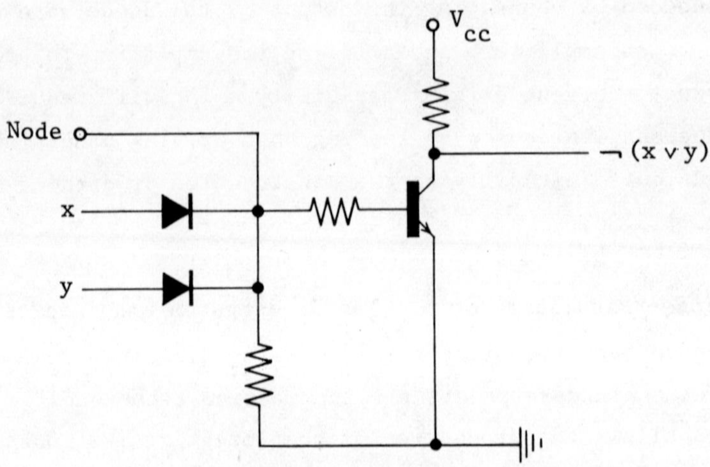

(b) A transistor-transistor logic NOR gate

Figure 5.3 Examples of diode-transistor logic.

5.2.4 *Transistor-transistor logic.* Diode-transistor logic was the first type of integrated circuit to be commercially available; however it suffered from being rather slow in comparison with the best speeds that could be achieved using discrete components and so Transistor-Transistor Logic (TTL) was introduced as a higher speed development. The slow speed

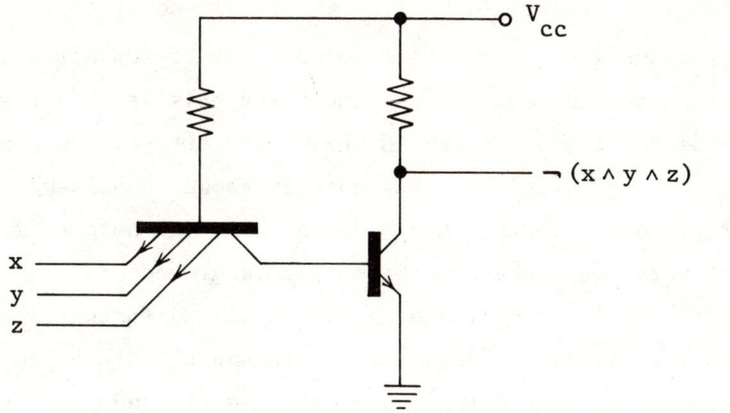

(a) A transistor-transistor logic NAND gate.

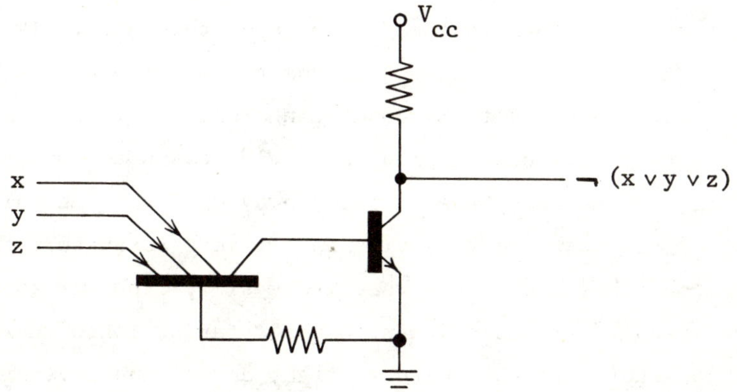

(b) A transistor-transistor logic NOR gate.

Figure 5.4 Examples of Transistor-transistor logic.

of DTL is attributable largely to the stray capacitances associated with the separate diodes driving into the base of the transistor forming the inverter. Using integrated circuit technology it is possible to fabricate a multi-emitter transistor, in which the multiple emitters perform the same logical function as the diodes of figure 5.2. The resulting circuits are illustrated in figures 5.4(a) and 5.4(b). The multi-emitter transistor on the left in each case forms either the Boolean product or sum of its inputs and this is then inverted by the second transistor which drives the output. In practice rather than the simple output inverter shown, a balanced output stage would probably be used, in which the output impedance is kept very small whether the output is ground or V_{cc}. Note that with TTL it is no longer possible to add further inputs by coupling via diodes to a node. TTL and DTL are often used in combinations, since their switching levels and power requirements are very similar; TTL is faster, but slightly more expensive.

5.2.5 *Emitter coupled logic*. Although TTL is faster than DTL, it still suffers in speed because of the relatively long times required to dissipate space-charges within the transistor. A transistor which is fully conducting contains large numbers of carriers in its base region, and only ceases to conduct when all the carriers have migrated away from the central region of the transistor leaving no carriers to support the conduction; this process is relatively slow. The way to still higher speeds is found by using *non-saturating* logic in which the transistors are not switched right across the switching region from the fully conducting to the fully non-conducting state, but work within the switching region, thus avoiding the necessity to sweep out the carriers. A simplified circuit is shown in figure 5.5. While all the inputs x,y,z are near to ground, none of the associated transistors conducts heavily, the voltage V_{ref} applied to the base of the output transistor ensures that that transistor conducts, and the output voltage is thus near to ground. Applying a sufficiently positive signal, say 0.8V to any one of x,y or z will cause the associated transistor to conduct, carrying the emitter of the output transistor above V_{ref}, shutting off this transistor,

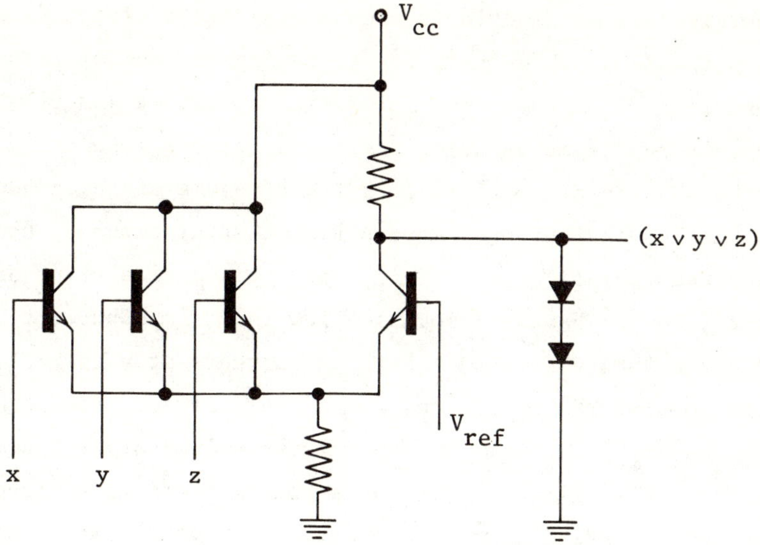

Figure 5.5 An emitter-coupled logic OR gate.

and allowing the output to rise towards V_{cc}. The reference voltage V_{ref} is typically 0.4V and is generated on the same integrated circuit by using a transistor stablilised voltage divider across the supply voltage (not shown). The chain of diodes at the output ensures that the output never rises above about 0.8V, which is a sufficient swing to drive a similar gate. Because the voltage swings are so small, and as the input transistors all operate in their active switching region the circuit can be made very fast; however the very small voltage swings also mean that such circuits are easily affected by noise on the input lines.

5.2.6 *Circuits using field effect transistors.* The circuits discussed so far use junction transistors whose production requires the deposition of many layers of accurately controlled thickness and composition. This leads to a relatively high failure rate in the manufacturing stages. The detection of these failures and the scrapping of rejected assemblies both lead to a high price for the finished product. An alternative technology uses metal oxide semiconductor/field effect transistors (MOS/FET) which call for fewer layers and for less precise control of the doping of these layers. A junction transistor functions by using one input (to the base) to control the density of carriers in a fixed volume of semiconductor which carries the current between two other electrodes, the emitter and the collector. This leads to a device which draws current into the base and so has a low input impedance, typically a few thousand ohms, requiring currents of a few milliamps to control the operation. In a field effect transistor one of the inputs is used to control the volume of semiconductor which contains a fixed density of carriers; this is achieved by having a narrow *channel* of very lightly doped semiconductor between the current source and the current sink (figure 5.6). Adjacent to this channel but insulated from it is a layer of very highly doped semiconductor. Applying a voltage to the electrode which forms the top face of this region effectively causes it to expand or contract at the expense of the lightly doped region, and so reduces or enhances the current flow through the channel. FETs are voltage operated rather than current operated, and have a high input impedance, in the order of hundreds of megohms; this high impedance allows a single output to drive very large numbers of inputs, which we shall see is advantageous in some applications. FET's also have low power requirements compared with junction transistors, but are relatively slow.

Figure 5.6(b) shows an FET three-input NOR gate; the inputs condition three FET's in series and a further three in parallel. With all inputs at ground, the three transistors in parallel are all turned off, while those in series are turned on, and the output point rises to very nearly the supply voltage. If any input rises to the supply voltage, its associated series FET is cut off, one of the parallel FET's is turned on, and the output falls very nearly to ground.

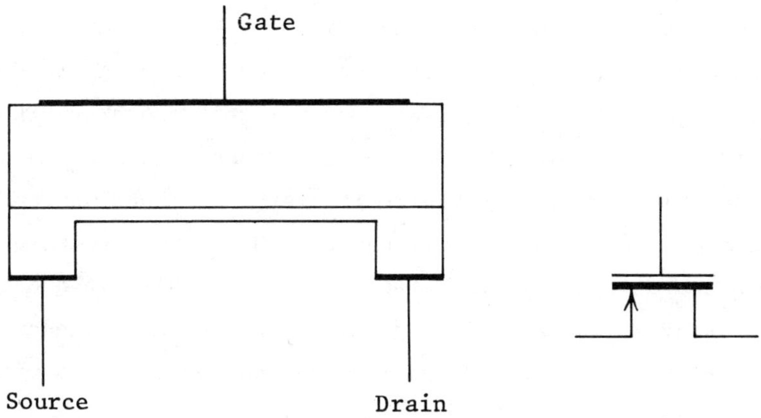

Figure 5.6(a) A field effect transistor.

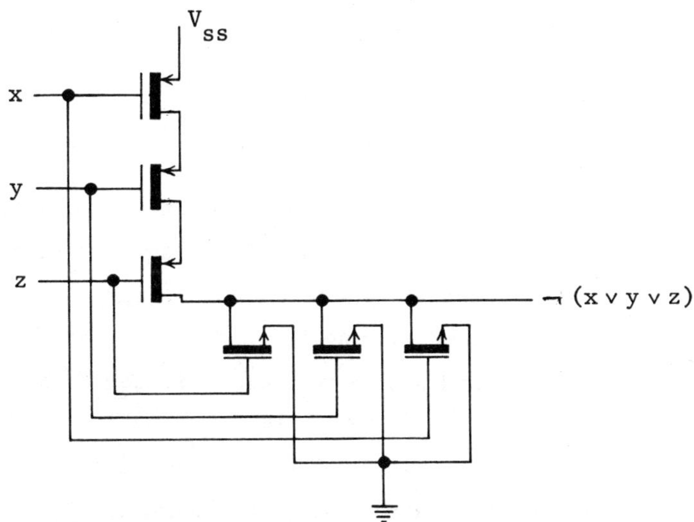

Figure 5.6(b) A field effect transistor NOR gate.

5.2.7 *Comparison of DTL, TTL, ECL and FET systems.* The four principal families of logic described can be compared in terms of four black-box properties; cost, power requirement, speed and noise immunity. The quality of a circuit is highest for lower cost, least power, highest speed and greatest rejection of noise.

The *cost* of a gate is determined by the unit cost of the

gate, but also includes consideration of the ease of assembly and interconnection. The interconnection technology is conditioned in part by the noise immunity; units such as DTL which are very tolerant of noise can be interconnected more readily than say ECL; however, ECL with its very low input and output impedances can be more easily matched on to the rather low impedances offered by transmission lines. Table 5.6 quotes the cost of a typical single gate, purchased on a standard dual-in-line package, and the cost per gate associated with a much more complex MSI or LSI assembly.

The *power requirement* of a gate is influenced to some extent by the speed required of it; within limits it is possible by using higher supply voltages, i.e. greater power, to improve the speed, or by allowing lower speeds to reduce the power. The power requirement quoted is an estimate of what one might normally expect.

The *speed* of a gate is measured by quoting the time between a change on one input which will change the output, and the corresponding change on the output. Since the rise and fall times will depend on the details of the circuit driven by the output, and also are often different for a rising output or a falling one the times quoted are again estimates for a circuit which is driving a short (few mm) connection to an input on a device of the same family.

The *noise immunity* is not easily quantified; it is possible for some families (e.g. DTL) to quote voltage ranges within which inputs 0 or 1 must lie for satisfactory operation. However, for FET's with their very low input power requirements such an approach may be misleading.

The table clearly shows the pay offs that are available to the system designer, in terms of price vs speed, power vs speed, and the benefits, especially, with FET technology, of using medium or large scale integrated circuits.

A consequence of the relatively high power requirement

of DTL, TTL or ECL is that there is a strict limit on the number of gates that can be fabricated on a single chip without running into severe problems of heat dissipation. A typical dual-in-line package can dissipate a few watts and thus can accommodate less than one-hundred DTL or TTL gates, only about ten ECL gates, but several thousand FET gates. Thus while DTL or TTL technology allows only relatively simple units in a single package, for example, a four bit parallel adder (see §5.6.1), FET technology allows a single package to contain say a 1,024 bit memory or a complete arithmetic processor handling 8-bit quantities.

Comparison of DTL, TTL, ECL, MOS systems

		DTL	TTL	ECL	MOS
Cost	one off	10p	20p	150p	35p
	MSI/LSI assembly	1p	2p	20p	0.15p
power per gate		50 mW	50 mW	200 mW	10 μW
speed		30 ns	7 ns	1 ns	60 ns
noise		excellent	good	poor	good

Table 5.6

5.3 *Functions, expressions and circuits*

A function of a set of variables associates a value with certain values of the variables; the set of variables are the *arguments* of the function, the set of all values of the arguments for which a resulting function value is defined form the *domain* of the function and the set of possible function values form the *range* of the function. A function may be defined in a rather general way; more usefully it may be possible to find an expression of the arguments which when evaluated yields the function value. It is important to grasp the distinction between a function and an expression. For example

$$e^x = \sum_{0}^{n} x^r/r!$$

purports to equate the exponential function (of a single argument x) with an expression in x (but which includes a new variable n). However, this expression may still be an acceptable approximation within certain parts of the domain and provided we can be certain that we are operating within that part of the domain the expression may well be more convenient than the function

$$e^x = \lim_{n\to\infty} (1 + \frac{x}{n})^n.$$

A single function may be approximated by many expressions; this is still true even where the defining function is given as an expression, for we may in general rearrange the expression in many ways and provided that in carrying out the rearrangement we do not break any of the rules of the algebra which we are using the rearranged expression will yield the same values as the original expression. The example of the exponential function involves a real function of real arguments, whereas we are more concerned with Boolean functions of Boolean arguments. However, the relationship between a function and an expression which computes values of that function within a domain is valid in both cases.

In a Boolean algebra it is possible to go further and to associate with any expression a *circuit* whose inputs are arguments and output a function value. The circuit contains functional units (gates) which compute the appropriate functions of their inputs and whose outputs serve as inputs to further gates*. Such circuits will appear in the remainder of this book, and can serve as a very convenient method of describing a system. On such a circuit connections are represented as a continuous line. The connections frequently cross and the convention is that where lines cross and connect a 'blob' is marked. If no blob is present, no connection (i.e. no passage of a signal value) occurs.

The most common gates are AND or OR gates, or NAND or NOR gates. These are represented by the symbols shown in figure 5.7 for two input gates. More inputs can be added as required. Note that the open circle implies inversion of a signal.

For example, suppose we wish to compute a function of two arguments which is 1 if one and only one of its two arguments is a 1. Suitable expressions are

$$\begin{aligned} f(x,y) &= (\bar{x} \wedge y) \vee (x \wedge \bar{y}) \\ &= -((x \vee \bar{y}) \wedge (\bar{x} \vee y)) \\ &= (x \vee y) \wedge (\bar{x} \vee \bar{y}) \end{aligned}$$

which yield three circuits as in figure 5.8. It is important to realise that each of the three circuits of figure 5.8 (see page 151) computes the *same* function of the variables x and y although they achieve this by evaluating quite different expressions. Clearly the three circuits are of roughly com-

---

* It is possible to generate the circuit for computing an expression quite automatically. The expression is mapped into a tree, whose nodes are gates and whose branches correspond to connections from one output *up* a branch as an input to the next node - the output appears naturally as the root of this tree. The details can be found in 'Information Representation and Manipulation in a Computer', by E.S. Page and L.B. Wilson.

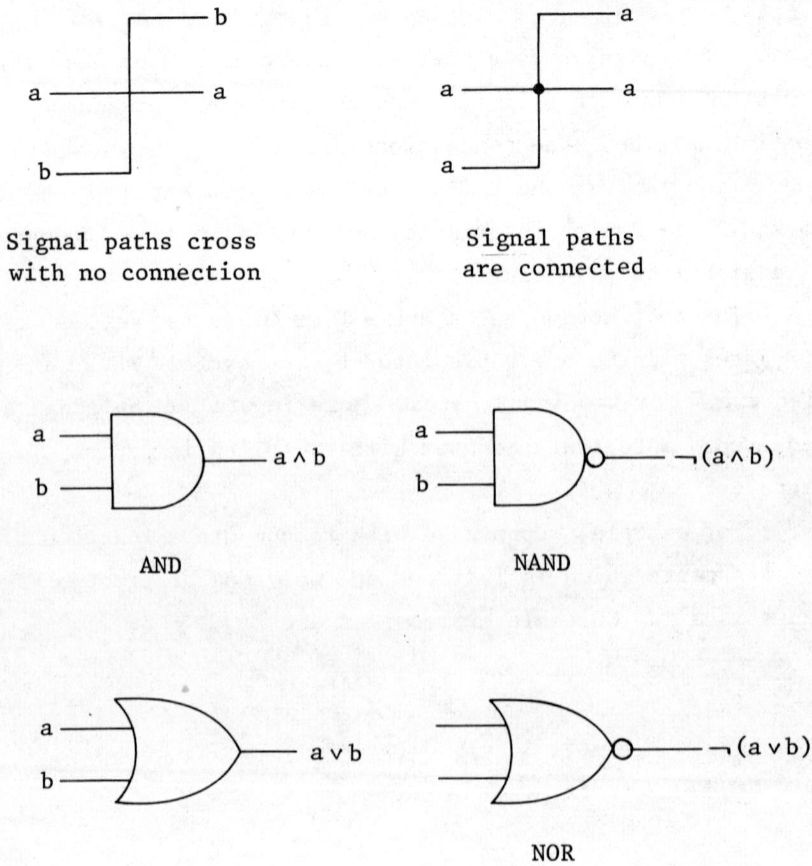

Figure 5.7 Decision circuit conventions.

parable complexity and hence would cost about the same to construct; perhaps less clearly they would all operate at about the same speed. It is possible to produce rather more formal definitions of the cost and speed of a circuit, and using these definitions, techniques can be arrived at for deciding which among many alternative circuits (i.e. expressions) equivalent to a given function is the cheapest and fastest. This topic is dealt with fully in Reeves', and we shall not pursue it any further here. Rather we shall concentrate on circuits currently in use for performing some of the more common operations on a digital computer.

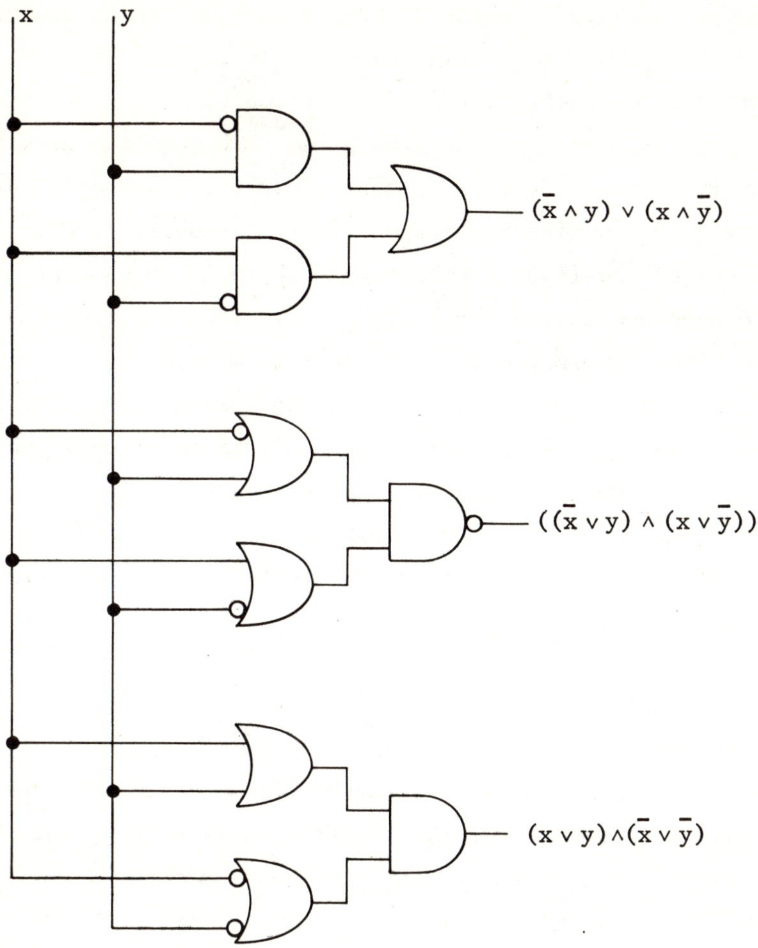

Figure 5.8 Three different circuits computing the same function.

5.4 *Sequential networks*

In carrying out any operation on a digital system we design circuits which operate on stored encodings of the quantities we manipulate, and as we have seen we shall regard this as being formally equivalent to computing a Boolean function of a number of Boolean variables. The Boolean variables will be encoded as 1/0 values of two state memory elements and it is convenient to make a careful distinction between a *decision circuit*, which contains NO storage elements, and a *sequential network* in which storage elements form an essential part of the complete circuit. A decision circuit does not contain any feedback, in which a function of the output of a gate appears as an input to that gate. A sequential network almost invariably contains feedback loops of this sort. In theory, decision circuits respond instantaneously to changes of values of the input variables and there is no concept of time dependence in their behaviour. (In practice there is a finite time between a change of input to a gate and the corresponding change of output, but we shall in general ignore this.) A sequential network contains decision circuits, but also contains memory elements, and its behaviour is essentially a function of time. We can illustrate this by considering one of the simplest forms of circuits with feedback, often referred to as a 'latch'.

5.4.1 *A simple example*. The circuit in figure 5.9, (see page 153), contains a pair of two input NOR gates, in which the output of each gate serves as one of the two inputs to the other gate. Suppose that the inputs r,s are both 0, and that the output of one of the gates, the upper one say is a 1 as shown. The presence of a 1 as an input to the lower NOR gate ensures that its output is a 0, giving two inputs of 0 on the upper gate and ensuring an output of 1. If the output of the lower gate were to be a 1, then this same argument could be repeated, interchanging 'lower' and 'upper'. Thus a pair of NOR gates as shown can remain indefinitely in a state where one gate outputs a 1 and the other a 0; there are two such states and they are both stable.

If we consider a situation in which both gates output a 0, then we shall find that each gate has both inputs as 0, leading to an output of 1 from both gates. Similarly, if both gates output a 1 then both have inputs of 1, leading to an output of 0 from both gates. Thus either of these conditions

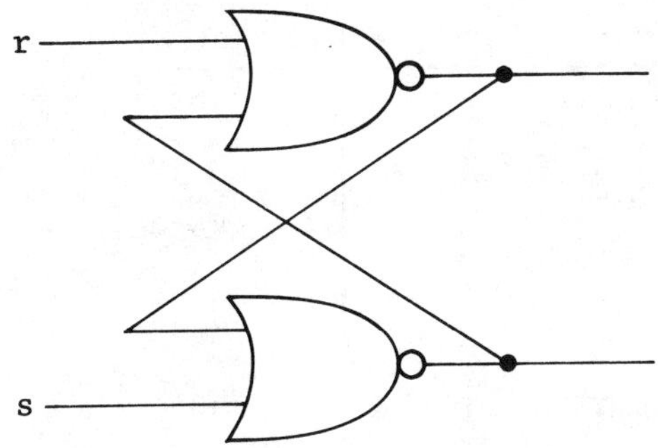

Figure 5.9 A latch (simple flip-flop).

is unstable, and in practice the circuit will collapse to a stable state where one output is 1, the other 0.

Suppose now a transient signal of 1 is applied to the input r, while s is held at 0; regardless of the other input to the upper gate, its output will fall to 0 for the duration of the 1 on r, and the output from the lower gate will rise to 1 and thus hold the circuit stable. Thus we can force a 1 on the output of the lower gate by applying a transient 1 on the input r; this 1 is then 'latched' into the circuit. Similarly we could apply a transient 1 to input s which would latch into the circuit leaving a stable state with 1 on the upper gates output. If we raise both inputs to 1, both outputs will fall to 0 and stay there until one of the inputs falls to 0; whichever 1 on the inputs falls latest will define the new state.

We can draw up a truth table (table 5.7) for such a circuit, which defines a function. The inputs to the function are

the value of q - the output of the upper gate
the value of r - the input to the upper gate
the value of s - the input to the lower gate

and its value is

the value of q′- the output of the upper gate
after both of r,s become 0

The truth table is shown overleaf.

q	r	s	q′
0	0	0	0
0	0	1	1
0	1	0	0
0	1	1	?
1	0	0	1
1	0	1	1
1	1	0	0
1	1	1	?

Table 5.7

where the query implies that the value of q′ is not defined when both r and s are simultaneously 1.

The latch circuit just described can equally well be thought of as an implementation of a flip-flop, but discussed now in terms of a logical description with signals of 0,1, rather than as the physical description of chapter 2.

5.4.2 *Clocked flip-flop*. We shall assume that wherever we are discussing a sequential network the memory elements it contains are based on this simple latch circuit. In practice, the flip-flops used in registers associated with a processing activity will be rather more complicated. In particular such a flip-flop almost invariably uses the gated form of circuit shown in figure 5.10. In this circuit, the clock input is connected to a source of clock pulses, that is to a device which produces a stream of 1→0→1→0 transitions. The time between these is chosen so as to allow all the decision circuits associated with the sequential network to reach a steady state again following the changes in the values of their inputs. The clock inputs may all be driven from a single external source of signals, or may be derived from within the network itself.

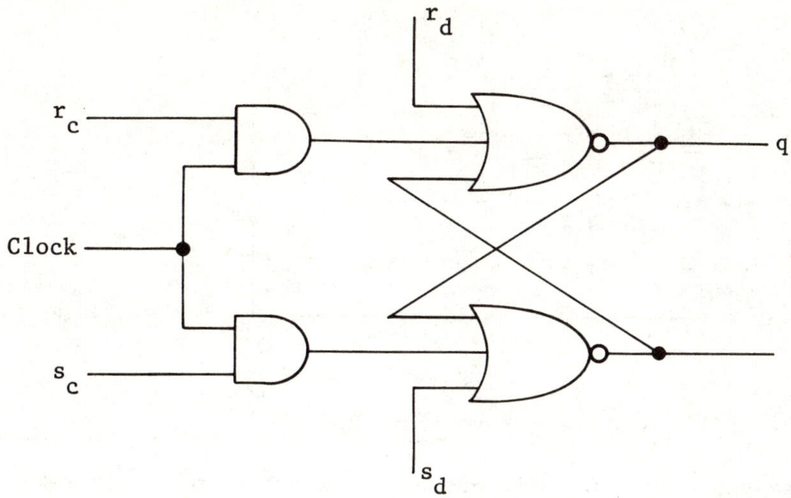

Figure 5.10 A flip-flop with clocked and direct inputs.

In either case, the inputs to the flip-flop will only be effective during the clock pulse, and the behaviour of the whole sequential network can be discussed in terms of its states immediately following the 1→0 transitions of successive clock pulses. The flip-flop includes two inputs which are not governed by the clock signals and which allow the state of the flip-flop to be set independent of the appearance of a clock signal.

5.4.3 *Master-slave flip-flops.* A further refinement still is outlined in figure 5.11. (See page 156.) This contains two flip-flops. During a clock signal, i.e. when the clock signal is 1, the inputs to the first flip-flop are gated into that flip-flop, whose outputs are simultaneously disconnected by the inverted clock signal at the AND gates between the master and slave flip-flops. When the clock signal falls to 0, the AND gates, between the master and the slave receive 1's at their clock controlled inputs and the state of the master flip-flop is transferred into the slave. The advantage of such a flip-flop is that transfer into the flip-flop occurs as the clock

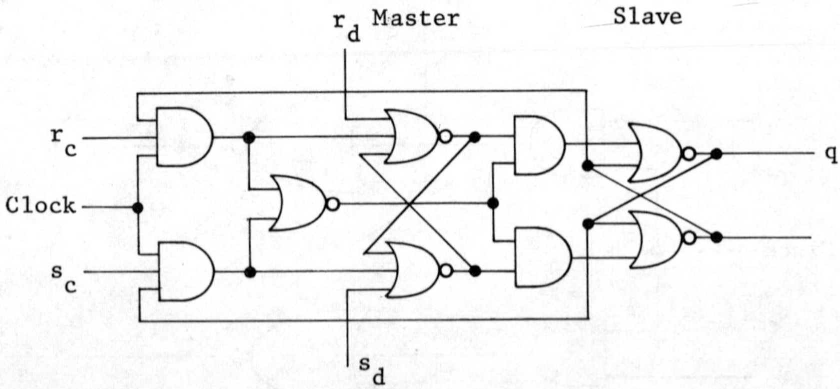

Figure 5.11 A master-slave flip-flop.

pulse rises from 0 to 1, but that the output does not take up its new value until the clock pulse falls from 1 to 0. This allows very straightforward interconnection in some of the circuits which will be discussed later. Such a flip-flop can readily be manufactured using normal integrated circuit techniques at virtually no greater total cost than the simple latch of figure 5.9.

We now consider the implementation of some typical computing circuits, using the functional units which we have described. In carrying out this description we make use of the conceptual framework outlined by figure 1.1. We consider first mapping the abstract concept which we wish to manipulate into some encoding on two digits (0,1); we then consider the mathematical action we wish to implement and use this to define functions which relate the outputs of our computing circuits to their inputs; using the techniques of Boolean algebra we can convert these functions into expressions which we can in turn convert to decision circuits.

We shall find it convenient to differentiate between operations which apply to representations of objects which a programmer wishes to manipulate such as numbers or character strings, and those which apply to components of the system on which these operations are implemented. (We have already met several of these latter, for example, interfaces and control circuits associated with storage devices.)

5.5 *Encodings of numbers*

In current computing systems numbers are encoded almost invariably as either strings of decimal digits each represented by a character, or in what is normally referred to as 'binary'; within these two major groupings many subdivisions exist.

5.5.1 *Character decimal encodings.* In character form a number X is encoded as an ordered string of p decimal digits d_i in the form

$$X = \sum_{0}^{p-1} d_i \, 10^i \qquad 0 \leq d_i \leq 9$$

where each digit d_i lies in the range 0 to 9 and is usually in turn encoded as four binary digits b_{i0} to b_{i3} such that

$$d_i = \sum_{0}^{3} b_{ij} \, 2^j \qquad d_{ij} = 0,1.$$

The decimal number 1973 encoded in this form would appear on 16 binary digits as

i	3	2	1	0
j	3210	3210	3210	3210
b_{ij}	0001	1001	0111	0011
d_i	1	9	7	3
$d_i 10^i$	1000	900	70	3

Table 5.8

There are obvious attractions in this encoding. In particular conversion to or from the external form such as printing on paper is relatively straightforward. However, as we shall see, by comparison with the technique of using binary numbers, there are severe drawbacks when designing circuits to manipulate numbers encoded in this way.

5.5.2 *Binary encoding*. In binary form a number X is encoded as an ordered string of p binary digits x_i in the form

$$X = \sum_{0}^{p-1} x_i \, 2^i \qquad x_i = 0,1$$

where each digit x_i is either 0 or 1. The decimal number 1973 would appear as

i	10	9	8	7	6	5	4	3	2	1	0
x_i	1	1	1	1	0	1	1	0	1	0	1
$x_i 2^i$	1024	512	256	128	0	32	16	0	4	0	1

Table 5.9

At first sight this is much less easily dealt with. However, consider what happens if we wish to add two numbers, encoded either both in character decimal form, or both in binary. For a pair of decimal digits in character decimal form we have an addition table

$$s = x + y \quad 0 \leq s,x,y \leq 9$$

of the form shown opposite

y \ x	0	1	2	3	4	5	6	7	8	9
0	0	1	2	3	4	5	6	7	8	9
1	1	2	3	4	5	6	7	8	9	0*
2	2	3	4	5	6	7	8	9	0*	1*
3	3	4	5	6	7	8	9	0*	1*	2*
4	4	5	6	7	8	9	0*	1*	2*	3*
5	5	6	7	8	9	0*	1*	2*	3*	4*
6	6	7	8	9	0*	1*	2*	3*	4*	5*
7	7	8	9	0*	1*	2*	3*	4*	5*	6*
8	8	9	0*	1*	2*	3*	4*	5*	6*	7*
9	9	0*	1*	2*	3*	4*	5*	6*	7*	8*

Table 5.10

Here the * by a result indicates that there is to be a unit carry into the next more significant digit position. For a binary number we have the much simpler table for

$$s = x + y \qquad s,x,y = 0,1$$

y \ x	0	1
0	0	1
1	1	0*

Table 5.11

Clearly we can expect the circuit for table 5.11 to be simpler than that for table 5.10!

5.5.3 *Excess three encoding.* An alternative form of encoding a number in character decimal form has been used with a view to simplifying matters slightly; this again encodes a number in the form

$$X = \sum_{0}^{p-1} d_i \, 10^i \qquad 0 \le d_i \le 9$$

but encodes each digit d_i on four binary digits in the form

$$d_i = \sum_{0}^{3} b_{ij} \, 2^j - 3 \qquad b_{ij} = 0,1.$$

This 'excess-3' encoding has the marginal advantage that if one adds two digits then the result will exceed 16 (i.e. will overflow four binary digits) at exactly those points in table 5.10 where a carry to the next most significant digit is required.

5.6 *Operations on unsigned binary numbers*

We shall restrict our further discussion to operations on binary numbers. We consider initially the operations of addition and multiplication on positive integers. Our reason for the restriction to positive integers is simply that the operations of addition and multiplication of positive integers always yield results which are positive integers; later we shall extend our definitions to cover encodings of numbers which may be fractional or negative.

Suppose $$X = \sum_{0}^{p-1} x_i \, 2^i \qquad x_i = 0,1$$

and $$Y = \sum_{0}^{p-1} y_i \, 2^i \qquad y_i = 0,1$$

are two p-digit positive integers. We shall devise circuits to compute their sum

$$S = \sum_{0}^{?} s_i\, 2^i$$

and product

$$P = \sum_{0}^{?} p_i\, 2^i$$

the undefined upper limit to the sums for S and P implying that at this stage we are not concerned as to the number of digits in the results.

5.6.1 *Addition.* To compute the sum of two numbers we define a set of partial sums S_0, S_1 ... by means of the recurrence

$$S_0 = 0 + x_0 2^0 + y_0 2^0$$

$$S_1 = S_0 + x_1 2^1 + y_1\, 2^1$$

$$S_r = S_{r-1} + x_r 2^r + y_r 2^r.$$

Clearly S_{p-1} equals S the sum of X and Y. We now rewrite these equations in the form

$$S_0 = (0 + x_0 + y_0)\ 2^0 = C_1\ 2^1 + S_0 2^0$$

$$S_1 = (C_1 + x_1 + y_1)\ 2^1 + S_0 2^0 = C_2 2^2 + S_1 2^1 + S_0 2^0$$

$$S_r = (C_r + x_r + y_r)\ 2^r + \sum_{i=0}^{r-1} S_i 2^i = (C_{r+1} 2^{r+1}) + \sum_{i=0}^{r} S_i 2^i.$$

The sum of all the terms $\sum_{0}^{r-1} S_i 2^i$ can never be as large as 2^r, and so at each stage we need consider only the term $(C_r + x_r + y_r)2^r$; the digits S_i are the digits of the result and once evaluated are always unaffected by later stages of the process. Each stage except the first thus involves adding together three digits of equal weight, to produce two digits, one the digit of that weight in the sum and the other the carry digit of twice that weight. The addition table will have eight entries, as shown

$2^r c_r$	$2^r x_r$	$2^r y_r$	sum	$2^r s_r$	$2^{r+1} c_{r+1}$
0	0	0	0	0	0
0	0	2^r	2^r	2^r	0
0	2^r	0	2^r	2^r	0
0	2^r	2^r	$2x2^r$	0	2^{r+1}
2^r	0	0	2^r	2^r	0
2^r	0	2^r	$2x2^r$	0	2^{r+1}
2^r	2^r	0	$2x2^r$	0	2^{r+1}
2^r	2^r	2^r	$3x2^r$	2^r	2^{r+1}

Table 5.11(a)

the three left-most columns are the inputs to the sum, the central column gives the arithmetic sum, while the two right-most columns show the arithmetic result expressed as the sum of two terms, one S_r of weight 2^r and one C_{r+1} of weight 2^{r+1}. We can rewrite table 5.11(a) in terms of integers having only values 0,1 by multiplying the inputs by 2^{-r}, and the outputs S_r, C_{r+1} by 2^{-r}, $2^{-(r+1)}$ respectively. When we do this we produce table 5.11(b). (See page 163), which contains only 0,1 entries. We can now treat this table as if the 0,1 were Boolean quantities, and use it to define functions S_r, C_{r+1} which give the encoded results of the arithmetic operations on the three quantities x_r, y_r, c_r. These functions have indefinitely many expressions equivalent to them, any of which we may implement so as to evaluate the function. A particularly interesting

C_r	x_r	y_r	S_r	C_{r+1}
0	0	0	0	0
0	0	1	1	0
0	1	0	1	0
0	1	1	0	1
1	0	0	1	0
1	0	1	0	1
1	1	0	0	1
1	1	1	1	1

Table 5.11(b)

form arises if we define a pair of auxiliary functions ps, pc (the partial sum and partial carry) of two inputs

$$ps(x,y) = (x \wedge \bar{y}) \vee (\bar{x} \wedge y)$$
$$pc(x,y) = x \wedge y.$$

It is then easy to show that

$$S_r(C_r,x_r,y_r) = ps(ps(x_r,y_r),C_r)$$

and

$$C_{r+1}(C_r,x_r,y_r) = pc(ps(x_r,y_r),C_r) \vee pc(x_r,y_r).$$

The functions ps,pc are readily realised by a 'half adder' as shown in figure 5.12(a), (see page 164) and two half adders and an OR gate allow the construction of a full adder, as in figure 5.12(b).

Figure 5.12(c) shows a serial adder constructed from a full adder and a single flip-flop, which implements addition using the recurrence relations derived above. The digits of

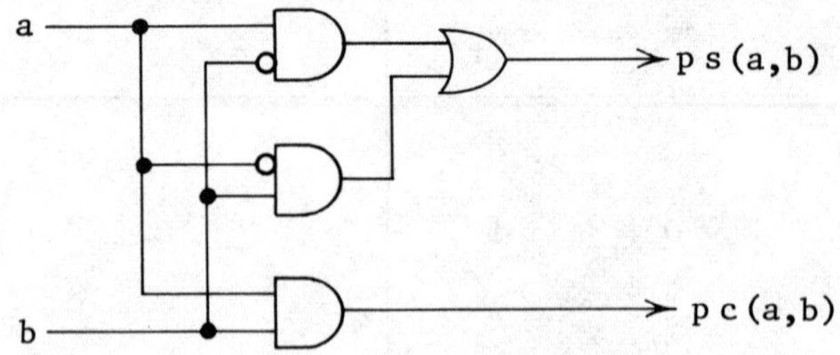

(a) A half adder

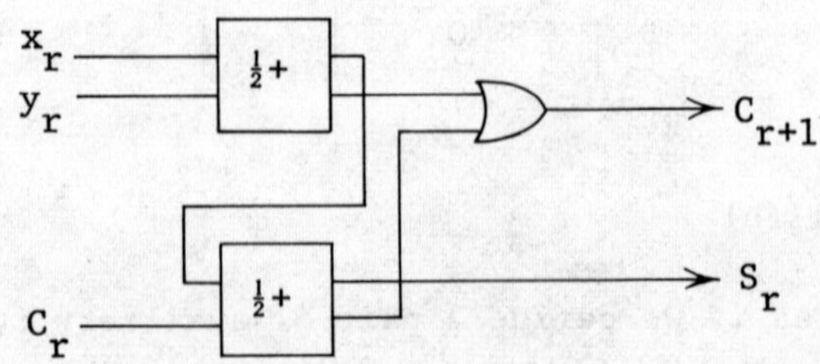

(b) A full adder

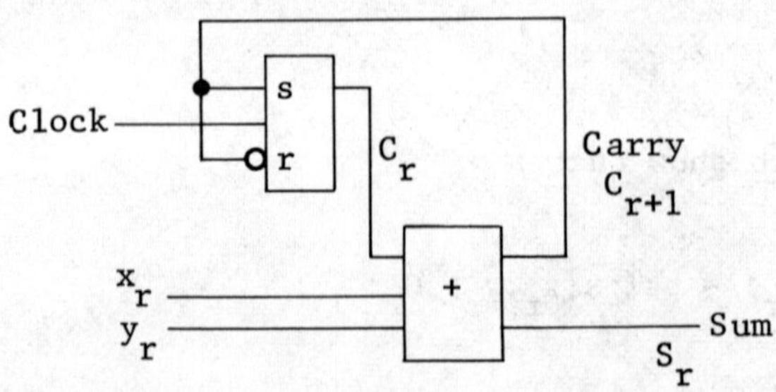

(c) A serial adder made from a full adder and a flip-flop

Figure 5.12 The adder.

the two numbers X,Y are presented in sequence on the lines x_r, y_r; the digits arrive at equally spaced times determined by the clock signal, the r-th digit arriving at the time of the r-th clock pulse, the least significant digits arriving first. Thus at the r-th clock pulse the inputs to the adder

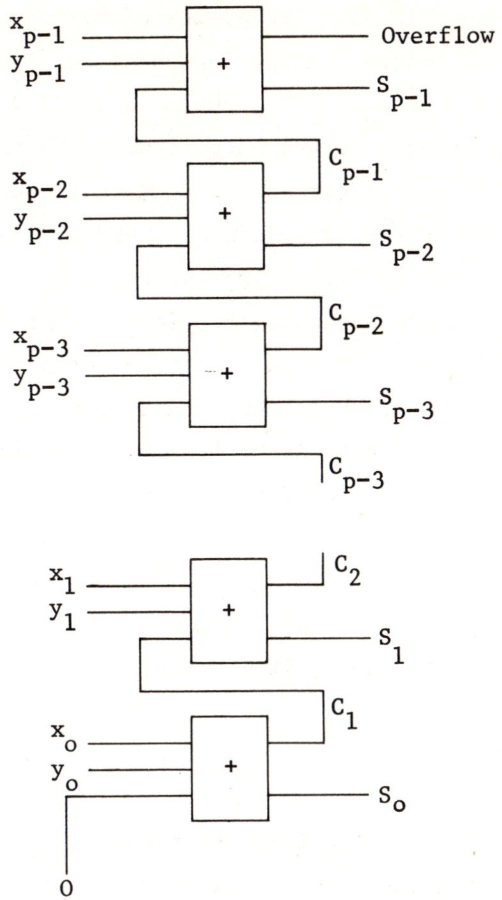

Figure 5.12(d) A parallel adder with 'ripple-through' carry propagation.

are x_r, y_r and the result of the carry from the previous addition C_r. The sum digit S_r is passed to the sum output line, and the carry C_{r+1} is clocked into the flip-flop ready to be presented to the adder at the next digit time. Initially the flip-flop is cleared to a 0, corresponding to $C_o = 0$.

A 'parallel adder' is made of a row of full adders, the carry output of each being fed in as an input to the next most significant position; the input in the least significant adder is held permanently at 0, as indicated by the 0 in the first term of the recurrence relation for the sum. Such an adder is shown in figure 5.12(d). The digits of X,Y are presented simultaneously to the corresponding inputs of the adders, and the outputs appear as shown. In practice X and Y would be held on flip-flop registers, and the outputs would be transferred to a flip-flop register. A common arrangement is one in which X is held in a register the 'accumulator', and Y is held in a register which holds a word read from store; the sum of X and Y is transferred into the accumulator. This can be achieved by the circuitry of figure 5.13. The store buffer b_0-b_{p-1} holds the word read from store, while the accumulator holds the word a_0-a_{p-1}; their outputs serve as inputs to the full adders and the output from the full adder is routed back as an input to the accumulator. When the 'clock' line is pulsed, the sum A+B will overwrite A in the accumulator. An adder in this form is rather slow, as the carry digits may have to propagate through many stages of the adder. It is possible to design adders in which carry digits are generated over large groups of digits simultaneously.

5.6.2 *Multiplication*. To form the product P of a pair of numbers X,Y a sequence of partial products is generated using the recurrence

$$P_0 = x_0 \times Y$$
$$P_1 = x_o 2^1 \times Y + P_0$$
$$P_r = x_r 2^r \times Y + P_{r-1}.$$

Clearly P_{p-1} is equal to the product of X and Y. Again, at each stage the term $x_r 2^r \times Y$ contains no terms smaller than 2^{r-1}, so that the r least significant digits will remain unaffected. The multiplication can be achieved using four registers each containing p binary digits and a single parallel adder capable of adding together two p digit quantities. Two

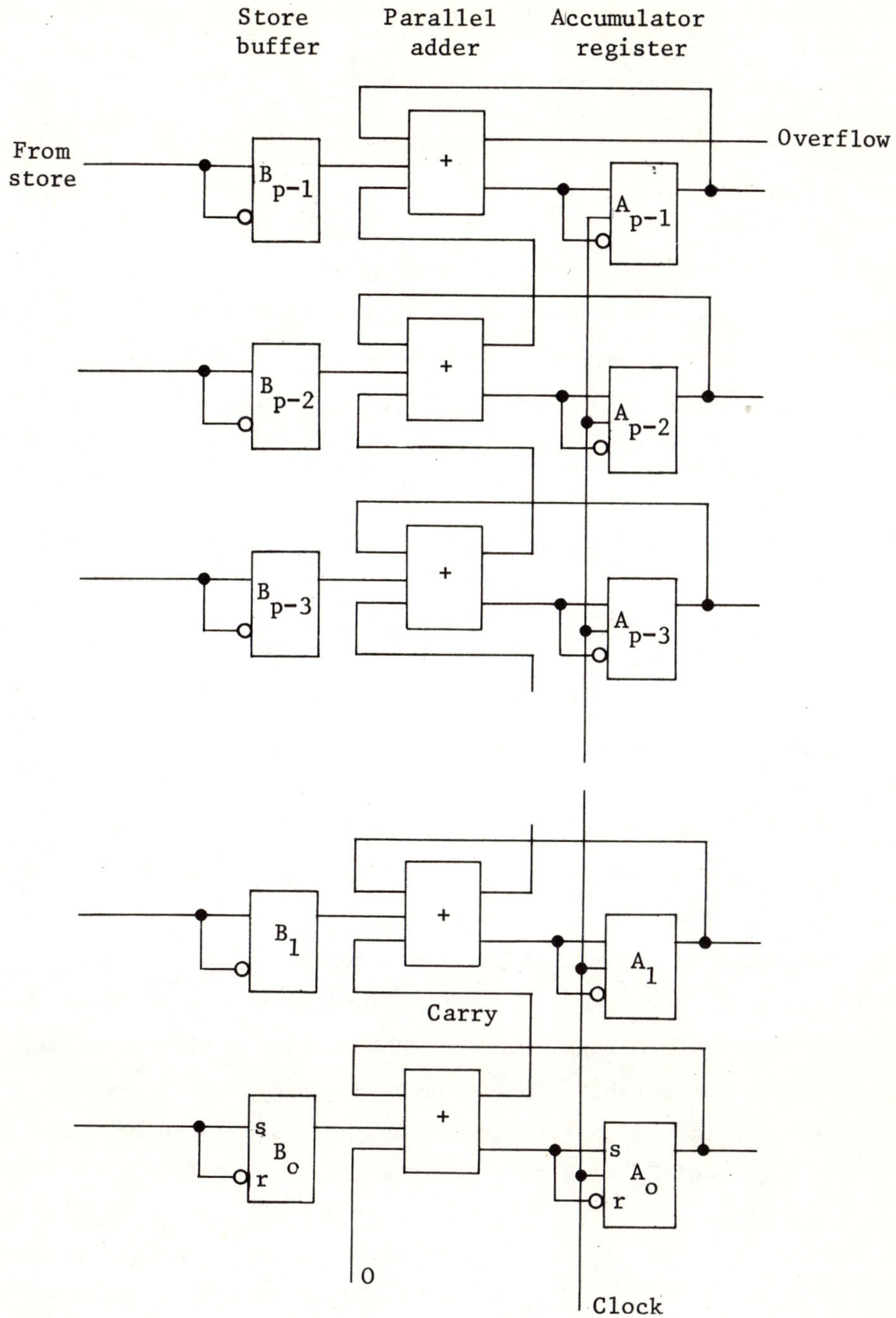

Figure 5.13 A simplified accumulator.

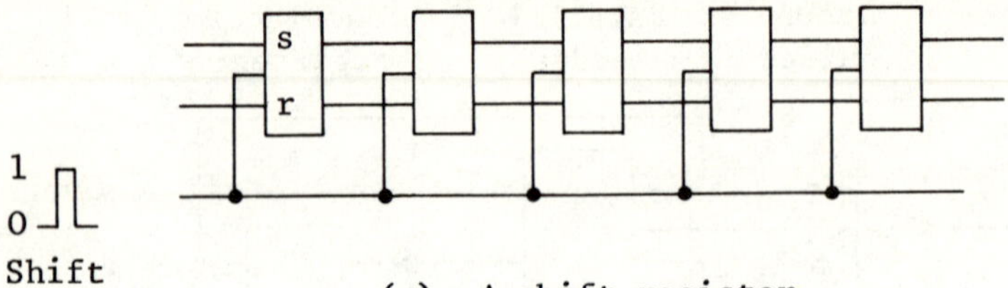

(a) A shift register

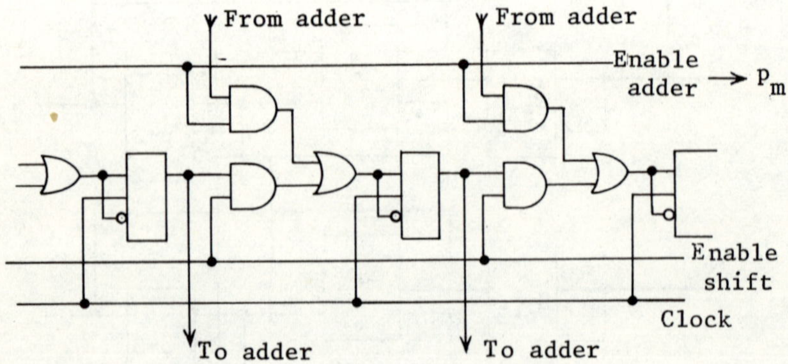

(b) Digits within the register P_m

Figure 5.14 A serial/parallel multiplier.

registers P_m,P_ℓ are wired as a shift register (figure 5.14(a)) - each flip-flop has its outputs connected as inputs to its right-hand neighbour. A pulse on the line labelled 'shift' will cause the contents of each flip-flop to be copied as the new value of its right-hand neighbour. It is also necessary to allow the output from the adder to enter into P_m, which holds the more significant half of the partial products and the digits of P_m will thus be arranged as in 5.14(b). A steady 1 applied to the line 'enable shift' allows a pulse applied to the clock line to shift the contents one place to the right; similarly a steady 1 applied to the line 'enable adder → P_m' allows a pulse applied to the clock line to transfer the outputs of the parallel adder into the register P_m overwriting the previous value.

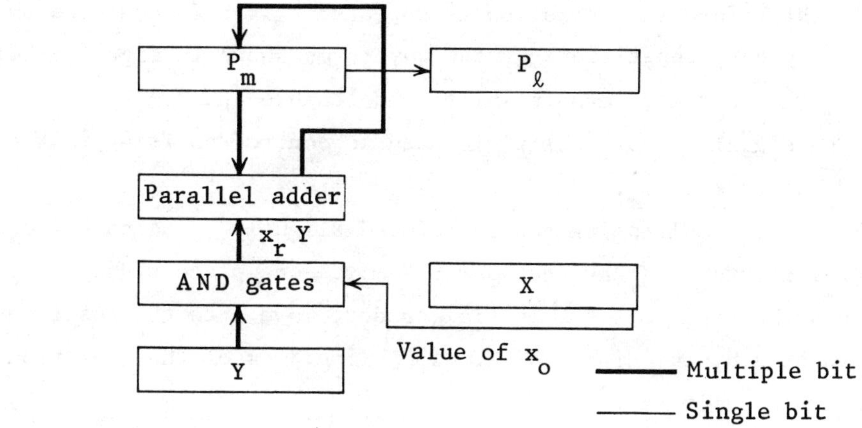

(c) Data paths within the multiplier

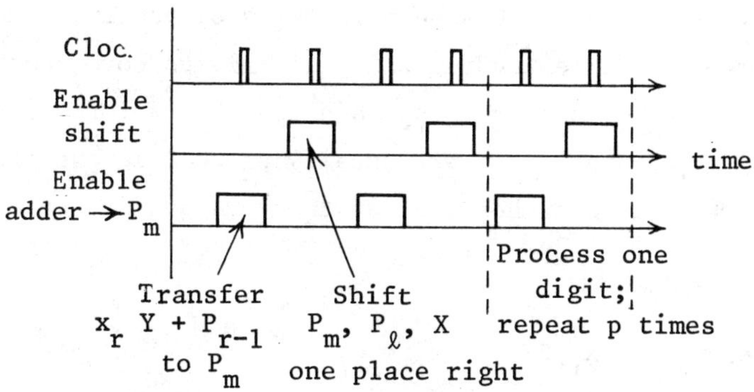

(d) Control signals to be applied to the multiplier

Figure 5.14 A serial/parallel multiplier.

The multiplier, figure 5.14(c), operates as follows. Initially P_m, P_ℓ are cleared to all 0's; X holds the digits of X, and Y the digits of Y; the connection between Y and the adder is via p AND gates. One input on each of these gates is the current value of x_0, the other the value of the r-th of Y, y_r. Thus the outputs from the AND gates are 0 if $x_0 = 0$, and Y if $x_0 = 1$, i.e. they are the products $x_r \times Y$. The successive partial products are developed in P_m, P_ℓ by adding $x_r \times Y$ to the previous product, then P_m, P_ℓ and X are all shifted one place to the right before the operation is repeated. This is achieved by applying p repetitions of the waveforms shown in figure 5.14(d) to the 'clock', 'enable shift' and 'enable adder → P_m' lines. The signal 'enable shift' is used to control shifting in X and P_ℓ as well as P_m.

The multiplier can be reduced slightly by using P_ℓ to hold the digits of X; at each shift X moves one place right in P_ℓ and the digits of the partial product move into the positions vacated by the digits of X. The principles of the operation remain unaltered.

5.7 *Encoding of signed numbers*

The discussion so far has been in terms of positive quantities; we now consider extending this, firstly to cover both positive and negative integers, and then to allow for fractional quantities. Signed quantities are usually encoded in one of three forms. If X is a number greater than or equal to zero then we have

$$X = \sum_{0}^{p-1} x_i \, 2^i \qquad x_i = 0,1.$$

We encode a negative quantity by using one extra binary digit x_p and using one of three forms

(1) Sign and modulus. We use $x_p = 0,1$ according as the quantity to be encoded is positive or negative

$$X = (-1)^{x_p} \sum_{0}^{p-1} x_i \, 2^i, \qquad -(2^p-1) \leq X \leq 2^p - 1.$$

(2) Ones' complement. We use a weighted code in which x_p has weight $-(2^p - 1)$ and

$$X = -(2^p-1)x_p + \sum_{0}^{p-1} x_i \, 2^i, \qquad -(2^p-1) \leq X \leq 2^p-1.$$

(3) Twos' complement. We again use a weighted code

in which x_p has weight -2^p and

$$X = -2^p x_p + \sum_0^{p-1} x_i 2^i, \qquad -2^p \leq X \leq 2^p - 1.$$

Notice that in each encoding $x_p = 0,1$ according as the quantity is positive or negative. Two tables illustrate this; the first gives the three encodings of the numbers -4 to +3 in a three binary digit coding; the second shows the three interpretations of the 8 three binary digit combinations.

There are advantages associated with each of these conventions. The sign and modulus convention deals very easily with multiplication and division, where the sign digit of the result is the 'not-equivalence' of the sign digits of the operands, and the magnitude of the result is simply the value of the result when the operands are treated without regard to their signs. However, addition and subtraction are rather complicated. The ones complement convention raises difficulties when carries propagate into the p-th digit position at any stage, and requires special arrangements in the adder at this position. Multiplication and division are also complicated. The twos complement convention raises fewer problems when carries propagate into the p-th digit, and multiplication and division are no more complicated than for ones complement. One of the principal difficulties with sign and modulus or ones' complement conventions is one that appears most trivial; both these conventions have *two* encodings for zero, one for +0 and the other for -0. In practice, nearly all current systems use twos' complement notation (some systems offer the user more than one convention!) and we shall concentrate on this convention.

5.7.1 *Negation of signed numbers.* It is frequently necessary to negate a signed quantity. Suppose that X is an integer; let -X be the quantity such that X + (-X) = 0 (in fact this

Number	Sign & Modulus	Ones' Complement	Twos' Complement
-4	not possible	not possible	100
-3	111	100	101
-2	110	101	110
-1	101	110	111
0	000	000	000
1	001	001	001
2	010	010	010
3	011	011	011

Table 5.12 Encodings of the numbers -4 to +3 in three different conventions.

		Number Represented	
Pattern of binary digits	Sign & Modulus	Ones' Complement	Twos' Complement
000	0	0	0
001	1	1	1
010	2	2	2
011	3	3	3
100	-0	-3	-4
101	-1	-2	-3
110	-2	-1	-2
111	-3	-0	-1

Table 5.13 Numbers encoded by eight combinations of three binary digits in the three conventions.

is really the definition of the negation of X) and let $\bar{X}$ be the quantity

$$\bar{X} = -2^p \bar{x}_p + \sum_0^{p-1} \bar{x}_i 2^i,$$

where X is encoded as the twos complement number

$$X = -2^p x_p + \sum_0^{p-1} x_i 2^i$$

and the digits of $\bar{x}$ are the inverses of the digits of X. If we add X to $\bar{X}$, the result will be the number containing 1's in every binary digit position, i.e. the number -1 in twos complement form. Thus

$$X + \bar{X} = -1$$

from which it follows that

$$-X = \bar{X} + 1.$$

[The student is advised at this stage to refer back to figure 1.3, and to attempt to classify at which levels on that diagram the various stages of this argument are taking place! The quantity X here has quite deliberately been treated at some points as a number, and at others as an encoding of that number according to a particular convention.]

Thus if we have a signed quantity in a register, we can negate that quantity by taking the inverse of each binary digit and adding 1 to the result.

5.7.2 *Construction of an adder/subtractor.* We can now extend figure 5.13 to act as an adder or a subtractor. We assume that we wish to form either

$$S_+ = X + Y$$

or

$$S_- = X - Y$$

where X is available on lines X_o to X_p, and Y is held in the p+1 flip-flops Y_o to Y_p. The line C carries a control signal which is 1 if we are to evaluate S_+ and 0 if we are to evaluate the difference S_-. The circuit in figure 5.15 operates as follows. If C = 0, the lower of the AND gates will be enabled, allowing the digits of $\bar{Y}$ to enter the full parallel adder, and the carry into digit 0 will be a 1, i.e. we shall supply $\bar{Y} + 1$ as the second argument and the digits S_r form $X + (\bar{Y}+1) = X-Y$ on the outputs of S. If C = 1 the upper gate is enabled, and the digits of S_r will represent X + Y. A 1 on the clock will transfer the result into the register A.

5.8 *Fractional numbers and floating point numbers*

It has been emphasised that a pattern of binary digits encodes a number according to a convention; change the convention and the number encoded will also be changed. The numbers so far discussed have been regarded as integers, and the digits of the number have had weights which were powers of 2 increasing from 2°. It is perfectly in order to regard the weights of the binary digits as being *any* powers of 2, including negative powers, and in this way numbers which are wholly fractional, or are mixed having both an integral and a fractional part can be represented using the convention

$$X = 2^c \left(-2^p x_p + \sum_0^{p-1} x_i 2^i\right).$$

The value of c, the binary exponent is at the discretion of the programmer. For additive operations, the value of c is in fact quite immaterial. However, when multiplication or division are carried out, the resulting quantity will require shifting by an amount c so as to bring its representation into the correct form.

Keeping track of the value of c is a straightforward operation, and virtually all systems offer an encoding known

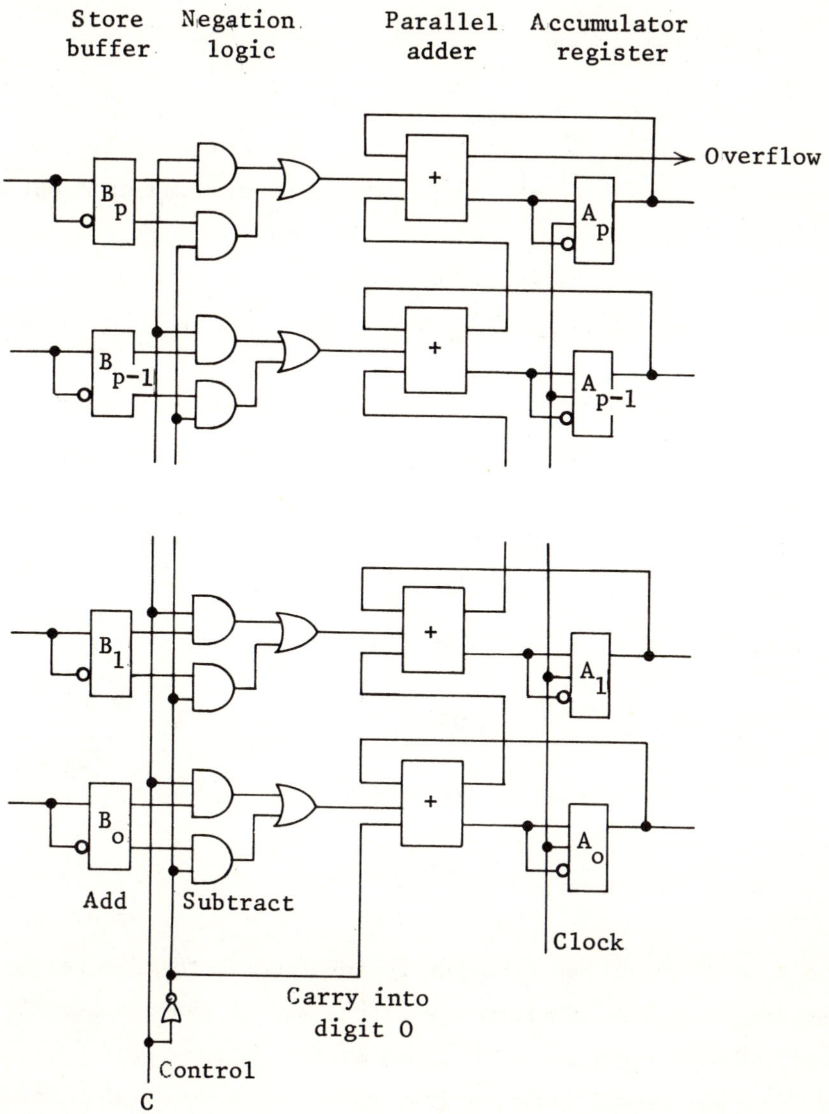

Figure 5.15 Accumulator with addition or subtraction.

as 'floating point', in which the computer hardware administers these operations. A floating point number F is encoded as *two* quantities, a mantissa f and a characteristic c, chosen such that

$$F = f \times 2^{c}.$$

(On some machines the characteristic c is an *octal* exponent i.e.

$$F = f \times 8^{c}.)$$

The two quantities are packed into a single word in store; for example a 48 bit word might be subdivided as

$d_{47}.d_{46}$ f d_8	d_7 c d_0

in which d_{47} to d_8 hold f in the form

$$f = -1 \times d_{47} + \sum_{8}^{46} d_i 2^{i-47} \qquad -1 \leq f < 1$$

and d_7 to d_0 hold c in the form

$$c = -2^{7} \times \bar{d}_7 + \sum_{0}^{6} d_i 2^{i} \qquad -128 \leq c < 127.$$

The sign digit of the exponent is inverted so that in this encoding zero has the form 0×2^{-128}, and is thus an all 0's word. Clearly f and c as defined are not unique, for we can encode the same number by multiplying f by a power of 2 and adjusting the exponent accordingly. To overcome this, it is usual to arrange for a 'standard form' in which f is to be as large as possible; this can always be achieved by arranging that d_{47} and d_{46} are not the same, except in the special case when $d_i = 0$ for all values of i, i.e. the number zero.

5.8.1 *A floating point arithmetic unit.* We conclude with a brief description of an arithmetic unit for manipulating numbers in such a floating point form. For simplicity we shall cover only addition, subtraction and multiplication. All operations on floating point numbers fall into three fairly distinct phases.

(1) preparation of operands
(2) main operation
(3) standardisation of result.

The arithmetic unit contains two separate sub units, one to operate only on exponents, the other on fractions. For addition or subtraction the three phases involve

(1) subtract the smaller exponent from the larger, and shift the fraction associated with the smaller exponent this many places to the right
(2) carry out the addition (or subtraction) on these fractional quantities
(3a) if the result is all 0's set the exponent to -128
(3b) if the result is non-zero and $d_{47} = d_{46}$, repeatedly shift it to the left and subtract 1 from the larger exponent each time, until $d_{47} \neq d_{46}$.

The outcome leaves the result in the shift register and the exponent processor. For multiplication the algorithm is equally simple.

(1) add together the exponents
(2) multiply the two fractions
(3) if $d_{47} = d_{46}$, repeatedly shift to the left and subtract 1 from the sum of the exponents until $d_{47} \neq d_{46}$.

Again the result is left in the shift register and the exponent processor.

5.9 *Order codes and addressing*

We have concentrated so far on describing the manipulation of encoded numbers. We now turn to consider techniques for the definition of single operations, and of sequences of operations within a digital system. The essence of a stored program digital system is that the precise sequence of operations to be undertaken is defined in a flexible manner, and that this sequence can be readily changed. To achieve this, the system has available a limited repertoire of rather primitive operations, each of which carries out a specific action on specific operands, and more complicated operations are built up as strings of these limited operations. Normally instructions will be executed in the order in which they are held in store; however, from time to time this sequence may be broken and resumed at some other location. The system thus requires three quite different types of operation to be available

(1) operations which are applied to the operands which are encodings of objects that exist in the real world

(2) operations which refer not to encodings of objects in the real world, but are concerned solely with organising the sequence of operations

(3) operations which refer not to encodings of objects in the real world, but to the selection of one such encoding from many.

5.9.1 *Operations applying to external data.* The first type of operation can be thought of as containing two quite distinct types of information; one type defines the *operator* that is to be applied to the representations of the external objects; the other defines the *operands* to which this operator is to be applied. In general the operands will be held either in locations in store, or in registers of the processor, and it is then necessary to specify which locations in store, or which registers, are supplying operands and which locations or registers will hold the result. Instruction codes can be classified on the number of addresses that each instruction contains, and on whether these addresses refer to locations in storage or to registers in the central processor. The following list indicates the range of possibilities, without being in any way exhaustive.

3-address order codes Each order is of the form

$$\text{Op} \quad X_1 \quad X_2 \quad X_3$$

where Op defines the operator, and X_1, X_2, X_3 are addresses. The effect is to set the result of applying the operator to the contents of locations X_1 and X_2 as the new contents of location X_3.

2-address order codes Each order is of the form

$$\text{Op} \quad X_1 \quad X_2$$

where again Op defines the operator and X_1, X_2 are addresses. The effect is to leave the result of applying the operator to the contents of X_1 and X_2 as the new contents of X_2. A rather special case of this form is where X_2 is a register of the processor. Bear in mind that typically a system will have, say 2^{16} locations in store, but only 8 registers; specifying a word in store thus requires 16 bits whereas specifying a register requires only 3 bits.

1-address order codes The 2-address order code can be thought of as being derived from the 3-address order code by allowing the location of the result to be implicitly defined. The 1-address order code takes this approach a little further, by using a processor containing only a single register for arithmetic working, and defining instructions as

$$\text{Op} \quad X$$

where X is a location in store. The operation is applied to the contents of this word and to the contents of the single register, leaving the result either in the register, or in the location in store, depending on the operation.

Zero-address order codes The zero-address order code carries the approach of allowing operands to be implicitly defined to the ultimate conclusion, in which operands and results are located in registers of the processor! In such an order code, instructions simply take the form

Op

specifying an operator. The system will draw the operands from registers of the processor, and return the result to a register in the processor. At first sight such an organisation is eccentric; however, it turns out that if the registers involved are arranged in the form of a nesting store then such an organisation has some very great advantages. In particular, it is relatively simple to generate code for a system organised in this way when writing a compiler to convert from a 'high-level' programming language. It is clearly necessary in such a machine to include some operations which allow data to be moved between main storage and the nesting store.

5.9.2 *Sequence control operations*. The operations which are concerned with sequence control and with control of the selection of operands again require the specification of operators and operands. For sequence control the primary 'operand' is basically the address in storage of the next instruction to be obeyed. The operator defines the conditions under which control should proceed sequentially to the next instruction, or should proceed to the location specified by the operand; typically the decision as to whether or not to branch will depend on for example the sign of contents of an arithmetic register of the processor. It is also common to provide instructions which branch unconditionally to a specified location and store the address of the present instruction in a processor register or which branch to the location specified by a register in the processor. Such an instruction is valuable in organising the entry to a sub-routine, and the subsequent return from the subroutine to the point from which the subroutine was first called. Again, on some systems, the storing of addresses on subroutine entry and their retrieval on exit is conveniently administered by means of a nesting store.

5.9.3 *Data selection operations*. The third class of operations deals with the control of the selection of an encoding of a particular object from many such encodings. On many systems this can be achieved by 'modification'. On such systems the central processor will contain one or more modifier (or index) registers; these registers have an associated unit which performs a limited amount of arithmetic, on integer quantities, and their prime use lies in the dynamic modification of the addresses of operands. The address of the operand can be modified, by having the contents of one (or sometimes more than one) of the modifier registers added to it before the address is used. This modification takes place after the instruction has been read from storage, and affects only the executed instruction - the instruction in store remains in its original form. To allow effective use of this facility, the order code will include instructions for setting up the contents of modifier registers, and branch instructions which can sense the contents of registers.

5.10 *A simplified processor*

We can now describe the overall form of a straightforward central processor unit (CPU). We shall assume a machine using a mixture of zero and 1-address orders; the zero address orders perform arithmetic on the contents of a nesting store forming part of the CPU, while the 1-address orders control the fetching and storing of operands, the operations on a single index register, and conditional and unconditional branching, including subroutine entry and exit which again uses a nesting store.

The processor contains five main registers, two nesting stores and two arithmetic units (figure 5.16)

(1),(2) SAR, SBR are the *S*tore *A*ddress *R*egister and *S*tore *B*uffer *R*egister; they hold the address of a word in store, and the word to be written to, (or just read from) store respectively. Together with the relevant control signals these two registers form the interface to the store.

(3),(4) ANI and INS are the *A*ddress of *N*ext *I*nstruction and the *INS*truction register; they hold the address of the instruction currently being obeyed, and the instruction itself.

(5) IND is the *IND*ex register, used in modification.

The two nesting stores ANS and BNS are used respectively for temporary storage of quantities which are encoded representations of external objects, and for storing addresses associated with subroutine entry and exit. One arithmetic unit ARITH is connected to the nesting store, for arithmetic manipulation of representations of external objects, and the other B+ to INS and IND for modification.

The main data paths within the processor are shown in figure 5.16.

We shall assume a machine with a thirty-two bit word, in which instructions of either eight digits (for zero address instructions) or twenty-four digits (for one address instructions) are stored; each word holds only one instruction, on digits d_{31} to d_{24} for zero address instructions or d_{31} to d_8

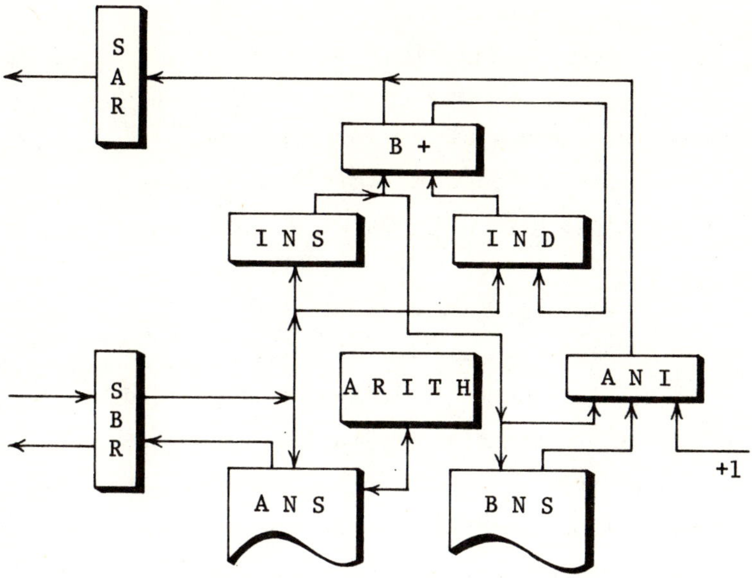

Figure 5.16 Main data paths within a simple processor.

for one address instructions. Digit d_{31} = 1/0 according as the instruction is 8/24 bits long. (In practice one would pack instructions up so as to fill words; the achievement of this would merely complicate description and so we ignore it.) The two formats are thus

d_{31}	d_{30} - d_{24}		
1	Operator		zero address
d_{31} d_{30}	d_{29} - d_{24}	d_{23} - d_8	one address
0 M	Operator	Address	

In one address instructions d_{30} is 1/0 according as the address d_{23}-d_8 is/is not to be modified. The operator is defined by digits d_{29}-d_{24}.

The execution of an instruction involves four major phases

(1) fetch instruction from store

(2) construct operand

(3) execute operation

(4) return results to store

and these phases can again be further subdivided

(1) Fetch instruction from store.

The actions here are

(1) transfer ANI to SAR

(2) initiate a store read

(3) transfer ANI +1 to ANI

(4) await completion of store read

(5) transfer SBR to INS

at the end of this sequence the address in ANI will have advanced to that of the next instruction, and the instruction which is to be obeyed will be held in the INS register.

(2) Construct operand.

The possibilities here are

(a) this is a zero address instruction and the operands are in the top of the ANS

(b) this is a 1-address instruction in which the digits d_{23}-d_8 of INS plus the contents of IND if d_{30} of INS is a 1 are the operand, or an address in store to which a result is to be returned.

(c) this is a 1-address instruction in which the quantity defined in (b) above is not the operand but the address in the store which holds the operand.

These three possibilities are indicated by

(a) d_{31} of INS = 1

(b),(c) the particular value of digits d_{29}-d_{24} of INS.

Bearing this in mind the construction of the operand takes the form

(1) if d_{31} (INS) = 1 exit from this sequence

(2) form $(d_{23}-d_8)$(INS) + d_{30}(INS) $\wedge$ (IND) in B+

(3) if $(d_{29}-d_{24})$(INS) indicate that the result of (2) is the operand or is an address for a write to store exit from this sequence

(4) transfer the output of B+ to SAR

(5) initiate a store read

(6) await completion of store read.

At the conclusion of this sequence the operand is available either as the output from the adder, or is available in the SBR.

(3) Execute operation.

The possibilities here are too numerous to discuss in detail; however in line with our classification of basic instruction types they can be thought of as

Zero address instructions - for all these the operands are in the top cells of the ANS and results of the operation are returned to the top cell of the ANS. The details of the actual implementation of more straightforward arithmetic operations have already been discussed.

Sequence control instructions - for these the operand is the outcome of step (3) in the operand construction phase above. This operand may be the address to which a branch is to be made if some condition is satisfied; the corresponding operation is simply achieved. If the condition is satisfied the output of B+ is transferred directly to the register ANI, overwriting the address of the next instruction, and then the system enters the fetch next instruction phase. For entry to a subroutine, the output of the contents of ANI (which now points to the instruction *after* the subroutine entry) are placed in the top cell of BNS and then the output of B+ transferred to ANI.

Index register instructions - for these the operand may be the result of step (3) or step (6) in the operand construction phase. The range of instructions available would include means of setting a value into IND, achieved by transferring the output of B+ or of SBR into IND, or of incrementing or decrementing the value of IND, again by transferring the output of the adder into IND.

Operand movements to/from ANS - these are instructions which load the top of the ANS with an operand, or transfer the contents of the ANS to store. For loading the ANS the operand may yet again be the result of step (3) or step (6) in the construct operand phase, and the actual operation is achieved by transferring either the output of B+ or the contents of SBR as appropriate into the top cell of the ANS. Storing from ANS is treated in the next phase.

(4) Return results to store.

This phase is only invoked for those instructions in which the operand requires a result to be written from the top cell of the ANS into store. The address in main store will have been constructed as the outcome of step (3) in the construct operand phase; this is transferred to SAR. The top cell of the ANS is transferred to SBR and a write to store initiated. This completes the operation.

5.11 *Some miscellaneous circuits*

We have discussed in some detail circuits which operate on encodings of numerical information. We now consider some miscellaneous circuits which are required at various points within any computing system.

5.11.1 *Decoders*. A frequently encountered situation is one in which a register contains an encoding of a number held on p binary digits, and one wishes to convert this to a signal of 1 on one of 2^p output lines and 0 on the remaining 2^p-1 lines.

Such a circuit is known as a one-of-n decoder, and will be used for example to determine which instruction has been placed in the INS register of a processor, or to select the X or Y line in a ferrite core store. For small values of p a circuit such as that of figure 5.17(a), (see page 188) would be used; this decodes the 16 possibilities for a four-bit register, by using 16 four input AND gates, each one of which responds to a different combination within the register. When the number of bits in the register becomes large the fan-out required from each bit becomes very large; clearly for p bits the fan-out of each output of each flip-flop is 2^{p-1}. For DTL, TTL or ECL the maximum fan-out is usually less than sixteen, and thus decoders of the form shown in figure 5.17(a) are impracticable when more than say five bits are involved. For FET circuits much greater fan-out, as high as several hundred, may be possible, and one may be able to extend the circuit to decode directly as many as ten bits. More commonly, one would use a two level decoder such as figure 5.17(b); this decodes eight bits into one of 256 possibilities. The circuit uses two separate four bit decoders such as those in figure 5.17(a); each line of each one-of-sixteen decoder drives one input on sixteen two input AND gates. (For obvious reasons figure 5.17(b) omits much of the detail!)

5.11.2 *Multiple equivalence units.* When processing character data, such as names and addresses, the number of valid operations is very small. A common one is the detection of equality or inequality. One can achieve this by treating the character string as if it were an encoding of an integer and testing for arithmetic equality by performing a subtraction and checking for zero. However, many processors allow a test for equivalence via a special purpose unit. A similar unit is required in the control unit of a drum (or disc) to detect equality between the current angular position of the drum (disc) and that of the information to be transferred.

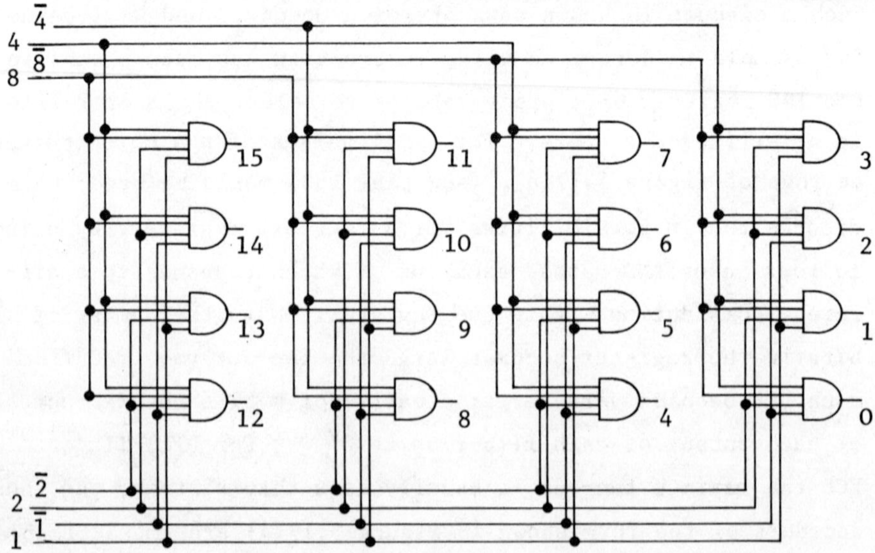

Figure 5.17(a) A 1-of-16 decoder.

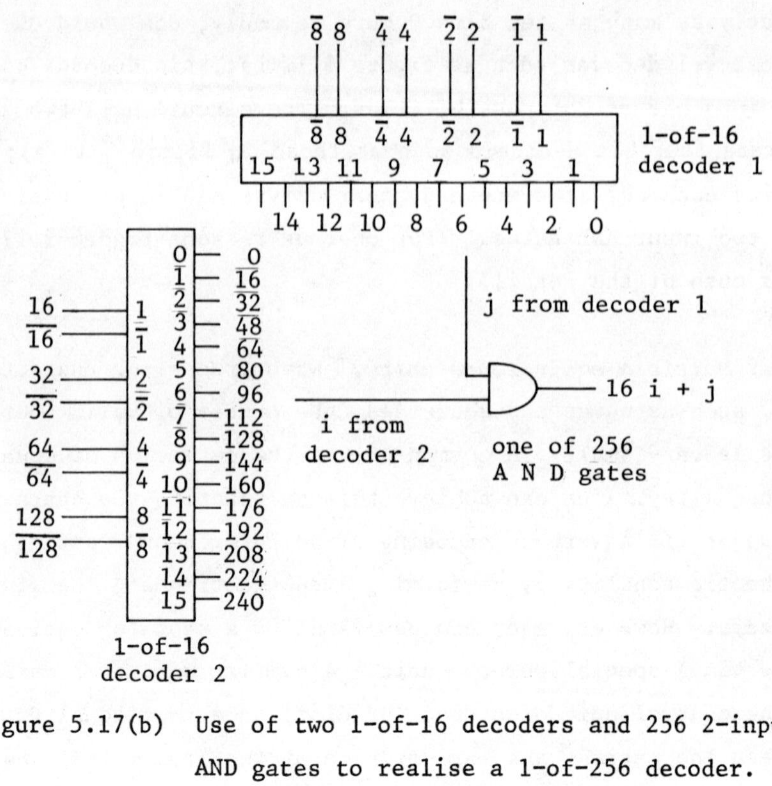

Figure 5.17(b) Use of two 1-of-16 decoders and 256 2-input AND gates to realise a 1-of-256 decoder.

The corresponding circuit is easily derived by noting that two character strings are the same if and only if all the bits in corresponding positions are the same. The circuit consists fundamentally of half adders (used in this case to perform a 'not equivalence' evaluation) whose sum outputs are all fed to a single multi-input OR gate. This OR gate has output of 0 if the character streams are identical and 1 if they differ anywhere.

5.11.3 *Counters.* It is often convenient to use counters which can be incremented or decremented for example to control a process which must be repeated a predetermined number of times, or to indicate the address of the next instruction to be obeyed. One form of such a counter is shown in figure 5.18. This is an 'up-down counter', capable of holding a binary number; it has two input lines, one of which is held at a steady 1 or 0 to indicate counting up or counting down, while the second carries $0 \to 1 \to 0$ transient pulses, each one of which causes the counter contents to increment or decrement by one. In addition to these inputs the circuit shown includes a facility for inputting a predetermined value, indicated by the lines labelled 1, 2, 4, 8 when the 'load' line is raised to a 1 and then lowered to 0. In practice a counter such as this would probably also include circuitry for disabling all the inputs so as to allow the value on the up/down line to be changed without inducing spurious changes in the value held on the four flip-flops.

5.11.4 *Nesting stores.* We can combine a four bit up/down counter, a four bit one-of-sixteen decoder and a sixteen word flip-flop store to produce a sixteen word last-in-first-out or nesting store. A block diagram of such a store is shown in figure 5.19, (see page 191). A word is added to the store by setting the up-down line to 1 (i.e. count up) and allowing

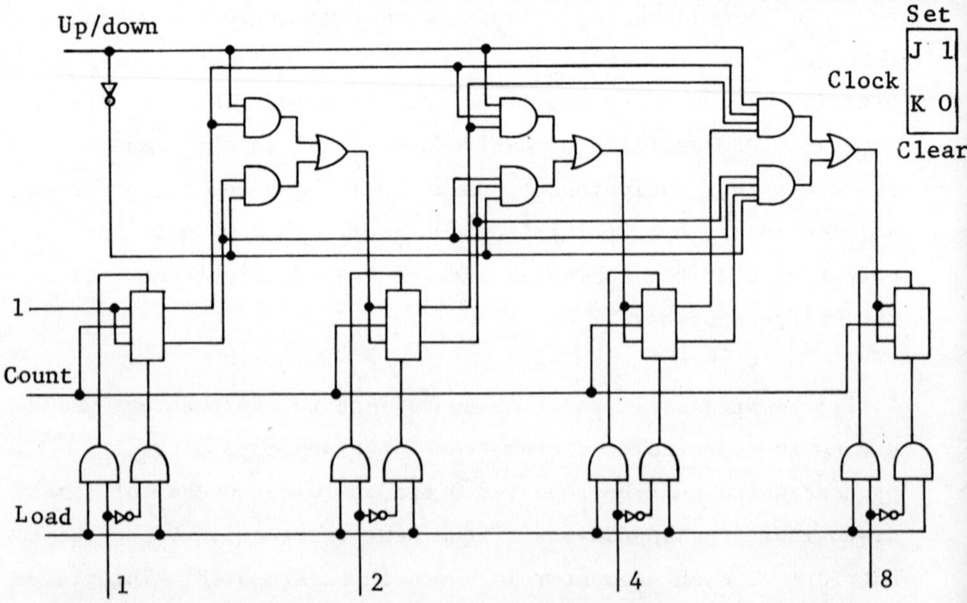

Figure 5.18 Up/down counter with presetting.

one pulse on the count line of the counter, whose contents will now point to the next free word in the store; the contents of the counter are decoded to point to the selected word via the decoder. The new contents of the selected word can then be written into store by driving the clock on the store which will transfer the digits of the word from the input lines to the selected word in the store. To read a word out, the read line is enabled, which places the contents of the word selected by the counter on the store output lines. When the acceptor signals that these outputs have been received, the up/down line is set to 0 (i.e. count down) and one pulse is applied to the count line of the counter stepping it back to point to the previous word. Clearly, this store can easily be extended to be of any depth by extending the number of digits in the counter and decoder and by adding extra words to the store.

5.11.5 *Associative store.* Rather as we can combine a store and a counter to produce a nesting store, we can combine

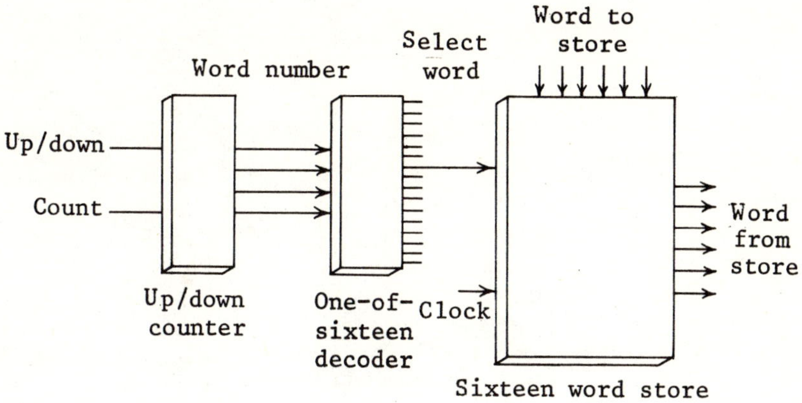

Figure 5.19(a) Block diagram of a nesting store.

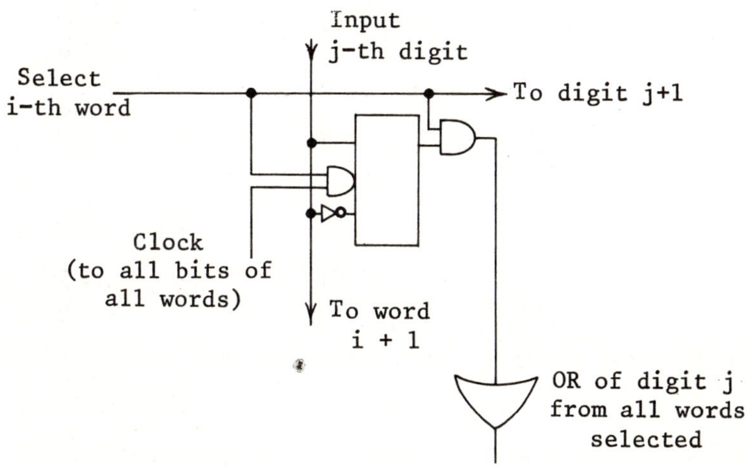

Figure 5.19(b) The j-th digit of the i-th word in the sixteen word store.

several multiple equivalence units and some storage to produce an associative store, as indicated in figure 5.20. The store now contains words divided into two parts. The left-hand part contains the addressing information, while the right-hand part contains the information associated with a given set of addressing information. When an address is presented on the lines at the top left-hand side the address is simultaneously compared with all the addressing information in the

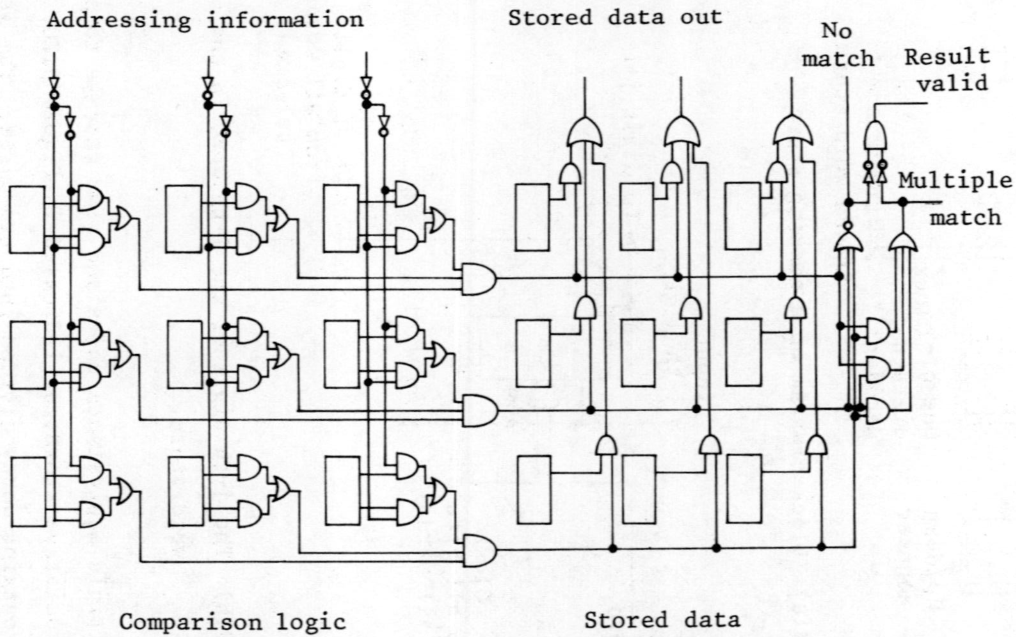

Figure 5.20 An associative store (for simplicity only the reading logic is shown).

address parts of the stored words. There are three possible outcomes

(1) there is no equivalence between the address presented and any of the stored addresses

(2) there is equivalence between the address presented and several of the stored addresses

(3) there is equivalence between the address presented and exactly one of the stored addresses.

In the first two cases the associative store signals a 1 on the appropriate line, i.e. 'no match' or 'multiple match' and the output lines are undefined; only with third case, when both 'no match' and multiple match' remain at 0, are the outputs defined as being the information part of the word whose address part corresponds with the presented address.

Writing to the associative store may take one of two forms. One may wish to overwrite the information part of the word (if any) whose address part matches the address presented on the address lines. A more common form of writing is to select one of the words in the store and to overwrite its entire contents. Where writing is to an existing address then it can only take place when there is a match between the address presented and exactly one address part within the store. Where writing is to a selected word no such check is made.

5.12 *Summary*

In this chapter we have discussed the mechanisms for processing information which is represented digitally; the information represented could be classified as referring to external data existing in some 'real' world outside the digital system, or as referring to the selection from a whole set of internally stored information a particular item, or as being concerned in some way with the precise operations to be applied to the information to produce the representations of the required results. We have not discussed how the information is stored, except temporarily within registers of the processor, nor how it is communicated to the processor, nor how it is converted between the external and internal representations.

Equally important, there has been no discussion of how the whole complex of subsystems which together constitute an information processing system is co-ordinated and organised. In the next chapter, we turn from our detailed examination of the black boxes which are the individual units of the system and examine how this synthesis is achieved.

5.13 *Bibliography*

The following suggestions for further reading are made.

Logical Design of Switching Circuits (Nelson, London, 1968), by D. Lewis, is mostly concerned with Logic design, but it includes descriptions of alternative forms of logical element in chapter 8.

Semiconductor Logic and Switching Circuits (Merril, Columbus Ohio, 1966), by S.L. Oppenheimer, contains detailed descriptions of the discrete component versions of many types of logical element, but predates the introduction of integrated circuits.

Logical Design of Digital Computers (Wiley, New York, 1958), by Montgomery Phister, is a good introduction to logic design as applied to computing equipment, although after 15 years the actual implementation of the logical elements is outmoded.

Computer Hardware Theory (McMillan, New York, 1972), by W.J. Poppelbaum, gives very detailed mathematical treatment of the functioning of many semiconductor devices, and is recommended only to those wishing to reach an advanced level.

Elementary Electronics (Harper and Row, London, 1967), by D.H. White, contains an informal, non-mathematical description of the behaviour of junction diodes and transistors (but not of FET's), and describes the functioning of many circuits.

Digital Systems Logic and Circuits (Allen and Unwin, London, 1968) by B. Zacharov, contains much information on the basis of logical design, and a descriptive treatment of discrete component circuits, especially tunnel diodes.

5.14 *Examples*

(1) Write a survey of the properties of TTL, ECL and some representative kinds of MOS logic, having regard to the complexities of integration which are available, as well as performance and power consumption.
(University of St. Andrews, 1973)

(2) Describe one of the methods commonly used for representing signed integers in present day digital computers. What are the maximum and minimum values which may be represented using your method? What important rules apply to the performance of addition and subtraction in this representation?

The following two integers have been printed in their binary coded decimal (BCD) representation. Convert them to a normalised floating point representation using 6 bits for the mantissa and 5 bits for the exponent. Using this representation form their sum. Pay attention to correct rounding at all stages.

0001 0001 1001

0010 0000

(University of Leeds, 1974)

(3) Draw a circuit diagram for a half-adder, using three gates. Show by means of a truth-table that the sum (s) and carry (c) outputs are given by:

$$c = a \cdot b \qquad s = (a + b) \cdot \bar{c}$$

where a and b are two inputs.

How can a full adder be made from two half-adders and an OR gate? Draw a block diagram indicating how a 3-bit parallel adder can be made from 2 full adders and one half-adder. (University of Leeds, 1969)

(4) What does the term *weighted code* signify? Write down the representation of integers in the ranges 0 to ±8 using 'negbin' weighted code which has radix -2 and the digits 0 and 1.

The circuit used to add a general pair of digits from two negbin numbers has four inputs (2 input digits, 2 carries in) and three outputs (sum digit, 2 carries out). Bearing in mind that addition is associative and commutative, construct a table giving for each possible input combination the corresponding outputs. Use this table to perform in negbin the following additions showing clearly any carry digits used:

2+4 -5+(-6) 7+7.

Comment briefly on the relative merits of negbin and binary arithmetic units as computer components.
(University of Leeds, 1972)

(5) Ternary digits are represented in a certain binary logic system with 0, 1 and 2 encoded as 00, 01 and 10. A subcircuit H is provided having inputs corresponding to two ternary digits x,y and outputs corresponding to the ternary sum digit s and the carry c of the arithmetic sum x+y. Show how H may be augmented by further logic to form one stage of a parallel ternary adder.
(University of Leeds, 1971)

(6) State the definitions of the:

1. ONES Complement
2. TWOS Complement
3. SIGN and MODULUS

methods of representing signed integers.

Using your definitions prove that the following method of finding the TWOS Complement of an integer k is valid for all values of k except one (what is this value of k?)

'Taking the binary representation of the integer k retain all the less significant bits up to and including the least significant ONE bit, then invert all the remaining bits.'

Invert means replace 0 with 1 and 1 with 0.

Using the rule stated above and the 'logical' machine instructions only, write a function to find the number of ONE bits in a computer word.

(University of Essex, 1972)

(7) In what ways is it less efficient to represent integers as 'packed decimals' rather than as binary integers?

A new machine is to be based on a three-state device. Integers within this machine will be represented as

$$x = \sum_i t_i 3^i$$

where each t_i = -1,0, or +1, denoted by $\bar{1}$ 0 1 respectively.

(a) write down the representations of 0, +17, -31 in this system using four-place numbers;

(b) how can numbers in this system be negated?

(c) approximately how many places would be required to represent numbers as large as -10^{40}, to an accuracy of about 12 decimal places?

(University of Leeds, 1969)

(8) What techniques are used to represent numbers in a digital computer? Pay particular attention to the representation of signed numbers, and to situations in which the range of values to be represented may be very large.

A computer for use with sterling currency uses 17 bits thus

4 bits	4 bits	5 bits	4 bits
x	l	s	d

where x, l, s, d represent units of £10, £1, one shilling and one penny respectively and where

$0 \leq x \leq 9$

$0 \leq l \leq 9$

$0 \leq s \leq 19$

$0 \leq d \leq 11$

What is the largest amount that can be represented in this way? Compare this with the largest amount that can be represented in units of one penny using 17 bits. Outline briefly how the adder for this machine might be constructed. (University of Leeds, 1967)

(9) Show how the assignment statements:

(i) x:= a+b

(ii) x:= a×(b+c)-d/e

can be coded for machines with

(a) 1-address

(b) 3-address

(c) 0-address (with 1-address fetch and store instructions)

order codes.

x, a, b, c, d, and e represent core store locations. You can assume that the machines have suitable instructions for +, −, ×, / and also fetch and store instructions where necessary.

If one byte is needed to store a function code and two bytes to store an address, calculate the number of bytes occupied by each of your six pieces of code, and the number of core cycles needed to obey each one. (Ignore the core cycles needed for instruction fetching.)

Comment *briefly* on the relative merits of the three types of addressing.
(University of Leeds, 1972)

6 · Systems architecture

6.1 *Information processing systems properties*

This final chapter draws together the ideas already presented and discusses the design of an information processing system. Any information processing system aims to allow the processing of a flow of information with the minimum cost and maximum reliability; it is probably fair to add that not all systems meet these objectives. In practice large information processing systems tend to be very complex, and it is helpful when discussing the system to consider each type of activity in which the system is engaged in virtual isolation from other activities, considering the interactions between activities only where this cannot be avoided. We shall see that on many systems the actual time for which the system is actively processing a particular activity is relatively short compared with the real time which elapses, and we are compelled to consider systems in which many activities are known to the system at any time, though only a few of them may be active at any one instant.

Clearly such a system will tend to be

modular containing units (of either hardware or software) which are designed to function in isolation, communicating with other units only via well defined interfaces.

parallel operating containing units which because they function in isolation, and interact only infrequently, may all be operating simultaneously.

We shall also find that because there are units which are running in parallel that we shall require mechanisms for *process protection* to ensure that no unit interfaces with the running of any other unit unless authorised to do so

process synchronisation to ensure that where several units are required to collaborate they do so in an orderly and disciplined way.

Our emphasis will be on the hardware aspects of these four features of the system, but we shall find it necessary from time to time to discuss the associated software.

6.1.1 *Modularity.* At the end of chapter 1 we gave a brief description of the major elements comprising an information processing system; we now return to this and consider it from the point of view of the types of activities that it can support. These can fall loosely under five main headings:

(1) Local batch processing
(2) Remote batch processing
(3) Interactive terminal processing
(4) Transaction processing
(5) Real time processing.

These categories are not exhaustive and it is possible to find many jobs which overlap several categories, but they serve as a useful subdivision. It is probably helpful to give a *brief* description of each type of work.

(1) *Local batch processing:* the running of complete jobs (e.g. the compilation and execution of a user's program) whose input and output take place on peripheral devices interfaced directly to the computing system.

(2) *Remote batch processing:* the running of complete jobs whose inputs and outputs are via remotely sited peripheral devices interfaced via a communications subsystem on the main computing system.

(3) *Interactive terminal processing:* the handling of subsections of a complete job via a keyboard device through which the user exchanges messages with the system. For

example, the user may wish to edit the text of a program which he has stored within the system, compile the program, and then supply data via his keyboard to the program and receive results on his character display before supplying further data.

(4) *Transaction processing:* the maintenance by a large number of users of a shared set of data, each transaction producing changes in the shared data. An obvious example here is an airline reservation system in which the users are travel agents and airport staff who are accessing data describing the reservations for travel on the various routes that the airline operates. Notice that users of interactive terminals are running their own programs operating on their own data, users of a transaction processing system are running a single (very large) program operating on a single (again very large) set of data.

(5) *Real time processing:* the processing of data derived from some ongoing process to produce results which are used to control the behaviour of the process. It is quite conceivable that there will be human intervention in the input of data, or the subsequent return of control signals; for example in the control of the cutting of rolled steel strip into lengths required by customers it is possible to feed to the computer information on the lengths of strip available and the lengths required and to return to the operator instructions as to how to cut the strips to minimise wastage. More difficult problems arise where there is no human intervention, either because of the time scales involved or because of hostile environments.

In principle, a single computing system might accommodate all these types of activity simultaneously; in practice this is not at all common.

It is good practice to consider the design of the system

as consisting of modules, each module consisting of some software running on the hardware of the system. Some modules will clearly be highly specific to a particular type of work; for example, the module which handles input from a card reader in a local batch processing system is specific to that style of processing. Other modules may well be common to more than one type of work; for example, the compiler which handles local batch processing, remote batch processing and compilations from interactive terminals may well be a single module of the system, with a common interface to the modules which handle input or output associated with these different types of processing.

The software details of these modules are not our concern at present, except in as much as they affect the hardware design. The software of the modules leads to changes in hardware design in various ways; the hardware may be altered because the software requires that alterations be made in order to cope with the presence of many simultaneously active modules; or the hardware may be altered because the alterations make easier the generation of suitable software. Before we discuss these hardware changes in detail we look more closely at the notion of many modules operating simultaneously.

6.1.2 *Parallel operation of processes.* We have seen a number of instances in which the performance of a system was improved, at the cost of having extra equipment, by the introduction of many units operating simultaneously to replace one unit used repeatedly. One such example was in the printing of output. In these earlier examples of parallel operation greater speed of operation was achieved for a given type of operation by the introduction of more functionally similar units each capable of basically the same operation. We are now discussing a slightly different form of parallel operation in which a speeding up of the overall system is achieved by allowing functionally different units, carrying out different operations, to operate simultaneously. To achieve this, the units must each be capable of autonomous operation, and the modules of the previous section must be constructed in such a way that they can drive these autonomous units and keep them operating simultaneously.

Each module is thought of as a combination of both hardware and software. The software consists of stored instructions and stored data, and clearly the module therefore requires a certain amount of storage. The stored instructions are used to drive a 'processor' of some sort; we use 'processor' in quotes because the processor may be either an arithmetic processor such as we discussed in chapter 5, or it may be an interface between storage and an input/output device, an interface between storage and a communications channel, or an interface between one form of storage and another (e.g. between core store and magnetic disc). In each case a 'processor' contains registers whose contents are changed as the arithmetic unit or interface operates; there will be times, when an arithmetic unit has completed one operation, or when an interface has completed a transfer of data, at which it is possible to record the contents of *all* the processor's registers in storage. If, at some later point in time, *all* the processor's registers' contents are reinstated, then the processor can continue processing as if nothing had happened. It is therefore possible to think of a module as defined entirely by stored information; while the module is actually driving any of the processors which are present in the system some of the stored information will be held in the registers of those processors that the module is driving. At other times, when the module is not actually driving any processor, all the stored information can be held in conventional storage. However, much the most common situation will be one in which a particular module is driving only one processor; as the processor finishes some particular operation on behalf of that module, it will be possible for that module to become active on some other processor and for that processor to become active on behalf of some other module.

We shall refer to the modules as 'processes' from now on. A process is defined by

(i) the stored instructions which define the algorithms for that particular process

(ii) the stored data on which the algorithms are being carried out

(iii) the stored information defining the register contents of processors associated with that process, but which are currently not active

(iv) the stored information held in the registers of processors associated with that process, and which are currently active.

The first three classes of stored information can be held in any suitable storage medium - the fourth class *must* be held in the appropriate registers of the active processors. It is possible to have one copy of the stored instructions operating on several different sets of data in the last three classes, each set corresponding to a different realisation of what is basically the same process.

Clearly, it is necessary to have some form of supervisory activity present in such a system, responsible for transferring information from processor registers to storage when a process ceases to use a particular processor, and from storage to processor registers when the process is about to become active on a processor. It is necessary to provide for protection, to ensure that storage associated with one process is not overwritten by the activities of some other process. It is necessary to provide for communication and synchronisation of processes, to allow one process to pass data to another process and to reactivate the process to which data has been passed when the transfer of data is complete. Finally, it is necessary to provide means of ensuring that processes which are sharing processors do so in such a way that they do not interfere with one another's activities.

The next two sections describe some of the hardware that is associated with the provision of these various facilities within a system.

6.1.3 *Process protection*. A system containing a number of concurrently operating processes requires protection mechanisms to deal with errors; these errors may occur within a program written by a user, within a part of the system software, or within a unit forming the hardware of the system. There are also some systems in which there is a requirement to protect against malice on the part of a user who may be writing a program, or operating a terminal in a transaction processing system. Protection against accidental error is fairly readily achieved; protection against malice on the part of a user is possible though with some difficulty; protection against malice on the part of the author of system software or designer of hardware is virtually impossible.

It is worth explaining that 'protection' in this context means not an absolute certainty that one process can never corrupt the storage or interfere with the processors of some other process, but that the probability of such damage is reduced to an acceptable level. Protection may also carry an element of security to ensure that unauthorised reading by one process of the data of some other process is effectively prevented.

A process is largely equivalent to the stored information defining the current state of that process, and this information is held either in storage or in the registers of active processors. We shall see in section 6.2 how the mechanisms which are needed to allow the effective administration of storage can ensure that the information about a process that is held in normal storage can be protected from access by other processes, and in this section we consider only the problem of ensuring that an active processor does not have its registers corrupted by some other process. Processors invariably contain a register whose contents specify the instruction in store which that processor is obeying or will obey next; they also contain registers which indicate the position in store of data to be accessed or at which results are to be stored. Notice that all these remarks apply to a 'processor' which is controlling an interface just as much as to an arithmetic processor. It is possible to extend the storage protection of section 6.2 to ensure that all the accesses to store generated by an active processor are valid. We therefore only require a means of ensuring that a processor cannot directly overwrite the registers of another processor. In fact, there is in general an asymmetry between the arithmetic processors and the interface processors in this respect; the arithmetic processors are regarded as being in command of the interface processors, and can overwrite their registers by executing appropriate instructions, whereas the interface processors cannot directly overwrite registers in the arithmetic processors, except by means of an 'interrupt' as described below. It is therefore possible to associate with each arithmetic processor a status register which defines certain classes of operations (for example, those which overwrite registers in interface processors, or change the status register of an arithmetic processor) as being illegal when in that status. At all times, the Boolean sum of the Boolean products of the outputs of the instruction decoder with a signal derived from the status register which is a 1 if a given instruction is illegal in that status, is monitored and causes an interrupt whenever an illegal instruction is encountered.

An interrupt is rather akin to a forced entry to a subroutine, and on many arithmetic processors is implemented using much of the same logic. It forces the program counter to a predetermined value, storing the present value of the program counter, and resets the status register to a value which allows the processor to obey all possible instructions. From then on, the software thus initiated is responsible for determining the cause of the interrupt and for taking appropriate action. (On some systems, the forced value of the program counter is different for different causes of an interrupt.)

The first action of the software thus entered will be to preserve all the registers of the interrupted arithmetic processor in store; then having handled the interrupt, the software will select a process to restart on the arithmetic processor, reinstate the registers appropriately (including the processor status register) and finally return control to the new process.

When the interrupt is caused by an attempt on the part of the code currently being executed by a processor to gain access to resources denied to the currently active process, the software that handles the interrupt will terminate the offending process and arrange for a suitable message to be output. Generally such failures are attributable to a programming error by a user of the system; they may arise from an error in the coding of a part of the operating system, or very exceptionally from a hardware malfunction. It is usually possible to discover by software the exact nature of the offending process and to take appropriate action. The details are not our concern.

Interrupts more commonly arise by requests from interface processors for attention by the main processor. Such attention will be required in a variety of circumstances. In a large system virtually all interfaces will handle multi-character transfers of actual information; however, there will frequently be transfers of small amounts of information associated with the organisation of the multi-character transfers (for example, track and position selection on a magnetic disc, or information concerning the success or otherwise of a transfer). In all cases, it is common at the completion of a transfer for the interface to require further attention before going on to deal with the next transfer. This is usually achieved by causing an interrupt in an arithmetic processor, which will then enter software to recognise the cause of the interrupt and to inform the process whose transfer has now completed that it is free to proceed. On some very large systems, the more straightforward situations of this kind may be handled entirely via hardware in the unit controlling the interface, and only exceptional cases, such as a failed transfer, will produce an interrupt.

There are two other sources of interrupts found on a computing system; a 'clock' and some means of allowing the human operator to initiate actions. The clock interrupt is generated periodically, so as to ensure that for as long as the system is switched on, it can be guaranteed to enter the interrupt handling software at least on every clock interrupt. This ensures that the system can never find itself in a state of complete suspension of all activities and with no processor active anywhere - it also allows the system to maintain a reasonably accurate record of the passage of real time. For a system involved in true real time work it is likely that one of the input devices on the system would be a digital clock.

The operator in charge of the system can also generate an interrupt wherever he wishes. The software activated will allow the operator to intervene in the system, for example to remove faulty units from the list of available devices and return them when they are repaired, or to abort programs which are known to be malfunctioning.

6.1.4 *Process synchronisation.* We picture a system as containing a number of processes, each process proceeding by utilising storage, which it occupies exclusively, and processors which it uses intermittently, to achieve its particular function. The protection hardware outlined in the previous section is designed to ensure that as far as possible no one process interferes with others. However, from time to time it is necessary for processes to communicate; this communication takes two basic forms.

(1) *cooperation* - where several otherwise independent processes cooperate in a 'producer/consumer' manner. A typical example might be the processing of punched card images read into core store buffer areas; the card reader, and the process which drives it, can be regarded as a producer (of core images) while the processes which remove card images from the buffer area are consumers. Clearly, it is necessary to ensure that the consumer processes do not overtake the card readers ability to load card images into the buffer area - equally clearly the card reader process must not be allowed to load a fresh card image into a buffer area whose contents have not yet been successfully processed by a consumer process.

(2) *exclusion* - where several otherwise independent processes use a single shared resource. An example is the shared use by many processes of a single arithmetic processor. A much less obvious one is the shared use by many processors of a single copy of a piece of stored code for which there is a restriction that only one processor may be actively executing that code at any one time. This situation occurs in certain parts of the supervisory system on a multi-processor system, where it is essential that only one processor at a time should be allowed to update the stored information which defines the current status of the various processors in the system.

Dijkstra has described an extremely simple, yet powerful technique for dealing with problems of cooperation and exclusion based on the use of a 'semaphore'. A semaphore S can be manipulated by two operators P 'wait' and V 'signal' with the following effects. S can take any integer value. The operation P(S) 'wait for S' attempts to subtract one from the value of S; if this would leave S positive or zero, then the result of the subtraction is left as the new value of S and the process which carried out the P operation continues. However, if S was already zero, the process which attempted the P operation will be suspended, and will only attempt to repeat the P operation when S becomes greater than zero, as a consequence of a V operation.

The operation V(S) 'signal on S' is the converse of P(S), and adds one to the value of S. If S was already positive the process which carried out the V operation will continue; however, if S has now become zero, then some process which was awaiting the setting of the semaphore to zero will now be free to proceed, i.e. in effect to complete the P operation which first suspended it.

Clearly, the P operation has the effect of causing a process to await the availability of a resource, while the V operation signals that the resource has become available. Both P and V operations must be carried out without any form of interruption being possible until their operations are complete. In general P operations will be issued by processes and the corresponding V operations by the software which deals with interrupts associated with the termination of activities on interface processors.

6.2 *Virtual machine systems*

In this section we examine further the concept of an information processing system as a set of processes acting on stored information through the agency of various processors. We shall arrive at a system in which each major activity of the system can be considered as a hierarchy of processes which are realised on 'virtual machines' which are supported by the real resources of the actual system.

6.2.1 *Resources within a system.* We saw in section 6.1.2 that an information processing system contains two basic types of resource, storage and processors, and that it was possible under certain circumstances to stop and restart processors - when a processor is stopped the contents of its working registers can be transferred to storage and held there indefinitely, ready to be reinstated when the processor is restarted on behalf of that particular process. Thus a processor (used in the generalised sense of section 6.1.2) can be shared amongst several processes in a 'time-like' way. When an individual process takes control of the processor, it takes over the entire processor for an interval of time. When it relinquishes the processor it releases it entirely and all the information necessary to allow it to be restarted must be transferred to storage. We can contrast this with the way in which storage is allocated to a process. As we have seen the storage may contain three quite different types of information

(a) the instructions defining the process algorithm
(b) the data on which the process operates
(c) the stored contents of the registers of processors associated with this process which are not currently active.

All of this storage must be available for all of the time for which the process exists, even at those times when *no* processor is active on behalf of the process. Thus to service the storage requirements of a process it is necessary to allocate storage to it, and to leave the storage allocated for the entire life of the process. In most systems the storage allocated to a process in this way will represent a fraction of the total storage available in the system. We can think of the total available storage as a space, of which some part is separated off and made available to the process, and thus regard storage as being shared amongst processes in a 'space-like' way.

These two modes of sharing resources on a system are analogous to the ways in which a fast communications channel can be operated via a multiplexer to service a number of slower channels. In time-division multiplexing the whole fast channel is dedicated to meeting the needs of a single slow channel, and the fast channel is switched around amongst the slower channels. In frequency division multiplexing each slow channel has permanently allocated to it a fraction of the total bandwidth of the fast channel.

We shall see that any resource within a system can be subdivided amongst a number of competing demands in one or other of these two basic ways, i.e. either by dividing it in time or in space. The distinction between the two ways in which a resource divides is important when deciding how to manage the resource when the total demand for the resource exceeds the available supply. However, before we go on to consider the problem of resource management, we examine another facet of resource handling.

6.2.2 *Resource substitution*. The majority of programs which run on a computer read in data and output results; it is possible of course to write programs in which all the data are built into the program as constants although this is normally regarded as poor practice; it is difficult to conceive of any useful program which does not output results. Normally, input and output are relatively slow processes, in the sense that the average time taken to transfer a character across an interface is long conpared with the time required by the processor to handle the computation associated with that character. This discrepancy in speed between input or output transfer and the relevant processing is often further emphasised by the fact that input or output usually occurs in bursts, with intervening periods during which no transfer activity takes place.

If a computing system runs only one program at a time, then during input all other activities will cease until sufficient information has been transferred into the system to allow processing to resume. The same remark applies to output, where the processor will fill a buffer area with characters to be output quickly and processing must then cease while the relatively slow output device actually transfers characters. Many systems use 'spooling' as a technique to reduce the periods during which the processor is idle. For simplicity, consider a program which requires to read cards, via a card reader: before this program is run, a process is initiated which reads card images from a card reader into store, and then writes the card image on to backing store. When the program requiring cards to be read attempts to claim a card reader and subsequently to start reading cards, it is initially connected to the card-reading process, and each subsequent request to read a card transfers into the store of the program a card image (from backing store), which appears to the program exactly as if it had come in directly from a card reader.

In a similar way it is possible for output from a program to a line printer to be written to backing store as the program runs; subsequently the output which has accumulated on backing store is transcribed from backing store into store, and from there on to a printer.

The reason usually offered for using this technique is that it avoids leaving the fast arithmetic processor idle during the relatively slow input or output transfers. A moment's thought will show that this is a totally fallacious argument; in an environment in which a number of processes are simultaneously in store, if one process can not run on the arithmetic processor then some other process should be able to. Extra processor times are consumed in organising the transfers of card images to backing store and their subsequent retrieval into the store of the program concerned. These processor times are inevitably greater than the times in reading card images directly into the store of the program (note that there will be more than one processor involved, i.e. the arithmetic processor and the processor which supervises the card reader or the backing store device). Thus in total, extra processor time is used in this approach. The saving is one of store occupancy. The total store used by a program is measured not simply as say kilo-words, but as 'kilo-word seconds', that is as the accumulated product of store occupied (in kwords, say) by the time for which it is occupied (in seconds, say). Even this product may not be a direct measure of the demands on the system, in the sense that a very large program occupying store for a short time may be more difficult to handle than a smaller program occupying store for a longer time.

If we consider a program occupying store, and carrying out transfers directly with slow input/output devices, we shall find that it generates a certain amount of store use, measured in kword-seconds. If we now allow the same program to run, but with its input and output handled via the spooling technique outlined earlier, we find

(a) the storage use of the program is reduced, as the transfers between backing store and store are faster than those between slow peripheral devices and store, thus reducing the time for which the program occupies store

(b) the presence of the processes for carrying out the spooling activities generates extra store usage, by increasing the amount of store occupied.

In general a program occupies more store at any one instant than the process which drives a slow peripheral device, and the reduction under (a) above outweighs the extra overheads under (b) resulting in a net saving.

There is, however, a much more important aspect of the use of spooling. We have so far discussed the effect of spooling on a single program, although running in a multi-programming environment. If we have a multi-programming system and do not use spooling, then for each active program that requires a card reader, a real card reader must be attached to the system. If we adopt a spooling approach, we need only *one* card reader, and as many instances of the part of the

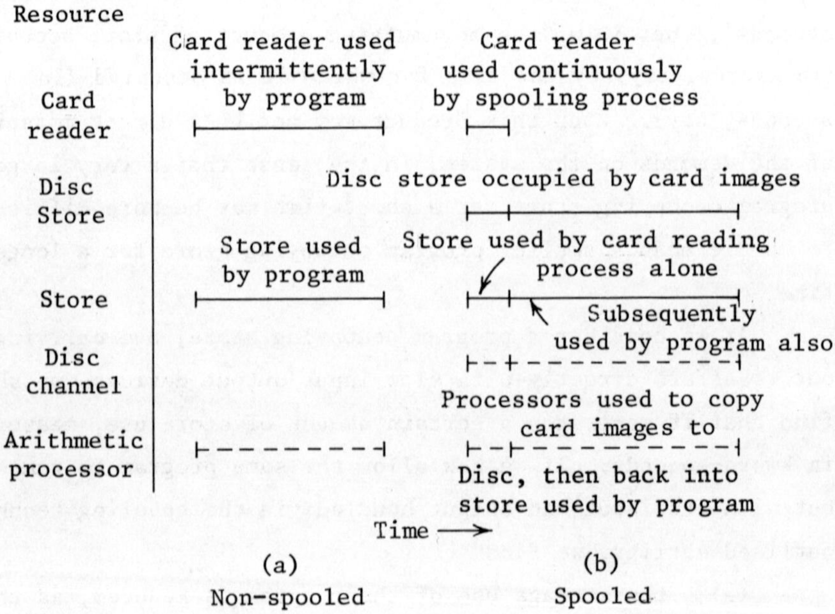

Figure 6.1 Non-spooled and spooled use of a card-reader.

spooling process which transfers card images from backing store to store as there are programs requiring card readers. What we are able to do is to substitute for each card reader requested:

(a) time on a real card reader and its controller
(b) space on a backing store device
(c) time on a backing store channel controller
(d) time on an arithmetic processor
(e) space in store.

Taken together these separate sets of demands on the available system resources can be regarded as a substitute for the single demand originally made by the program; and this substitution can be made much more flexibly, in terms of when they are required, than if we do not spool, as figure 6.1 illustrates. In this figure, demands on space-divisible resources are shown as a solid line, and on time-divisible resources as a dashed line. Notice that a card-reader, which can be regarded as store which can only be read, is regarded as a space-divisible resource, which must be allocated entirely to a process which is using it.

This notion of substituting one resource by a whole collection of resources can be applied not only to spooling for input and output devices but to many of the resources of a system. In the next section its application to a wide range of resources is discussed.

6.2.3 *Virtual machine systems*. The previous section discussed one form of resource substitution, in which a resource, in this case a card reader, was effectively supplied to a program by using a collection of other resources in addition to the card reader in such a way that the net effect as visible to the program was the same as that produced by the availability of a real card reader. This was possible because the program is concerned only with the changes produced in the store accessible to it by the actions of any of the processors of the system. If the changes produced in the store available to a process by a simulated resource are the same as those produced by an actual resource then the process concerned has no way of telling that the substitution has taken place. If such a substitution allows either a reduction of real resource usage, or greater flexibility in the scheduling of real resources, then it may well be worthwhile making this substitution.

We now consider systems in which every resource of the system may be supplied to any process either as a real resource, or by resource substitution. In each case the sole criterion as to whether or not this substitution is allowable is that the process concerned shall not be able to discover whether it is using a real resource or a substituted one. Since the only resources available to a process are storage of various kinds, and processors producing changes in the contents of storage, we need concern ourselves only with techniques for carrying out these two types of substitution. We are particularly concerned with any hardware which is either necessary to allow such substitution at all, or desirable on grounds of efficiency.

6.2.3.1 *Virtual processors*. The effect of a processor is to change the contents of the storage area of the process on whose behalf it is operating. We accept the slightly extended definition of processor, as applying to 'processors' which are supervising the activities of an input/output device (such as a reader or a printer) or a storage device (such as a drum or disc). Such 'processors' still produce changes in the storage area of the process on whose behalf they operate, by transferring into or out of designated areas of store. All processors are time-divisible resources. Also, any processor may be simulated by the use of a collection of resources which is operated in such a way as to produce the same net effect in the storage areas of the process as the resource which is substituted. There is one important restriction on this substitution, in the case of resources where a change of physical representation is involved and is the essence of the purpose for which that device is used (that is for input or output devices) or where data transmission is involved. When substitution of a device involving data transmission or change of physical representation takes place, the collection of resources to carry out the simulation *must* ultimately include at some time a real device of the type being simulated. Thus, the substitution in such cases can not remove the need for a real device, but only alter the time at which that need is met. There is also a constraint on the time at which the need is met, governed by the direction in which information flows into the storage area of the process. For input transfers the provision of the real device can only be advanced to an earlier time i.e. the use of the real input device must take place before, or at the latest, simultaneously with, the request for use of the input device by the process. For output transfers the provision of the real device can only be deferred to a later time, i.e. the use of the real output device must take place after, or at the earliest simultaneously with, the request for use of the output device by the process.

For processors where no physical change of representation or location is essential, there are no restrictions of the sort outlined above governing the resource that must be used. In practice of course, a simulated arithmetic processor required by a process will in general be simulated by a genuine arithmetic processor, and so on.

The extra hardware required to allow processor substitution is not great. A prime requirement is the means to ensure that only processes which are allowed access to real resources actually achieve access, and that any process which does not have access to a real resource will be prevented from gaining access. A method of doing this is to associate with each process a process name, and to associate with each processor the name of the process to which the processor is currently allocated. Clearly this technique requires the existence of a supervisory system which is responsible for scheduling processes into real processors, and for handling the consequences of attempts at unauthorised use of a processor by a process.

6.2.3.2 *Virtual storage*. When a programmer prepares the code for a process, he will initially be concerned with storage for the stored form of the instructions, and for the data on which these instructions apply. Depending on the type of programming system which is in use, and whether the language primarily concerns itself with data objects of the problem (problem oriented language) or with components of the system on which the solution will take place (machine oriented language) there will be a more or less automatic generation of addresses within the stored form of the instructions representing the process, each address being encoded as a string of binary digits. In this subsection we consider various ways in which such a string can be used to assess data held in a store.

We can think of this associating of the identifiers in the program with addresses as constituting a mapping between two spaces, a 'name space' and an 'address space'. The name space consists of the set of all possible identifiers available within a given programming language, and defines the domain within which all identifiers in the program must lie. This domain is in general very large or even infinite and in any given program the set of identifiers actually used will be a small subset of the total name space. The address space consists of the set of all possible addresses within the system. The mapping of the name space on to the address space is sometimes referred to as binding and it may take place in a number of stages. In increasing order of flexibility these are:

(1) the binding for a program is carried out during assembly or compilation. This is only possible if all the identifiers referred to within a program are defined within that program, and if all the addresses produced are in absolute hardware form.

(2) the binding for the program is deferred until a 'consolidation' (loading, link-editing) phase. In this way the program may be placed at different points within the store prior to execution. This allows a program to refer by name to objects which are defined outside the program. The consolidation process will collect for all objects not defined, but referred to, within the program, a definition from the environment within which the program

runs, and use this definition to carry out the final association of hardware addresses with identifiers.

(3) the binding for the program is deferred until program execution time. In this way, the program may be placed at different points within the store during execution. Basically, we can define the following techniques for this type of binding

(a) datum-limit - at program load time the supervisory system associates with each program a 'datum'. Word 0 of the program's address space is located at this datum and to convert from the address as held in the program to the absolute hardware address each address must have the datum added to it. Some machines allow more than one datum per process, for example one for the coding and one for the data. (Do not confuse datum-limit working with the process of modification described in chapter 5.) It is customary also to have a 'limit' which defines the maximum address within the program address space and is used to prevent processes addressing store not allocated to them. With datum-limit working a program or its data can be physically located anywhere in store, provided only that there is a contiguous range of addresses available which is sufficiently large to accommodate the information to be stored. Indeed it is common when using datum limit techniques actually to move information about in storage in such a way as to coalesce all unoccupied space into a single area. This can be done by ensuring that *all* activities associated with this area to be moved, including input and output transactions, are handled; the supervisory process can then copy the entire storage area to its new position, assign to the datum and limit registers their new values, and allow the process to restart in the normal way.

(b) segmentation - the user is allowed an address space which is greatly in excess of the store available on the processor. Typically his address will contain (s + w) bits in all where the first s bits define the 'segment' within which he operates and the remaining w bits define the address within the segment. The total addressable store will be less than $2^{(s+w)}$ words. As each address is extracted at execution time the first s bits are used to consult a *segment table*, the entries in which define whereabouts in the hardware store word 0 of that segment is to be found. The allocation of the addresses of the start of each segment is usually done permanently at program load time, but there are also systems in which the location of a segment can move during the existence of a program. Thus the binding here, as with datum limit, takes place at execution time, but is to some extent visible to the user. In this way segmentation differs from both datum-limit and paging (next section).

(c) Paging - the users address space again may exceed the totality of available store, and his addresses will contain (p+w) bits in all where the first p bits define the 'page' within which the address lies and w bits define the address within the page. However, whereas with segmentation w is liable to be quite large, and the addresses within each segment that are actually used form a small proportion of the total and lie in a 'solid' block at the low numbered end, with paging w is quite small and most of the addresses within a page are actually used.

Again the translation to an address involves transforming the page number into the hardware address at which the zeroth word of the page lies. This is achieved by an associative store in which the address part of the word contains the page number and the data part the address of the start of the corresponding page for each page in store. If there is a match between the page number and an entry in associative store, the address of the word within store is then readily found by addition of the w bits giving the word number within the page.

Again, paging leads to binding being completed at execution time. However, there are two great differences from segmentation. Paging is not visible to the user, who has no control over its working. Secondly, paging can be used to allow the user to access a store that is apparently much larger than is actually available. This is achieved by allowing a page that is not frequently in use to be transferred to backing store (usually a drum or head per track disc) and deleting its entry from the associative store. If this page is subsequently addressed, then when the associative store is addressed no match will occur between the p bits presented and any entry in the associative store - at this stage a special page fault interrupt is generated, and the corresponding page will be transferred from backing store into store.

When using a paging system, it is common to append to the page number within the associative store a group of bits which define the way in which the contents of the page can be used, that is for execution (as instructions) for reading (as data) or for writing (as data and workspace). These bits are checked on each access to ensure that a process uses store only as allowed by the supervisory system.

Some machines incorporate both segmentation and paging.

In a segmented system it is usually the case that all the addresses generated by a program can be accommodated in high speed storage. This is not true of paging which is a form of resource substitution. In this case, one is mapping a large virtual address space on to a small physical address space in high speed and expensive store, plus a large physical address space in low speed (and less expensive per bit) backing store, plus the use of some fraction of the capacity of a processor to organise transfers, plus a channel to the backing store. Clearly a process running on a paging system will run more slowly than the same process running on a machine in which all working is into high speed storage. However, the paging system with its smaller high speed store will have a lower initial cost than the non-paging system with the same total storage. When allowance is made for the processor and channel overheads associated with paging, the total cost of running the process on the slower paging system may well be less than the cost on the faster non-paging system. A more valid comparison is between paging and non-paging systems with the same configuration of both high speed store and backing store. Where the size of program is such that any program will fit into high speed storage, then the non-paging system is likely to show greater throughput. A paging system will be more effective where some jobs are so large that they cannot fit entirely into high speed storage, and some information must be put on to backing store. There is evidence to suggest that in these conditions, the control of transfers between backing store and high speed store will be more effectively achieved by paging than by the manual inclusion of overlays within the program. Paging is even more valuable in an environment in which large numbers of users wish to execute the same program using different data. Appropriate construction of the entries in page tables will ensure that all users have execute only access to a single copy of the coding, while each user has access to his own data set.

6.3 *Micro-programming*

The design and construction of a digital system can often be handled in two reasonably separate stages. In the first stage, the designer considers primarily the registers which the system contains, the functional units which take the outputs from one or more registers and process these to produce a result which will be transferred into a register to form its new contents, and the necessary pathways between registers and functional units which are required to allow the system to perform the tasks for which it is being built. In the second stage, the designer considers primarily the precise sequence in which functions of registers are transferred into other registers. Of course, during the first stage, the designer will bear in mind the functions and pathways that are required in the second stage, and in the second stage he may find it necessary to return and add new registers, new functional units, or new pathways to his design.

When a machine is contructed in this way, we can regard the definition of the sequence of transfers which form the result of the second design stage as constituting a 'program' for a very simple machine. Since this simple machine takes the program steps of the actual machine and breaks each of them down into a number of steps, this 'program' is often referred to as a 'micro-program'.

6.3.1 *Concepts of micro-programming.* To construct a system using micro-programming techniques we require some way of storing the individual micro-instructions which make up the micro-program. A micro-instruction will typically select one or more registers as inputs to a functional unit, or transfer the output of a function into a register, and a complete micro-program will contain a number of micro-instructions which are to be obeyed sequentially. As in a conventional machine order code, included in the micro-instructions will be some which allow changes in the sequence; unlike a conventional machine code, nearly all micro-instructions have an implied operand and do not require any form of address of an operand to be specified; again unlike a conventional machine code, it is often possible to allow several micro-instructions to execute at a given step in the sequence. For a given machine, the actual micro-program is unlikely to change, and the store in which the micro-program is held may be constructed as a read-only-store (ROS). Advantage may be taken of this to allow the use of a faster micro-program store, resulting in a faster machine. However, there are certain advantages in holding micro-program in rewritable store. A micro-program is constructed in much the same way as a conventional program, and we have already seen some examples of micro-programs in chapter 5, although at that time they were not presented as such. As in normal programming, the sequence of operations within a micro-program is very important. We may think of the micro-instructions as being held in successive words of a central store. A master oscillator or clock supplies regular pulses to the micro-program control unit, and at each clock time a word is read from the central store and the corresponding micro-instruction executed. Since at any clock time several operations may take place simultaneously, and since each operation implies all its operands, the amount of information required to specify an operation may only be a single bit, whose position in the word indicates the actual operation.

Clearly such a representation allows several operations to be specified within a single micro-instruction.

As a specific example we will consider the micro-program to control the multiplier of chapter 5 section 10; this contains four registers P_m, P_ℓ, X and Y and forms the arithmetic product X×Y in P_m, P_ℓ by accumulating p partial products using a p-digit parallel adder. In addition, the micro-program uses a number-generator which can supply an encoding of the number p, and an up-down counter which is initially loaded with the number p and decremented towards zero as each partial product is formed. The algorithm of the earlier section is modified slightly; as described earlier, the product of X_r the r-th digit of X with the number Y was formed by using p AND-gates having a common input x_r. We now use the value of X_r to control whether or not we add Y to the partial product (x_r=1) or whether we pass straight on to the next digit of X, omitting the addition (x_r=0). To implement this requires the following micro-operations:

$0 \to P_m$	clear P_m to all 0's
$0 \to P_\ell$	clear P_ℓ to all 0's
$rP_m \to P_m$	shift P_m one place right transferring the least significant digit of P_m to the most significant digit of $P\ell$
$rP_\ell \to P_\ell$	shift P_ℓ one place right
$rX \to X$	shift X one place right
$+ \to P_m$	copy the output of the adder into P_m (the inputs to the adder are P_m and Y).

The following operations are internal to the micro-program unit:

$(p) \to W$	insert the number p in the work register W

(W-1)→W   decrement W by 1.

The entire micro-program would be:

Step	*Operations*
1	$o \to P_m$; $o \to P_\ell$; $(p) \to W$;
2	*if* W=o *then goto* next instruction
3	*if* x_o=1 *then goto* step 5
4	$+ \to P_m$
5	$rP_m \to P_m$; $rP_\ell \to P_\ell$; $rX \to X$; $(W-1) \to W$; *goto* step 2.

Notice the presence here of multiple operations carried out in parallel (1 and 5) and of conditional and unconditional jumps (2, 3 and 5).

6.3.2 *Register transfer machines.* The multiplier unit outlined above would form part of a larger system, consisting of registers whose output can be supplied as inputs to various functional units, the outputs of which are in turn available as inputs to registers; it may also be convenient to use functional registers, for example the up-down counter described in chapter 5. Within such a system, operations are implemented as sequences of transfers of the contents of registers, and the outputs from functional units, into registers, and the machine is known as a 'register transfer machine'. The only additional equipment necessary to allow the construction of a register transfer machine is a means of selecting one register from several as an input to a function unit or register. This can be achieved by the unit shown in figure 6.2. This shows one digit position in a selector unit; the i-th digits of three separate registers A,B,C are supplied as inputs to three AND gates, whose other inputs are selector lines S_A,S_B, S_C of which exactly one is 1, the other two being 0. Clearly the output of the OR gate is one of A_i, B_i or C_i depending on whether S_A, S_B or S_C is a 1; a complete selector unit consists of a row of such sub-units one for each digit position, and allows us to select one of A, B, or C as the output f. As an example in the multiplier unit, the necessary paths are as shown in figure 5.14; notice that the AND gates of 5.14 are now replaced by the conditional micro-operation of step 3 above. In figure 6.3(a) we have redrawn figure 5.14(c), and figure 6.3(b) shows all the paths necessary for the i-th digit

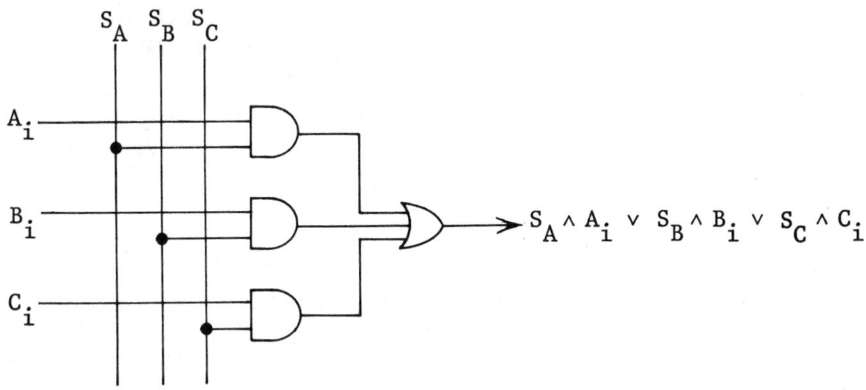

Figure 6.2 The i-th digit in a 3-input selector unit or multiplexer.

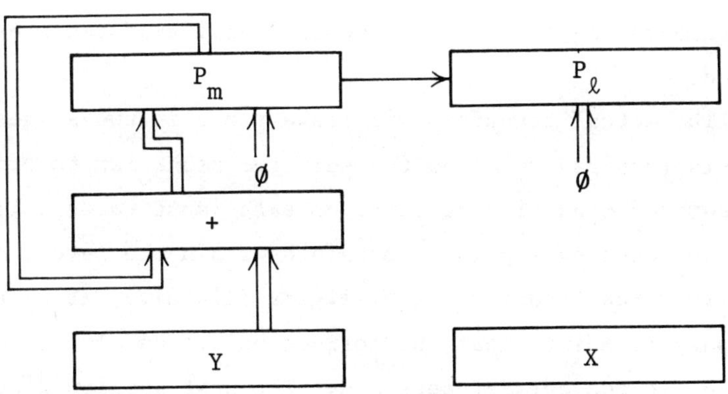

Figure 6.3(a) Data paths in a simple multiplier.

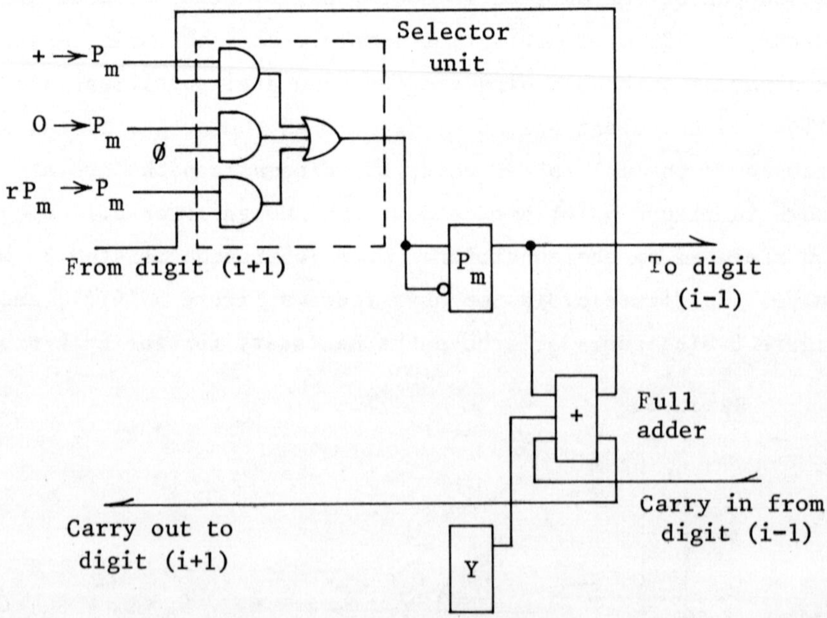

Figure 6.3(b) Connections on the i-th digit of P_m, Y and the adder in a simple multiplier.

of the adder and of register P_m. It can be seen that the input to P_m consists essentially of a selector whose inputs are all 0's, the output from the adder, and the digits of P_m displaced one position to the right, together with lines to select $0 \rightarrow P_m$, $+ \rightarrow P_m$ and $rP_m \rightarrow P_m$ respectively. For simplicity the special arrangements required for the endmost digits of registers are omitted.

The actual transfers will take place in two stages; a *level* is required to allow the selector mechanism to produce the required conditioning input on each input to each flip-flop, followed by a *pulse*, contained within the level, actually to perform the transfer. (Cf. figure 5.14(d).) It is also necessary to ensure that the correct pulses and levels are applied, in the correct sequence. The next section discusses how this is realised.

6.3.3 *Implementation of micro-programming.* We shall now outline two forms of micro-program control unit. One form uses a small read only memory (ROM), and a single counter, whose contents form the address within the ROM. Each word in the ROM contains three fields of information

(i) a group of single digit items whose state 1 or 0 indicates whether or not a particular micro-operation is to be performed, each possible micro-operation being controlled by a particular digit,

(ii) a group of single digit items whose state 1 or 0 indicates a condition which is to be applied so as to govern the transfer of the address part of the word as the position for the next micro-instruction,

(iii) a field whose value indicates the address in the ROM of the next word to be obeyed. This address may be conditionally transferred into the counter controlling the selection of micro-program words.

Clearly such a unit can easily be reprogrammed, simply by altering the contents of the ROM. For the example we have chosen the contents of the micro-instructions might be as shown in the lower half of figure 6.4(a).

An alternative faster form of micro-program control unit uses two registers and a rectangular array of AND gates. One register, the major cycle selector, is decoded and the output selects a row of AND gates defining the particular sequence of micro-instructions to be obeyed to implement a particular instruction. The other register, the minor cycle selector, functions as a shift register and selects successive columns, and advances through the sequence of micro-operations which constitute the instruction selected by the major cycle selector. Each AND gate in the array has inputs from the corresponding row and column in the major cycle (row) and minor cycle (column) selectors; it may also have an input from an

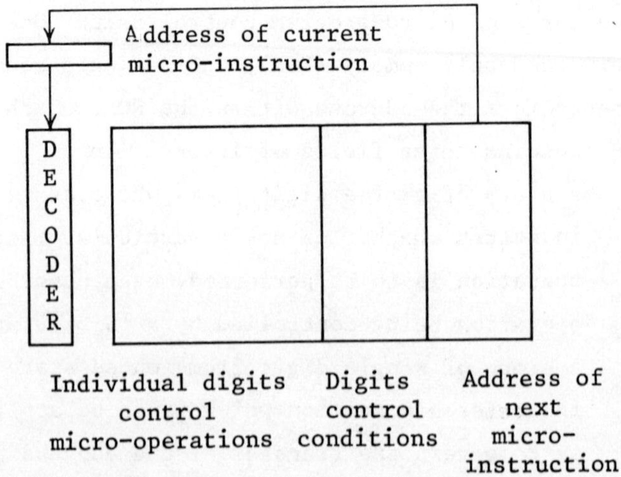

Step	$0 \rightarrow P_m$	$0 \rightarrow P_\ell$	$rP_m \rightarrow P_m$	$rP_\ell \rightarrow P_\ell$	$rX \rightarrow X$	$+ \rightarrow P_m$	$p \rightarrow w$	$w-1 \rightarrow w$	$w=0$	$x_o = 0$	Next step
1	1	1	0	0	0	0	1	0	0	0	2
2	0	0	0	0	0	0	0	0	1	0	Exit
3	0	0	0	0	0	0	0	0	0	1	5
4	0	0	0	0	0	1	0	0	0	0	5
5	0	0	1	1	1	0	0	1	0	0	2

Figure 6.4(a) Use of an ROM as a micro-program store.

external condition. The outputs of the AND gates are taken to the lines invoking the micro-instructions; where the same micro-operation may be invoked from several points in the array this will involve ORing the outputs from the relevant AND gates. It is possible to use an output to reset the position within a minor cycle, thus effecting a jump within the sequence, which can be governed by an external condition, or to select a new major cycle.

The micro-program in such a system is realised by hand

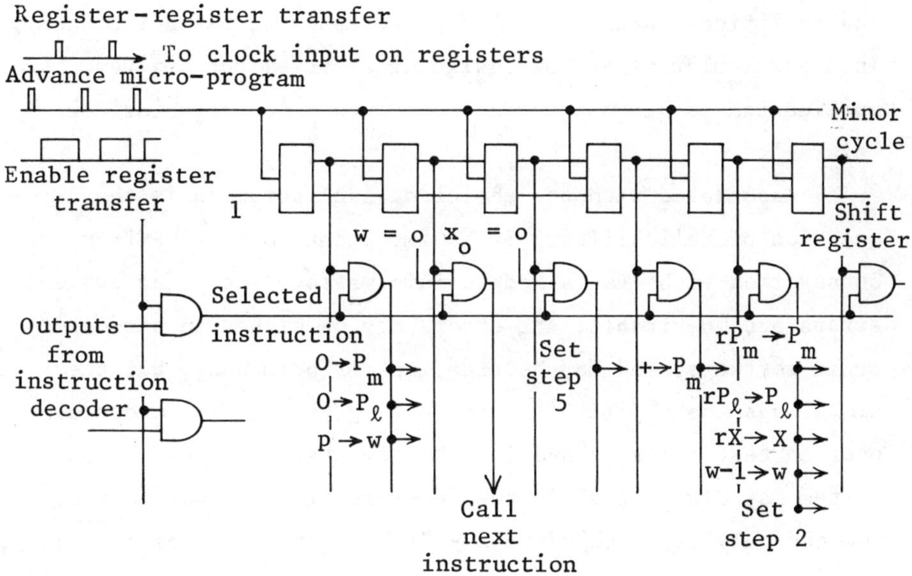

Figure 6.4(b) Use of an array of AND gates to generate a micro-program.

wiring from each AND gate and each point in the rectangular array leads to the OR gates controlling each micro-operation. This is very tedious and error-prone, and leads to a system which is very difficult to alter.

6.4 *Summary*

We started this chapter by stating one design objective for an information processing system as being minimum cost and maximum reliability. In the course of the chapter we have indicated ways in which the proper design of a system may well allow the sharing by many activities of scarce resources, and the substitution of cheaper resources of lower overall performance for more expensive ones of higher performance; both the sharing and the substitution can be carried out with a controlled degree of loss of total performance, and it is a matter of judgement as to the exact point at which one sacrifices further loss of performance to further economy. This particular aspect of designing a system for a given application is given a variety of names - 'configuring' or 'sizing'.

Associated with the choice of configuration is the question of reliability. It is important to realise from the outset that with even a modest information processing system, errors are inevitable; the errors may be either in hardware or in software, and may be transient or permanent, but they are always there. (It is worth noting that it is impossible ever to test a system and say "I know that it works" - the system may always fail in the interval since it was tested. One can only say with certainty "I know that it does not work", if a test fails, and if the test does not fail one can only state "I do not know that it does not work"). Reliability in a system with errors in it is assessed not simply in terms of the rate at which failures occur, assessed by such measures as 'mean time between faults', but equally importantly by the time to repair the system, assessed by 'mean time to recover' and by the amount of work spoilt by a break. This is especially true for interactive systems, where users are working directly with the system, as distinct from batch processing systems. In batch systems, where a user may expect his work back several hours after submission, a break of a few minutes may well be quite acceptable. For an interactive system a break of a few minutes may cause serious disruption to users, especially if after repair each user has to repeat much of the work that he had already completed.

The type of modular system described in this chapter lends itself very well to two different forms of resilience against the failure of system components. If all resources can be realised by substitution of other collections of resources, then the failure of one particular component can be disguised with varying degrees of success by transferring the activity which it was supporting on to other components. The opportunities for doing this are increased if the system contains more than one of each kind of component, though this redundancy of course increases the total cost of the system. At the same time, the modular nature of the system provides opportunities for the effects of errors to be localised to those processes whose data have been corrupted by the error; processes whose data are not corrupted can be restarted from the point they had last reached, with no loss of work completed so far.

In certain cases, the ability to localise errors to only a very few processes (or even to just one) can be combined with the ability to restart the entire system very quickly after an error, and to run the system without the faulty component, so as to yield an overall system which has a very high availability from the point of view of most users. It is likely that as computing systems and communications systems become further intertwined the computer system designer will be obliged to embed this philosophy, which is already common in telecommunications, deeply into the system.

6.5 *Bibliography*

Third Generation Computer Systems, ACM Computing Surveys 1971, vol. 3, no. 4, p. 175, by Peter J. Denning.

A tutorial article treating many aspects of the material covered in this chapter in more depth. This paper is accompanied by an annotated bibliography which is a valuable source of references to research papers for the reader requiring still more detail.

Concurrent Programming Concepts, ACM Computing Surveys 1973, vol. 5, no. 4, p. 223, by Pcr. Brinch Hansen.

Discusses a number of different approaches to the problems arising where many processes operate asynchronously.

The Structure of the THE Multi-Programming System, C.A.C.M.

vol. 11, no. 5 (May 1968), p. 341, by E.W. Dijkstra.
An outline description of a multi-programming system implemented on a small computer, making use of the P and V operations.

Process Structuring, ACM Computing Surveys 1973, vol. 5, no. 1, p. 5, by J.J. Horning and B. Randell.
A rather more theoretical treatment of the concept of a process and of the properties of collections of processes which are interacting. (The paper by J.K. Baer in the same number of the ACM surveys 'A Survey of Some Theoretical Aspects of Multiprocessing' is interesting, though it deals primarily with systems containing several identical arithmetic processors.)

Two other papers deal with 'deadlocks' which can occur in multi-programming systems:

Systems Deadlocks, ACM Computing Surveys 1971, vol. 3, no. 2, p. 67, by E.G. Coffman, Jnr., M.J. Elphick and A. Shoshani, and

Some Deadlock Properties of Computer Systems, ACM Computing Surveys 1972, vol. 4, no. 3, p. 179, by R.C. Holt.

The Growth of Interest in Microprogramming - A Literature Survey, ACM Computing Surveys 1969, vol. 1, no. 3, p. 139, by M.V. Wilkes.
An account of the early growth of the subject by the person principally responsible for its introduction, coupled with an extensive list of further reading.

Contemporary Concepts of Microprogramming and Emulation, ACM Computing Surveys 1969, vol. 1, no. 4, p. 197, by Robert E. Rosin.
Describes the application of microprogramming by a number of manufacturers to the problem of using one computing system to emulate the order code of another.

Virtual Memory, ACM Computing Surveys 1970, vol. 2, no. 3, p. 153, by Peter J. Denning.

A general account of the practical and theoretical development of the virtual memory concept, and includes an extensive bibliography.

6.6 *Examples*

(1) The control routine supervising a number of separate processes can normally perform some actions which no individual process can perform. Explain why this need be, paying particular attention to the allocation of resources to a process and the protection of each process's resources.
(University of Leeds, 1970)

(2) The following techniques are concerned with memory allocation; describe what each technique accomplishes giving any advantages or disadvantages:

(a) Static Relocation

(b) Dynamic Relocation using Paging

(c) Dynamic Relocation using Segmentation.

(University of Essex, 1973)

(3) Show how separate processes trying to update common information may fail to achieve the intended result if steps are not taken to ensure that each process completes its updating of such information before another process is allowed access to the information. Describe how the Dijkstra semaphore technique offers a solution to this problem. Give flow diagrams for the supervisor routines required to implement the two extracodes which each process should use when accessing such common information.
(University of Leeds, 1973)

(4) Explain fully the following techniques, why they have come to be used and how they may be implemented in practice.

(a) Paging

(b) Segmentation.
(University of Essex, 1972)

(5) A process running under a multiprogramming operating system can be thought of as running on its own virtual machine. Discuss ways in which an operating system can arrange to map the storage of the virtual machine on to the actual machine. Show how the choices open to the software designer are conditioned by the facilities provided by the address translation hardware. Also include in your discussion a consideration of the way in which different forms of storage protection hardware allow the integrity of a virtual machine's memory space to be maintained.
(University of Leeds, 1973)

(6) What is meant by binding a variable? Describe the various occurrences of binding in the passage of a program from algorithm to execution in

(1) a machine with a simple namespace

(2) a machine with segmentation

(3) a machine with segmentation and paging.

(University of Essex, 1971)

(7) A job is to be run on a batch-monitor computer system. You can assume that this job is completely processor-bound except for limitations imposed by the rate at which the data can be fed from the cards to the program run by the job. The job reads N+1 cards (numbered 0 to N). We denote the processor time used between requiring the data from cards n-1 and n by P_n. Calculate the total elapsed time T for the execution of the job as measured by the time from the read of card 0 starting and the read of card N terminating, for each of the following systems of input organisation:

(a) The reading of a card is only commenced when the

program requires the data.

(b) The system always starts the reader (autonomous) for card n+1 when the program asks for card n. (Equivalent to double-buffering.)

(c) The system spools the cards to tape and then reads from tape in the same way as b.

Show how the overall throughput of such a system can be improved by spooling at the expense of an increased time for a single job. Under what circumstances does spooling reduce turnround time over a simple batch-monitor?
(University of Leeds, 1974)

(8) Describe the function of the 'control section' of a digital computer.

A very simple digital computer has the following function parts:

(a) an instruction decoder
(b) an instruction register
(c) an instruction address register
(d) a storage address register
(e) a data address register
(f) main store with 1 μ sec cycle time
(g) an adder
(h) an A and B register used as inputs to the adder
(i) a CPU clock of 250 nsecs.

Show how information might flow from one function part to another in the execution of an add instruction. It may be useful in this question to use a language such as APL to describe the information flow.
(University of St. Andrews, 1974)

Index